Brick.
by

Brick by Brick

How LEGO
Rewrote
the Rules of
Innovation and
Conquered
the Global Toy
Industry

David C. Robertson
with Bill Breen

CROWN
BUSINESS

Published in the United States by Crown Business, an imprint of the Crown
Publishing Group, a division of Random House, Inc., New York.

www.crownpublishing.com

CROWN BUSINESS is a trademark and Crown and the Rising Sun colophon are
registered trademarks of Random House, Inc.

Crown Business books are available at special discounts for bulk purchases for
sales promotions or corporate use. Special editions, including personalized covers,
excerpts of existing books, or books with corporate logos, can be created in large
quantities for special needs. For more information, contact Premium Sales at (212)
572-2232 or e-mail specialmarkets@randomhouse.com.

Library of Congress Cataloging-in-Publication Data
Robertson, David C. (David Chandler)
    Brick by brick / David C. Robertson with Bill Breen.—First edition.
        pages cm
    1. LEGO koncernen (Denmark)   2. Toy industry—Denmark—Management.
    3. LEGO toys—History.   I. Breen, Bill.   II. Title.
    HD9993.T694L447 2013
    338.7'688725—dc23   2013004798

ISBN 978-0-307-95160-1
eISBN 978-0-307-95162-5

Printed in the United States of America

Book design by Ralph Fowler, rlfdesign
Jacket design by Michael Nagin
LEGO artist: Nathan Sawaya
Jacket photographs: Frank Longhitano

10 9 8 7 6 5 4 3 2 1

First Edition

To Gordon and Caroline,
from whom I learned the most
important lessons about LEGO
—DCR

Contents

Preface

I first approached the LEGO Group in 2007 while studying innovation efforts at companies in the United States and Europe. I'd surveyed fifty-six companies to understand their innovation management practices and planned to write a book about innovation and leadership, where I'd draw lessons and stories from many organizations and use those cases to illustrate how companies should manage innovation. After visiting LEGO, I wrote a case study that I hoped to use both in the classroom at the Swiss business school IMD and, later, in my book.

When I first taught my case study of LEGO at IMD in 2008 and 2009, I was taken aback by the outpouring of enthusiasm for the brand and its capacity to reawaken the sense of experimentation and play that resides within everyone. Subsequent interviews uncovered one fascinating aspect of the LEGO story after another. I realized that the LEGO management team had done more than just turn around the company; they had fundamentally rethought what "innovation" meant and how it should be managed and, by doing so, had rescued the company and boosted its performance to new heights. I saw that this case study was much more than a chapter in a book about innovation management—it was a full book's worth of stories and lessons: about a toy that touched the lives of millions around the globe for close to a century; about a much-beloved company that lost touch with its customers and its history and almost went out of business as a result; and about managers whose love for the company and perseverance saved it from ruin. What started as an academic book about innovation management became a much richer narrative of failure and recovery.

Since 2008 I've made more than a dozen trips to LEGO headquarters in Billund, Denmark (I highly recommend a June visit over one in January), where I've interviewed dozens of senior managers; sat in the bright white rooms of the Idea House and heard designers describe how they dream up new toys; pored over sketches and computer-generated designs that traced the evolution of some of the company's most compelling kits; visited the sprawling, noisy factories where millions of tons of plastic are molded into billions of bricks; and had a memorable meeting with Kjeld Kirk Kristiansen, a grandson of the company's founder and its chief executive for twenty-five years.

My trip around LEGO world also took me to FIRST LEGO League competitions in the United States and Switzerland, where I watched my son's teams compete against hundreds of other kids in frenzied robotics tournaments. In Fort Lee, New Jersey, I followed a team of LEGO designers and anthropologists as they tested their ideas for the next generation of kits with the world's most fickle, demanding consumers—nine- and ten-year-old boys. In a suburb of Chicago, Illinois, I met Adam Reed Tucker, who not only built a replica of architect Frank Lloyd Wright's iconic Fallingwater house entirely out of bricks, but transformed the replica into a kit and commercialized it through LEGO. In West Lafayette, Indiana, I met Steve Hassenplug, one of the greatest Mindstorms builders on the planet. And I traveled to Boulder, Colorado, where I met with some of the best game programmers and designers in the United States, who turned millions of lines of software code into the virtual worlds that constituted LEGO Universe.

At every turn, the company's leaders, employees, partners, and fans were remarkably candid about the mistakes that fueled its downfall, as well as the false starts and dead ends that accompanied its turnaround. Over its eighty-plus years, and particularly during the past decade, the LEGO Group has proven itself to be as resilient as its virtually indestructible bricks and as resourceful as the nine-year-olds who bring them to life.

Along the way I met dozens of LEGO employees, partners, and

fans who were consistently friendly, smart, thoughtful, and generous with their time. I would like to thank Henrik Weis Aalbaek, Henrik Andersen, Tormod Askildsen, Phil Atencio, Erich Bach, Zev Barsky, Jamie Berard, Torsten Bjorn, Karsten Juel Bunch, Steve Canvin, Dan Elggren, Peter Espersen, Greg Farshtey, Helle Friberg, Ulrik Gernow, John Hansen, Mark Hansen, Lena Dixon Hjoland, Søren Holm, Cephas Howard, Niels Sandahl Jakobsen, Birthe Jensen, Jacob Kragh, Kjeld Kirk Kristiansen, Jens Lambak, Allan Steen Larsen, Kim Yde Larson, Soren Torp Laursen, Erik Legernes, Henrik Taudorf Lorenzen, Søren Lund, Phil McCormick, Sine Moller, Jai Mukherjee, Gitte Nipper, Mads Nipper, Henrik Nonnemann, Lars Nyengaard, Jette Orduna, Fleming Østergaard, Lisbeth Pallesen, Niels Milan Pedersen, Christoffer Raundahl, Jan Ryan, John Sahlertz, Ronny Scherer, Poul Schou, Chris Sherland, Mark Stafford, Robert Stecher, Bjarne Tveskov, and Jill Wilfort from LEGO; Jesper Ovesen and Henrik Poulsen from TDC; Howard Roffman from Lucasfilm; Mitch Resnick from the MIT Media Lab; Jonathan Smith and Tom Stone from TT Games; Christian Faber from Advance; Scott Brown, Peter Grundy, and Ryan Seabury from NetDevil; and Peter Eio, Steve Hassenplug, Bill Hoover, Jake McKee, Megan Nerz, Poul Plougmann, Robert Rasmussen, Megan Rothrock, and Adam Reed Tucker.

Per Hjuler and Paal Smith-Meyer, my collaborators on earlier work on the LEGO story, have been invaluable in understanding the culture and practices at LEGO. This book builds on the insights that they provided. Cynthia Day, Duff McDonald, and Michael Watkins offered encouragement and feedback along the way—I am grateful to you all.

Within LEGO, Jan Christensen from the PR group and Jørgen Vig Knudstorp, the CEO, have been unfailingly supportive at every phase in this book's development. Both were always able to find time to help and to answer questions. Without their support this book would not have happened.

Thanks to Mary Choteborsky, my editor at Crown Business. Mary was consistently positive, helpful, and insightful. Her push to bring out the lessons in the LEGO story has made this a substantially better book.

Three final thank-yous. First, to Bill Breen, the writer who helped create this book. Bill participated in most of the interviews and contributed to the development of many of the core ideas in the book; his clear, powerful voice is on every page. A special thank-you also to Carol Franco, my agent and friend. I hope this is only the first book in a longer collaboration. And, finally, to Anne, who had to endure the emotional ups and downs, the financial sacrifices, and the constant absence of her husband. Thanks for all your love and support.

You hold in your hand the result of five years of study and thinking about LEGO. By telling the story of the company's near death, remarkable rebirth, and stunning recent success, I hope you will find examples that will guide you in your efforts to improve your company's innovation. I have tried to pull together the lessons from the company's recent successes and failures so that you can build a better future for yourself and your company, brick by brick.

Brick by Brick

Introduction

When the Bricks Click

BEHOLD THE LEGO BRICK, THAT HARD-EDGED, CANDY-colored bit of plastic that's bedeviled barefoot parents the world over. By itself, a single discrete, modular brick is inanimate, lifeless—or at least dormant. Only the eight little knobs atop the rectangular block and the three hollow tubes underneath hint at its potential.

Snap two of those inert, inorganic blocks together, however, and suddenly you open up a world of nearly infinite possibilities. Just six bricks yield more than 915 million potential combinations. With an unlimited supply, you could build a supercomputer made up of sixty-four Raspberry Pi PCs and a thousand LEGO bricks, a full-size Rolls-Royce aircraft engine (152,000 bricks), a lovingly detailed recreation of the 2012 London Olympics (250,000 bricks), or a life-size two-story house with a working toilet and shower (3.3 million bricks), as others have already done. In the fifty-plus years since it was patented, the little LEGO brick has ignited the imaginations of millions of children and adults—and become a universal building block for catalyzing creativity.

With the possible exception of Apple, arguably no brand sparks as much cultlike devotion as LEGO. Über-nerd Jonathan Gay credits the LEGO brick for helping him invent Flash animation and thereby light up the Web. Google cofounder Larry Page once built a fully functioning inkjet printer out of LEGO bricks; Google managers now use bricks in some of their Mensa-level hiring tests. Maestro clothing designer Eileen Fisher has praised the brick for its capacity to fuel creative play. In his BBC series *Toy Stories*, British TV raconteur James May gushed that the brick embodies "geometry, mathematics, truth."

LEGO lust isn't limited to famous alpha creatives. Thousands of LEGO acolytes come together at conventions that are held every month of the year in cities around the globe. These tribal assemblages range from the mainstream (the Netherlands' LEGO World, which annually pulls in more than seventy-five thousand kids and their families) to the fringe (Munich's LEGO Graffiti Convention, a freak-and-geek-fest of brick-themed street art). The Internet abounds with LEGO gathering places such as LUGNET (aka the LEGO Users Group Network), a global forum for LEGO fans; MOCpages, where builders show off more than 350,000 LEGO "My Own Creations"; Brickshelf, a fan-created site that features close to two million images as well as a thriving market for LEGO kits and pieces; and Brickipedia, a LEGO wiki that encompasses nearly twenty-four thousand pages of reviews and forums. YouTube alone is stuffed with more than nine-hundred thousand clips showcasing over-the-top LEGO creations, with robots that solve Rubik's Cube in mere seconds and a LEGO-based animation of English comedian Eddie Izzard's hilarious send-up of Darth Vader, which has drawn more than nineteen million views.

Along with Coca-Cola and Disney, LEGO has ranked at the top of a Young and Rubicam survey of the world's most recognized brands. In 2007, the Reputation Institute declared LEGO the world's most respected company. In 2010, a wide-ranging survey of more than three thousand adults between the ages of twenty and forty declared the LEGO brick "the most popular toy of all time."

Nearly everyone, it seems, loves LEGO. Or at least, everyone seems to know it. When *Fortune* decreed LEGO the toy of the century, the magazine half joked that with more than two hundred billion bricks scattered across the globe, "it seems safe to assume that at least ten billion are under sofa cushions [and] three billion are inside vacuum cleaners." That number has since tripled, as billions of new pieces pour out of LEGO factories every year (approximately thirty-six billion in 2010 alone). LEGO factories annually churn out bricks at the rate of more than five times the world's population. There are now some eighty LEGO bricks for every man, woman, and child on the planet.

And yet, although most everyone has encountered LEGO, far fewer are familiar with the organization that stands behind it. Wall Street largely ignores the family-owned LEGO Group, which is headquartered in Denmark's hinterlands. Given that LEGO is closely held, the Street's disregard is somewhat understandable. What's more perplexing is that aside from those in the toy industry, a surprising number of business journalists and analysts have paid scant attention to one of the world's most creative companies.

Over a four-year period, from 2009 to 2012, *Fast Company* magazine's annual accounting of the "50 Most Innovative Companies" cited the unimpressive (Microsoft), the unsurprising (Facebook), and the unsung (MITRE), as well as corporations based outside the United States (Samsung, Nissan), but not the makers of the iconic brick. Likewise, the LEGO Group didn't crack the "most innovative" lists at *Bloomberg Businessweek*, *Forbes*, or *MIT Technology Review* for 2010 through 2012.

Why should they—and we—give LEGO and its innovation strategies a closer look?

By any measure, LEGO has been relentlessly innovative for much of its eight decades. First and foremost there was the creation of the brick, which found its way into the hands, heads, and hearts of four hundred million people the world over. And then, year after year, the LEGO Group's idealistic, imaginative approach to play helped it conjure compelling toys that rarely retreated to the back of kids' closets. The company's values and creativity put it in an unmatched position within the toy industry: kids loved the brick because it was fun, and parents loved it because it was educational. That combination helped LEGO amass decades of unbroken sales growth.

But as LEGO approached the end of the twentieth century, changes in kids' lives challenged the brick's primacy. Toyland became a far less forgiving place to do business, as aggressive competitors fought fiercely for the growing legions of kids enamored with video games, MP3 players, and other high-tech wonders. LEGO, largely an analog enterprise, found itself fading in a faster-moving, far more competitive digital world.

To catch up, LEGO rolled out an ambitious growth strategy that was built upon some of the past decade's most widely heralded theories for sparking innovation. It sailed for untapped, "blue-ocean" markets; it concocted "disruptive" innovations; and it opened up its development process to the "wisdom of the crowd." But while those prescriptions for twenty-first-century innovation might have worked wonderfully for other companies, they almost sank LEGO. In 2003, just three years after both *Fortune* magazine and the British Toy Retailers Association had crowned the brick the toy of the century, the

LEGO Group announced the biggest loss in its history. Its extraordinary collapse led many observers to wonder whether LEGO, one of the world's most cherished brands, would survive as an independent enterprise.

Transforming LEGO

In fact, a new leadership team pulled off one of the most successful business transformations in recent memory. One by one, LEGO reinvented those academic prescriptions for innovation, synthesized them into a world-class management system, and reemerged as a powerful, serial innovator. LEGO created the world's first line of buildable action figures, fueled by a riveting story line that played out over a nine-year span. It launched a line that included an "intelligent brick," allowing kids (as well as many skilled adults) to build programmable LEGO robots. In another first, LEGO rolled out a series of board games that could be built, broken apart, and rebuilt.

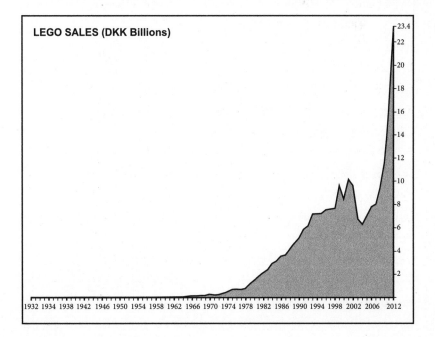

LEGO opened up its development process, enabling legions of fans to go online and post their own customized DIY LEGO sets. And it reimagined its core lines of classic LEGO sets, keeping them real while making them modern enough for twenty-first-century kids.

The result: LEGO emerged from its near-death experience as the world's most profitable and fastest-growing toy company. From 2007 to 2011, all through the worst of the global recession, the LEGO Group's pretax profits quadrupled, far outstripping the titans of the toy industry, Hasbro and Mattel, which were mired in the single digits over the same period. From 2008 to 2010, LEGO grew its profits faster than Apple, despite competing in an industry with few barriers to entry, aggressive global competition, fickle customers, a production cost disadvantage, and no patent protection on its

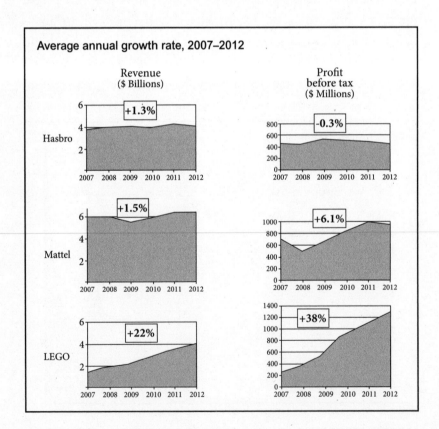

core product—the LEGO brick. LEGO achieved those results not by breaking with business convention but by building within it.

Business literature is rife with examples of daring, rule-busting outfits whose heretical management practices are celebrated for unleashing organic growth. For example, there's Google, where developers are free to devote up to 20 percent of their time to any project of their choosing. There's Gore-Tex maker W. L. Gore, whose boss-free work environment, where almost no one has a title, has helped it produce a profit for more than fifty consecutive years. And then there's the Brazilian manufacturer Semco, whose radical (and often successful) experiments in employee self-management—like those of Google and W. L. Gore—have been studied by legions of consultants and academics.

No doubt these business renegades are inspirational. But their precedent-breaking management systems are not easily transferable. For many companies, building a newfangled innovation model from the ground up—while struggling to nail quarterly performance targets and fend off competitors—is not a viable option.

LEGO is an inspired innovator, but it doesn't operate out on the fringes of business experience. There's no 20 percent time at LEGO, and there are plenty of titles. Having seen how some of the business world's most popular strategies for unleashing innovation almost destroyed their company, the LEGO Group's leaders instead built a clear framework for guiding every kind of innovation effort, from improving today's offerings to inventing tomorrow's markets.

The LEGO system for managing innovation also stands in stark contrast to Apple's (or at least to the way that Apple's is portrayed in the business press). Where Apple's innovation management system was built around the brilliant but often difficult Steve Jobs, with Jobs the final arbiter of when a product was good enough to take to market, the LEGO system is far more decentralized. The Apple model, while inspiring, is hard to follow: find a peerless innovator, promote him to the top of the company, and give him the power to make the big decisions. LEGO CEO Jørgen Vig Knudstorp asserts that he could leave his company for three months and its innovation process would continue unabated; although he was intimately involved in many decisions early in its development, he and other executives designed the process to work smoothly without significant input from him.

This book digs into the LEGO Group's practical approach to everyday innovation and shows how it helps the company's leaders resolve the seemingly irreconcilable trade-offs confronting every organization: How can a company give people the room to innovate while retaining focus? How can it allow autonomy while ensuring accountability? How can it deliver over the short term while building for the long term? Above all, how can it work within the limits of business orthodoxy and still deliver a no-nonsense plan for expansive growth? In other words, how can a company innovate *inside* the box? By deftly managing those tensions, LEGO has consistently created breakout products, even in especially challenging times.

We've also set out to trace the LEGO Group's extraordinary journey—from humble toy maker to a giant on the brink of collapse and back—which offers lessons both salutary and cautionary on the savviest ways to innovate, lead, and win. Along the way, we recount the creation of some of the LEGO Group's most iconic toys and introduce you to the designers and developers who are imagining the next generation of LEGO play experiences.

Additionally, we unveil the stories behind the company's most successful recent launches, as well as the management innovations that gave the toys' creators the freedom and the responsibility to live up to their full potential. And we show how LEGO took the most widely heralded prescriptions for managing innovation, reinvented them, and integrated them into a system that has sent its sales and profits soaring.

By chronicling the LEGO Group's reinvention of innovation, our aim is to help you yoke your organization's disparate innovation efforts into one all-encompassing system. Whether you're leading a start-up, a business unit, or a multinational corporation, we believe the LEGO Group's innovation-management system can help you coordinate the different types of innovation initiatives you take on and work more effectively with your most passionate customers and outside partners. Our goal is to make continuous innovation less of an abnormality and more of the new normal.

Having devoted a few words to describing the book's major themes, we want to offer a few brief thoughts on what the book is *not* about. Although the pages that follow offer many details and take-aways, we have purposely avoided laying out a blueprint for innovation and goading you to follow it. You won't achieve similar results by simply grafting the LEGO Group's innovation system onto your company's operations. And we absolutely don't recommend repeating the toy maker's mistake of waiting until a brush with bankruptcy forces management to embrace deep-seated change. No doubt, when it comes to shaping the future of your team or company, you would rather avoid the wrenching pain of a turnaround and instead blaze your own, trauma-free trail. Our intent is to identify signposts and guide your efforts, not direct them.

Like every LEGO enthusiast, you must bring your own imagination and experience to the game and figure out what's best for you and your company. After all, it's up to each of us to make the bricks click.

Part One

The Seven Truths
of Innovation
and the LEGO
Group's Decline

Stacking Up

The Birth of the Brick

We've got the bricks, you've got the ideas.

—LEGO catalog, 1992

NESTLED AMONG THE FARMLANDS OF DENMARK'S FLAT Jutland Peninsula, the tidy community of Billund, home of the LEGO Group's head offices, is in every sense a town that was built on the brick. Billund, residents say, is "three hours from anything"—a long, exhausting drive through windswept farms to either Copenhagen or Hamburg, the nearest major cities. One in four residents of this isolated hamlet owes his or her livelihood to LEGO. And with each passing hour, the LEGO Group's worldwide reach extends outward from Billund, as another 2.2 million bricks roll off production lines at the company's sprawling network of factories.[1]

Billund itself is a toy town, you might say. The LEGOLAND theme park's castle and towers are the most striking feature of the town's horizon. The neat rows of yellow-brick houses, topped with red-tile roofs, have the symmetry and stolidity of a little LEGO streetscape. So does the brick-inspired lobby of the LEGO Group's headquarters, where gigantic LEGO studs and tubes protrude from the floor and ceiling. In every conference room, there's a clear plastic bowl filled with LEGO bricks. On nearly every desk, there's an array of extravagant LEGO creations. Watching staffers bustle along the neon-red and yellow hallways, it's easy to imagine them as LEGO minifigures, with those sunny skin tones and preternaturally happy faces. If there is such a thing as a factory of fun, it is here, in Billund.

And yet life was no fun and games in the Billund of the 1930s, when LEGO was just a start-up. Back then, the village was little more than a smattering of farm cottages scattered along a railway line, a place where farmers scraped out a hard living from the surrounding moors. In a letter written just after World War I, Billund was dismissed as "a God-forsaken railway stopping point where nothing could possibly thrive."[2] It would be difficult to dispute the writer's claim. The Great Depression had shattered the local economy, which was almost entirely based on agriculture. Photographs from the era show a sparsely populated Billund of humble cottages surrounded by desolate plains.

How, then, did LEGO defy the odds, ascend from a carpenter's small workshop on the Jutland plains, and arrive in almost every playroom the world over? How has it managed to consistently deliver products, year after year and decade after decade, that fire kids' imaginations? How was LEGO "built to last" for most of the twentieth century?

LEGO owes much of its enduring performance to a core set of founding principles that have guided the company at every critical juncture over its eighty-plus years.

First Principle: Values Are Priceless

Every venture, at its inception, is imbued with a core purpose and set of values that emanate from the founder, shape the organization's culture, and largely define its future, for good or ill. Amazon is famous for its "customer obsession" largely because its founder, Jeff Bezos, is hell-bent on making it the "world's most customer-centric company." Google's mission to "organize the world's information" reflects its founders' surroundings—Silicon Valley and Stanford University's School of Engineering—where an outsize pursuit of knowledge is highly valued. And in Bentonville, Arkansas, Walmart

Billund, Denmark, in the 1930s.

founder Sam Walton's frugality and competitive fire continue to define his company's core ethos of "always low prices."

Ole Kirk Christiansen, a master carpenter who founded LEGO in
Billund in 1932, instilled the company's quintessential value in its
name, a combination of the first two letters from two Danish words:
leg godt, or "Play well."* Reasoning that the more desolate the times,
the more parents want to cheer their children, an insight that sustained LEGO through the Great Depression and subsequent global
recessions, Ole Kirk used his carpentry skills to create high-quality
wooden toys—brightly colored yo-yos, pull animals, trucks. And
he framed the company's overriding philosophy, which holds that
"good play" enriches the creative life of a child as well as that child's
later adult life. This philosophy has sustained LEGO for the better
part of a century.

Over the decades, LEGO has refined and reinterpreted its mission: to infuse children with the "joy of building, pride of creation";
to "stimulate children's imagination and creativity"; to "nurture the
child in each of us." But on a fundamental level, the company's goal
has stayed remarkably consistent and is probably best expressed in
its current iteration: "to inspire and develop the builders of tomorrow." This collective desire—to spark kids to pursue ideas through
"hands-on, minds-on" play—can be traced to Ole Kirk's life-altering
decision to devote himself and his business to the development of
children. Looking back on the earliest days of his start-up, he later
wrote, "Not until the day when I said to myself, 'You must make a
choice between carpentry and toys' did I find the real answer."[3]

The LEGO Group's early years were shaped by hardship. Ole Kirk's
wife died the year he founded LEGO, leaving him with four young
sons to raise and a business in the balance. He remarried two years
later and guided his young company through the depredations of
the Great Depression and Germany's occupation of Denmark during World War II. Then, in 1942, a short circuit caused an electri-

---

* Christiansen named the company LEGO in 1934.

cal fire that consumed the LEGO factory, as well as the company's entire inventory and blueprints for new toys. The cumulative effect of so many setbacks nearly overwhelmed Ole Kirk; for a time, he contemplated giving up on his start-up. But out of a sense of obligation to the company's employees, he summoned the will to start over. By 1944, LEGO had a new factory, one that was designed for assembly-line production. The organization's tenaciousness—its capacity to push past obstacles in pursuit of success—can arguably be traced to Ole Kirk's stubborn determination to raise his company out of that fire's ashes.

Today, every person who's hired into the LEGO Group's Billund operations gets a tour of the small brick building, with lions flanking the front steps, where Ole Kirk and his family once lived. There, they learn of another bedrock value that the company's founder bequeathed to his company: the bar-raising principle that "only the best is good enough."

The motto grows out of a story that's entered LEGO lore. Back in the days when LEGO was still producing wooden toys, Ole Kirk's son Godtfred Kirk—who had worked for the company since he was twelve and would eventually run it—boasted that he had saved money by using just two coats of varnish, instead of the usual three, on a batch of toy ducks (see insert photo 1). The deception offended Ole, who instructed the LEGO Group's future chief executive to go back to the train station, retrieve the carton of ducks, and spend the night rectifying his error. The experience inspired Godtfred to later immortalize his father's ideal by carving it onto a wooden plaque. Today, a mural-size photograph of the plaque, which bears the motto *"Det bedste er ikke for godt"*—"Only the best is good enough"—graces the entrance to the cafeteria in the LEGO Group's Billund headquarters. It's a signpost that summons LEGO staffers to exceptional performance.

It's this melding of these two guiding principles—serving the "builders of tomorrow" and creating "only the best"—that separates LEGO from its competitors and helps it stand out in the global marketplace. Today, anyone who doubts the company's commitment to quality need only consider the effort and skill that go into fabricating the nearly indestructible LEGO brick, an object so durable and unforgiving that more than half a million people have "liked" the Facebook page "For Those Who Have Experienced the Pain Caused by Stepping on LEGO!"

Second Principle: Relentless Experimentation Begets Breakthrough Innovation

More often than not, game-changing innovation doesn't come from one all-encompassing, ambitious strategy. It comes from persistent experimentation, which increases the odds that at least one effort will get you to the future first. The business strategist Gary Hamel underlines this notion in *The Future of Management*, where he asserts, "Innovation is always a numbers game: the more of it you do, the better your chances of reaping a fat payoff."[4] LEGO gets this. It possesses enough creativity to place multiple bets on new innovations and enough tenacity to hang tough long enough to collect its winnings.

Even in its start-up years, LEGO restlessly experimented with new ideas, sometimes making big bets on untested technologies. In 1946, LEGO became the first toy manufacturer in Denmark to acquire a plastic injection molding machine, which cost more than twice the previous year's profits. (Family members had to dissuade Ole Kirk, at least temporarily, from buying another.) For a rural Danish carpenter who had spent all of his years working with wood, plastics presented a risky, life-altering challenge. The company's leaders then displayed an uncommon degree of perseverance by spending the better part of the next decade chipping away at a big idea: how to sculpt the LEGO brick.

In a first step, Ole Kirk and Godtfred, who in 1950 was named junior managing director of LEGO, modified British inventor Hilary

A LEGO molding machine from 1947.

Fisher Page's "Self-Locking Building Bricks"—plastic cubes with two rows of four studs, which kids could stack into little houses and other creations—by altering the size of the bricks by 0.1 mm and sharpening the corners. The result was the "Automatic Binding Brick," made out of cellulose acetate, which featured the little studs that top today's LEGO brick but was hollow underneath. Although the "binding" bricks were stackable, they weren't particularly sturdy once stacked. A child could layer the bricks into a wobbly house, but it took just a poke to crash the creation. Thus, retailers returned many Automatic Binding Brick sets unsold to LEGO. It didn't help that after a visit to the LEGO Group's Billund factory, the Danish toy-trade magazine *Legetøjs-Tidende* declared, "Plastics will never take the place of good, solid wooden toys." Despite consumers' low regard of plastic toys and some retailers' outright criticism, the Christiansens persevered.

Over the next decade, Godtfred continued to tinker with his "LEGO Mursten" (LEGO bricks). But the bricks still had problems bonding and often suffered from the "spring effect"—when you snapped two bricks together, they'd bind for a short time but then pop apart. Although LEGO continued to manufacture sets of bricks, they sold poorly, at most accounting for 5 to 7 percent of the company's total sales in the early 1950s.

It took years of failed experiments before Godtfred hit on the stud-and-tube coupling system, where the knobs that top one brick fit between the round hollow tubes and side walls underneath another brick. The tight tolerances and flexible properties of the modern brick, which is made from acrylonitrile butadiene styrene (ABS), allowed the studs and tubes to remain connected through friction. That design, patented in Copenhagen on January 28, 1958, delivered what LEGO continues to call "clutch power." When a child snaps two bricks together, they stick with a satisfying *click*. And they stay stuck until the child uncouples them with a gratifying tug. And therein lies the LEGO brick's magic. Because bricks resist coming apart, kids could build from the bottom up, making their creations as simple or as complicated as they wanted.

Born out of a seemingly unending series of experiments more than half a century ago, it is clutch power that makes LEGO such an endlessly expandable toy, one that lets kids build whatever they imagine. And it is the brick that became the physical manifestation of an entire philosophy about learning through play.

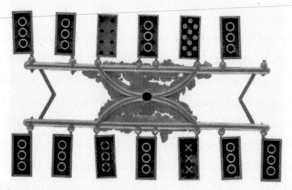

Early LEGO brick prototypes. Notice that the company experimented with different configurations to find the right "clutch power."

Although the brick was a breakthrough, it grew out of a long, hard slog. Godtfred's single-minded pursuit of a far-off goal in the face of adversity is a testament to his persistence, which is too often undervalued in business. Slow, inch-by-inch progress lacks the dramatic gratification that comes with a quick hit. But in the LEGO Group's case, it produced a winner.

In the years to come, tenacity and experimentation would continue to be prime ingredients in the company's recipe for innovation, as the company displayed an uncommon willingness to endure setbacks while testing promising ideas. Best-selling product lines such as Bionicle, LEGO Games, and the LEGO *Star Wars* video game series were each preceded by years of experiments that failed to pan out. Yet never was the LEGO Group's perseverance and determination rewarded quite so spectacularly as it was with the invention of the "real" (as Godtfred called it) brick, which would prove to be one of the toy industry's greatest innovations.

Third Principle: Not a Product but a System

The LEGO Group's breakaway success grew out of its ability to see where the toy world was heading and get there first. The company's first farsighted move came when it bet on plastic toys and the future of the brick. The second came when LEGO had the insight that it must evolve from producing stand-alone toys to creating an entire system of play, with the brick as the unifying element.

Long before the first computer software programs were patented, LEGO made the brick backward compatible, so that a newly manufactured brick could connect with an original 1958 brick. Thanks to backward compatibility, kids could integrate LEGO model buildings from one kit with LEGO model cars, light pylons, traffic signs, train tracks, and more from other kits. No matter what the toy, every brick clicked with every other brick, which meant every LEGO kit was expandable. Thus, the LEGO universe grew with the launch of each new toy. An early publicity campaign summed up the company's capacity for endless play (and limitless sales) thusly: "You can go on and on, building and building. You never get tired of LEGO." Decades before the rise of "value webs" and Apple's "brand ecosystem" of i-centered offerings, LEGO took a holistic view of its product family, with the ubiquitous brick as the touchstone.

The notion of a LEGO system of play came to Godtfred during a January 1954 trip to the London Toy Fair. Ole Kirk's health was declining, and Godtfred began to oversee more of the company's day-to-day management. On the ferry crossing the North Sea, he met up with a toy buyer from Magasin du Nord, the largest department store in Copenhagen. The buyer lamented that instead of delivering the one-off products that so dominated the market, toy makers should focus on developing a cohesive system where sets of toys were interrelated. Such a system would generate repeat sales. The suggestion stuck with Godtfred. After returning home, he spent several weeks working out the attributes that might define a viable system. He eventually identified six features, which he called the company's "Principles of Play" and issued to every LEGO employee:

1. Limited in size without setting limitations for imagination

2. Affordable

3. Simple, durable, and offer rich variations

4. For girls, for boys, fun for every age

5. A classic among toys, without the need of renewal

6. Easy to distribute.*

Using these principles as a benchmark, Godtfred then reviewed the company's wide-ranging portfolio of more than two hundred wooden and plastic products. He decided the LEGO brick came the

---

* There are several versions of the principles, which Godtfred revised over the years. This one is the most concise.

closest to conforming to all six attributes and represented the best opportunity for evolving a true system of play, one that would lend itself to mass production and massive sales.

Along with a small group of skilled designers, Godtfred spent the next year organizing the LEGO Mursten sets around a single, integrated town theme. The revised sets allowed children to create the homes and buildings that had long been featured in LEGO catalogs. The sets also let kids embellish the streetscapes—and thereby discover additional play potential—through a new array of vehicles, trees, bushes, and street signs. The great virtue of the LEGO System was its elasticity. That is, a parent could purchase a kit and then, at the kids' behest, accessorize it with any number of additional sets. Indeed, LEGO even came out with supplementary "parts packs" for just that purpose. Consisting of just one or two specialized pieces and fewer than fifty bricks, the packs were designed to be inexpensive, impulse add-ons for existing sets.

In a 1955 note to the company's sales agents, Godtfred highlighted the philosophy that continues to animate the LEGO System: "Our idea has been to create a toy that prepares the child for life, appealing to its imagination and developing the creative urge and joy of creation that are the driving force in every human being."

Despite Godtfred's lofty ambition for the set, the LEGO System i Leg (System of Play) was launched at the Nuremberg Toy Fair in February 1955 to decidedly mixed reviews. Commented one buyer: "The product has nothing at all to offer the German toy market." (Today, Germany ranks as one of the LEGO Group's leading markets in percapita sales, outpacing even the United States.) But the buyer from Magasin du Nord, who had suggested the systems idea to Godtfred some thirteen months earlier, was so taken with the set that he arranged a lavish ground-floor display for its Danish launch.

The launch took off, as System i Leg's early success in Denmark and its expansion into Germany nearly doubled sales in 1957 and again in 1958. More important, the set's promise pushed Godtfred to continue experimenting and eventually develop the modern brick with its stud-and-tube coupling, which quite literally made the System click. With the brick now conforming to Ole Kirk's exacting, "only the best" standard and the System of Play firmly established, LEGO quickly expanded its town- and street-themed sets, which included a gas station, car showroom, and fire station (see insert photo 2). Indeed, LEGO had hit on a virtuous cycle: as the System evolved and, in the years to come, took in new themes such as castles, space, trains, pirates, and much, much more, kids' capacity for "unlimited play" grew with it. The LEGO brick's promise was both infinite and irresistible: the more you buy, the more you can build.

Fourth Principle: Tighter Focus Leads to More Profitable Innovation

When Godtfred bet on the brick, he opted out of producing wooden toys. Dropping the toys that accounted for 90 percent of the company's product assortment could not have been an easy decision. But Godtfred believed that too many options could overwhelm a nascent effort to create a new kind of play experience—that, in fact, less can be more. Channeling his company's limited resources in just one area, the plastic brick, could lead to more and more profitable products getting to market. Freed from the distraction of having to create new kinds of wooden toys, designers could pour all of their talents into imagining new play opportunities for the brick.

The notion that a company should focus its resources on a clearly defined core business runs counter to much of the prevailing thinking about innovation, which holds that talented associates should have a broad canvas for creativity and be allowed to search for "blue-ocean" markets or develop "disruptive" technologies (themes we'll return to later). But Godtfred found that the LEGO System was flexible enough to allow a great deal of innovation within a very tight set of constraints. To him, every LEGO designer's idea was in scope, so long as that idea was built on the brick and conformed to the System of Play. In the years that followed, as designers improved their ability to extend the brick's DNA, they went on to create a dizzying array of profit-generating products, from DUPLO bricks for preschoolers and Technic rods and beams for advanced builders to the Mindstorms programmable brick and beyond. But all of those breakthrough products came from innovating "inside the brick." By strictly defining the boundaries of the company's core business, Godtfred gave his designers the chance to develop a set of world-beating competencies in *brick-based* creativity, which LEGO leveraged for years to come. "Less is more" is a principle that many companies forget—and which LEGO itself would forget at the end of the century.

Having bet on the brick, Godtfred continued to channel the company's efforts into a set of brightly defined boundaries. To protect the System's integrity, he limited the range of different shapes and colors of bricks that LEGO produced.* Seeking to ensure that every LEGO set was compatible with all other LEGO sets, the company's chief executive personally vetted every proposal for a new LEGO element.† Rejecting many more ideas than he accepted, Godtfred kept the number of different LEGO shapes and colors in check during the first twenty years of the brick's existence. His laserlike focus on doing just a few things extraordinarily well—such as designing solely for the brick—foreshadowed a key leadership lesson from another serial innovator, Steve Jobs, who famously quipped, "Innovation is saying no to a thousand things."[5] Knowing what to leave out—even when it's really good—can sometimes deliver far better results. Take, for example, the LEGO Universal Building Set of 1977. The set consisted of just a few dozen shapes in only seven colors. Even so, its simplicity and utility made it a bestseller.

Godtfred's stringent control over the range of different LEGO pieces forced designers to create within a limited palette of options.

---

* The original colors for the LEGO brick—the bright yellow, red, and blue—were sourced from the Dutch Modernist painter Piet Mondrian.

† A LEGO "element" is defined as a unique shape and color combination. A red 2×4 brick is an element; so too is a yellow 2×4 brick.

Although it might be counterintuitive, those luminous boundaries helped designers home in on what mattered, which in turn catalyzed their creativity. The 1975 catalog, for example, featured an impressive array of different toys, including an antique Renault car, as well as a helicopter, a Formula One racer, a family of three (with two dogs), a windmill, a Wild West town, a hospital, a train (with tanker, passenger car, and mobile crane), and a train station, all made from the same limited set of shapes and just nine different colors.

Betting on the brick was a risky strategy, as it made LEGO a one-toy company. The LEGO Group's many competitors only amplified Godtfred's eggs-in-one-basket gamble. By the mid- to late 1950s, there were dozens of manufacturers of architectural toys, including Minibrix (rubberized, interlocking bricks), Lincoln Logs (notched wooden logs), and Erector sets (small metal beams). For a time, each of those brands was a bestseller. But none amounted to an entire system of play. And so they faded. Only Godtfred grasped the potential of a tightly focused, endlessly expandable, and fully integrated system that was built around the brick.

Fifth Principle: Make It Authentic

At first blush, it's difficult to see how a universe composed of brightly colored chunks of ABS, the indestructible plastic that's used to manufacture LEGO bricks, can in any way be construed as authentic. After all, the inert plastic brick, as well as the miniature boats, cranes, doors, electric motors, flags, garages, hinges, hooks, and thousands of other elements that span the alphabet from Aqua Raiders to Znaps (a kind of beam), are the materials by which a child fabricates a fantasy LEGO world. It's a synthetic world of plasticized ninjas, dragons, the lost city of Atlantis, skeletons, treasure hunters, and a head-spinning array of other unnatural creations. And yet, for LEGO the appeal of what's real is, well, very real.

LEGO long ago figured out that kids' fantasy lives grow out of their real lives. That in fact, the everyday world that children observe is the feedstock for their imaginations. Well before the advent of the modern brick, one of Ole Kirk's top-selling toys was the plastic, life-like 781 Ferguson Traktor, modeled on the Massey-Fergusons found on many a postwar European farm. The logic was inescapable: if Dad's got a tractor, the child should have one, too—as well as miniature hoes, cultivators, and other implements that could be attached to the toy. Today, a quick trip through YouTube reveals more than a few clips, posted by grown-up LEGO devotees, of remote-controlled mini Massey-Fergusons custom-built out of bricks.

In the mid- to late 1950s, LEGO continued to make it real by producing a series of mini metal and plastic trucks that lovingly replicated such European auto models as Citroën, Mercedes, and Opel. The first sets to present the modern brick offered town and city features that were familiar to any suburban kid: a fire station, a church, even a VW car showroom and an Esso gas station (see insert photo 2). These and later kits reveled in the promise of one of the company's 1960s ad campaigns, which proclaimed that whatever you built with LEGO bricks, it's always "real as real."

In an increasingly shiny, fabricated world of concocted experiences, we hunger for the authentic. Kids as well as adults gravitate toward experiences that they sense are true and genuine. LEGO gets this. Even when LEGO ventures into a fictional universe that's "far, far away," as it does with its *Star Wars* sets, the effort is rooted in the real. When all of the kit's 274 pieces are fully assembled, a LEGO X-wing Fighter, to cite just one example from the *Star Wars* milieu, strikingly mirrors the real deal.

The word *authentic* is derived from the Greek *authentikós,* which means "original." And as we've seen, LEGO has cooked up its own recipe for originality. The LEGO brick is the first creation of its kind. The LEGO System of Play is unlike anything in the toy world. If you Google "fake LEGO," you'll get more than sixteen million results, a testament to the System's originality. LEGO is so genuine, it's spawned a universe of imitators and outright counterfeits. As LEGO demonstrates with product lines offering exotic worlds that are entirely fictional, such as Bionicle and Power Miners, what's authentic is not always "real." What *are* real are the connections that kids and kids-at-heart forge, with one another and with LEGO itself, when they make the bricks click. For many adult fans of LEGO, classic toys such as the Yellow Castle and Space Cruiser, which were unveiled in the late 1970s, summon powerful childhood memories and no doubt draw them to new LEGO offerings for *their* children. It's the primal, human-to-human relationships that LEGO fosters—through play, the Internet, fan events, and more—that have helped the brick endure for more than eight decades.

Sixth Principle: First the Stores, Then the Kids

When you walk around the LEGO headquarters in Billund, the company's respect for children is much in evidence. Flag-size banners of kids at play ring the company's design and development studio, where extravagant brick creations litter almost every desk. The company's slogans have included lines such as "Children are our role models" and "We believe in nurturing the child in every one of us." Such sayings can come off as more than a little cheesy. But the company's appreciation for children is as important a corporate asset as the brick itself. Because LEGO is a buildable toy that ignites the imagination solely through construction, it depends on kids even more than other toy outfits. Designers and developers understand that even their simplest toy, such as the stripped-down box of basic bricks, requires a child's hands and mind to bring the kit to life. So it's surprising to find that while kids are vital to LEGO, much of the company's attention goes to another constituency.

Although the LEGO Group's guiding mission is to develop children through play, it's the stores, not the kids, who rank first among the company's priorities. It was hardly a coincidence that a retailer—the buyer from Magasin du Nord—inspired Godtfred to concoct one of the company's foremost innovations, its System of Play. From the outset, Ole Kirk and Godtfred strove to build tight ties with the buyers who stocked LEGO toys. The LEGO Group's leaders knew that to connect with the kids, they first had to align with the stores.

The imperative that led LEGO to build close, personal ties with retailers was ingrained during the spring and summer of 1951. That year, the company's sales representatives told Ole Kirk there wouldn't be any new orders until retailers placed their Christmas purchases after the summer holidays. Out of concern that the company couldn't afford to manufacture toys that would be stockpiled for months, Ole Kirk decided to shut down the factory for the summer.

Godtfred, however, believed it would be a devastating mistake to suspend operations. Along with his wife, Edith, he drove to every toy buyer in southern Jutland and scored enough orders to keep the factory running through summer. The trip was so successful, he repeated it in other parts of Denmark. Before the year was out, Godtfred had personally visited nearly every buyer in the country.

LEGO expanded its network of retailers throughout the 1950s and '60s, moving into western Europe and the United States and collaborating with buyers to create eye-catching store displays. The company's 1963 catalog shows an impressive array of in-store materials available to retailers: a calendar, stand-alone racks of toys, hanging signs, lighted window displays, wall posters, display models, and even short movies designed to run in theaters before the main feature. From the outset, LEGO understood that winning repeat sales depended on appealing to the kids, but winning the first sale depended on supporting the retailers.

An aspirational mission. Relentless experimentation. Systems thinking. Discipline and focus. The appeal of the real. Inspiring the customer, prioritizing the retailer. By leveraging these six principles,

LEGO store displays from the company's 1963 retailer catalog.

LEGO embarked on a growth curve that extended its reach—throughout western Europe and on into the United States, Asia, Australia, and South America—and expanded its range of game-changing products, all through the 1960s. Among the highlights:

- In 1961, the company's bricksmiths invented the wheel, a simple round brick encircled with a rubber tire, with a bearing that was innovative enough to justify a patent application. Today, LEGO produces some three hundred million tires per year, more than Goodyear or Bridgestone.

- In 1967, LEGO unveiled DUPLO, a line of bigger bricks for preschoolers' little hands. Derived from the Latin word *duplus*, "double," DUPLO proved to be an irresistible gateway brick for LEGO. Because LEGO bricks clicked with the bigger DUPLO bricks, kids could graduate to LEGO when they outgrew DUPLO.

- In 1968, the first LEGOLAND theme park, in Billund, opened its gates. Featuring over-the-top attractions—such as the remarkably realistic, thirty-six-foot-tall Chief Sitting Bull, which required more than 1.75 million bricks—Billund's LEGO-LAND still pulls in close to 1.5 million visitors a year.

By the early 1970s, the LEGO Group employed one thousand staffers at its Billund headquarters and was responsible for nearly 1 percent of Denmark's industrial exports. But then its growth curve plateaued. The product lineup had grown a bit stale, make-or-break Christmas sales were dramatically dropping, and the company's direction had begun to drift, as Godtfred was not yet ready to cede leadership to his son, Kjeld Kirk Kristiansen. "Everything was put on hold for some years," remembered Kristiansen. "It was a period of uncertainty."[6]

No one at LEGO has more brick in the blood than Kristiansen, who grew up with the brick and is a living link to the days when the company's primary products were wooden toys. (Kjeld Kirk's surname was misspelled with a "K" on his birth certificate.) He and his sisters were the LEGO Group's first focus group for testing the brick's appeal; in 1950, his image appeared on the boxes of some of the LEGO Group's earliest plastic sets. Noting his sharp instinct for divining what most appeals to kids, former deputy Poul Plougmann called Kristiansen "the Steve Jobs of LEGO."

In 1979, Kristiansen was just thirty-one when he was appointed president of the company. A quiet, bespectacled man of medium height who frequently pauses to collect his thoughts before he speaks, he shuns the spotlight and shies away from taking any credit for the company's almost supernatural success from the late 1970s through the early 1990s. But it was Kristiansen who built a management organization around the LEGO System of Play and put the company

The only known photo of the three generations of LEGO leaders: Ole Kirk, Godt-fred Kirk, and Kjeld Kirk.

on a fifteen-year growth spurt, an expansion that saw LEGO double in size every five years. As a first step, he devised what he later called a "development model for the company," which sought to give the LEGO Group's designers a vivid sense of direction and consumers a clear choice.

Before expanding the company's offerings, Kristiansen laid the foundations for growth. Under his father, the company's product range had simply been lumped under the brand called LEGO System. Kristiansen set out to build a professional management system by dividing the LEGO Group's product lines into three groups: DUPLO, with its big bricks for the youngest children; LEGO Construction Toys, which took in the basic building sets that were the heart of the LEGO System; and a third category devoted to "other forms of LEGO quality play material" such as Scala, a new line of buildable jewelry for young girls.

"The thought behind [the reorganization] was twofold," he told us. "We wanted to make it much easier for consumers to find the relevant product offering for the child. And we wanted to make it much easier for our development and marketing people to work specifically within their own brand profiles, which in turn made it easier for them to see so many more possibilities."

The result was that a line such as DUPLO became a full-fledged brand in its own right. Relaunched in 1979 with the now famous red rabbit logo, DUPLO grew far beyond bricks to include train sets, DUPLO "people" with movable limbs, doll houses, and licensed characters from the likes of Disney and, later, *Winnie the Pooh* and *Toy Story*.

Kristiansen's second major innovation was to redefine and extend the entire concept of a System of Play. In the mid-1970s, the company had its core LEGO town sets that allowed kids to build full towns with houses, stores, cars, and gas stations. The company also had electric train sets, although the train cars were almost twice the height of the houses in the LEGO towns. In 1974, the company introduced "LEGO family" sets—a granny, mom, dad, and kids with movable arms. At the time, they were one of the company's bestsellers. But the figures measured in at a maximum height of over ten bricks, so big they wouldn't fit in the train sets and towered, like Godzilla, over the houses in a LEGO town. In 1978, working with a

Three sets from the mid-1970s: the LEGO Family, a LEGO train, and a LEGO house. Notice that the family is too large to fit in the train and towers over the house.

team of designers, Kristiansen came out with a revised line of miniature figures that were properly scaled to the System. Two years later, he followed up with a revised line of trains that were scaled to these minifigures.

Originally launched in 1975, the first of Kristiansen's little plastic people lacked arms or faces. The oversight was remedied three years later, when the LEGO minifigures, or "minifigs" as they came to be called, were rendered with a pair of black, unblinking eyes, an indelible smile, and an ultra-yellow skin tone. Ten years later, the Pirates line introduced the first minifigs with facial expressions, as well as hooks for hands and pegs for legs. With that, minifigs morphed into nearly anything that LEGO designers could think of: leering vampires, grimacing weightlifters, blissed-out cheerleaders, even famous fictional characters such as Batman, Yoda, SpongeBob, and many, many more. Because it brought role-playing to LEGO and dramatically animated its kits, the minifig might well be the company's most significant creation, second only to the brick. As of June 2013, more

The first LEGO minifigure, from 1978.

than 4.4 billion minifigs have rolled off the brick maker's production lines, more than the combined human populations of China, India, Europe, and the United States.

Kristiansen's third significant innovation was to push the notion of themed sets to the fore. Although LEGO already featured the Town line, he championed new themes, which added other dimensions to the play experience. "Instead of talking about children moving through age categories, we began to think about different play ideas," he recalled. "We were focused more on children's needs." With basic bricks, kids built whatever they imagined. With themed sets, kids created whatever the theme inspired. The building experience was less creative, but the play experience was more rewarding. The result was two of the company's greatest successes, Castle and Space.

Launched in 1978 with a single kit, the Castle line quickly grew into a medieval world of LEGO crusaders, dragon masters, and royal knights that continues to this day. Space took off the same year, and while it featured such endearing curiosities as putting mini LEGO astronauts in open, unprotected cockpits and giving them carlike steering wheels to direct spacecraft, the line became one of the most expansive themes in the company's history, with more than

The LEGO Castle set #375 from 1977.

two hundred individual sets (see insert photo 3). Equally important, Space and Castle cleared the way for other monstrously successful, homegrown themes such as Pirates and even licensed themes such as LEGO *Star Wars* and LEGO *Harry Potter*.

By melding minifigures with themed sets, Kristiansen created a far more immersive play experience. Kids treated their minifigs as analog avatars, imagining themselves as knights or astronauts as they built entire worlds out of bricks. The combination of storytelling (through themes) and role-playing (through the minifigs) electrified a new generation of kids and sparked a period of dramatic expansion for LEGO. Just consider: it took LEGO forty-six years, from its founding in 1932 until 1978, to hit DKK 1 billion in sales (about $180 million at the time). Over the next decade, the sales chart's slope rocketed upward, increasing fivefold by 1988.

To be sure, LEGO endured some significant failures along the way. Scala, the line of products for young girls, proved a flop and was dropped in 1981. And Fabuland, an ambitious product range aimed at young children and the first LEGO theme to be extended

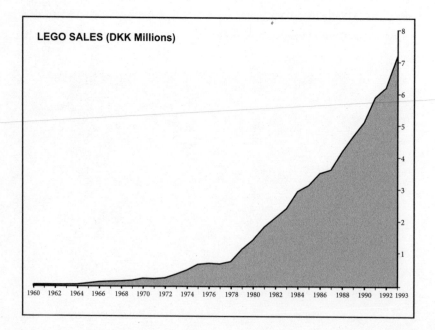

LEGO SALES (DKK Millions)

into books, clothing, and a TV series, never caught on and was killed in 1989, after a ten-year run. Even so, the LEGO Group's growth continued to accelerate. In 1991, LEGO saw an 18 percent jump in sales, at a time when overall toy industry sales rose by just 4 percent. In 1992, LEGO controlled nearly 80 percent of the construction toy market. By the mid-1990s, the small Billund carpentry business had grown into a group of forty-five companies on six continents employing nearly nine thousand people.

The ever-climbing growth in sales made the LEGO Group look great. But as the company entered the 1990s and its sales crested, LEGO began to confuse growth with success. LEGO had expanded its sales effort to target markets around the world—sets were now available to kids from Norway to Brazil—but the company's rapid globalization was not accompanied by sufficient innovation. Meanwhile, technological advances had begun to radically change the nature of play, as VCRs, video games, cable TV, and computers claimed an increasingly larger share of kids' lives. In a 2001 interview with *Fast Company*, Kristiansen conceded that by the mid-1990s, LEGO had become a slow company. "We were a heavy institution," he declared. "We were losing our dynamism, and our fun."[7]

In fact, LEGO, which was on the cusp of being declared the toy of the century, had grown self-satisfied and insular. And that left it flatfooted for its encounter with the rapidly accelerating changes in kids' lives.

2

Boosting Innovation

The LEGO Group's Bold Bid to Keep Pace with a Fast-Forward World

Our goal, for the LEGO brand to be the strongest among families with children, is within our grasp.

—LEGO Annual Accounts, 1999

THE LEGO VP'S ANGRY RETORT HUNG IN THE AIR LIKE acrid cigar smoke: "Over my dead body will LEGO ever introduce *Star Wars*."

It was early 1997, and Peter Eio, chief of the company's operations in the Americas, had just proposed to the LEGO Group's senior management team a collaboration that he'd been working on for months: that the company partner with Lucasfilm Ltd. to bring out a licensed line of LEGO *Star Wars* toys. The line would accompany the first installment of the long-awaited *Star Wars* prequel trilogy, which was coming out in the spring of 1999. Executives at Lucas loved LEGO and had long wanted to partner with the company. Executives in Billund were aghast. Eio had to struggle to keep his composure.

"Normally the Danes are very polite people," recalled Eio. "We never had huge confrontations. But their initial reaction to *Star Wars* was one of shock and horror that we would even suggest such a thing. It wasn't the LEGO way."

Star Wars skeptics had a point. In the four decades since the birth of the brick, LEGO had always gone its own way, eschewing partnerships and licensing agreements. It succeeded at almost every turn. Year after year, the company's master toy makers had unerringly divined what kids wanted next. Wheels, minifigs, trains, themed kits such as Space and Castle—for years, the LEGO Group's ever-expanding range fueled steadily surging sales. For proud, self-sufficient LEGO, the notion that it should license another outfit's intellectual property, even if the partner was an unstoppable hit maker such as Lucasfilm, was repugnant. So was the fact that if LEGO licensed *Star Wars*, it would have to play by Hollywood's rules. "It was almost as if LEGO didn't trust outside partners," said Eio. "The thinking was always, 'We'll do it ourselves. We can do it better.' "

Aside from the go-it-alone culture that pervaded Billund, the biggest obstacle to a Lucasfilm/LEGO licensing deal was the prospect of introducing attack cruisers, assassin droids, and other *Star Wars* armaments into the LEGO Group's milieu. Even today, LEGO continues to embrace one of founder Ole Kirk Christiansen's core values: to never let war seem like child's play. LEGO executives who opposed the deal feared that by aligning the company's squeaky-clean reputation with the *Star Wars* brand, it might well diminish its own. "The very name, *Star Wars*, was anathema to the LEGO concept," Eio asserted. "It was just so horrid to them that we'd even consider linking with a brand that was all about battle."

Despite resistance from LEGO managers, Eio believed that *his* battle—to persuade the company to marry the brick with the Force— was one he had to win. For Eio, the most compelling reason to do a deal with Lucasfilm was the danger of *not* doing one.

From his base at the LEGO Group's North American headquarters in Enfield, Connecticut, Eio was alarmed at how the United States was becoming a license-driven market at a far faster rate than Europe. Hit movies and TV cartoon series were spinning off countless licensed products, from Buzz Lightyear to Transformers, accounting for half of all toys sold in the United States. Heavyweight rivals Hasbro and Mattel were bulking up on licensing pacts with Disney and others, while LEGO hadn't deigned to get into the game. Eio feared that if LEGO didn't tap into the global pop culture phenomenon that was *Star Wars*, the future would catch it out and it would remain a licensing laggard.

Working with Howard Roffman, Lucasfilm's licensing chief, Eio launched an internal campaign to convince the LEGO Group's brain trust that *Star Wars* was more Ivanhoe than G.I. Joe—that despite its sci-fi trappings, the series presented a classic confrontation between good and evil, with little blood and no guts. Eio also suggested a proposal so sensible that no one could assail it: why not ask the parents? And so they did. LEGO surveyed parents in the United States and Germany to learn whether they'd say yes to a marriage between LEGO and *Star Wars*. U.S. parents overwhelmingly backed the idea; surprisingly, so did German parents, who at that time were the company's largest and by far its most conservative market.

Despite the approval of most surveyed parents, some LEGO executives still refused to countenance *Star Wars*. In the end, Kjeld Kirk Kristiansen, who was an ardent *Star Wars* fan and was buoyed by the polling, overruled his tradition-bound executives and gave the deal his imprimatur. And so launched one of the most successful and enduring partnerships in the toy industry's history. Released on the wings of the blockbuster *The Phantom Menace*, LEGO *Star Wars* was a staggering hit, accounting for more than one-sixth of the company's sales.

And yet, even at the very moment that Eio and his allies won the skirmish over *Star Wars*, sweeping changes in its competitive landscape put LEGO in grave peril of losing the wider war. The battle for *Star Wars* would prove to be just the first of several consequential debates that were boiling up within LEGO, as the company confronted

The LEGO *Star Wars* X-Wing Starfighter.

an increasingly disruptive world and a toy industry that was becoming more volatile with each passing year.

For decades, the LEGO Group's proven ability to twine education with imagination and creativity with fun gave it a near monopoly over the market for construction-based toys. Year after year, LEGO sets jumped off the toy shop shelves and the profits poured into the corporate coffers. In the 1990s, however, the brick's fairy-tale story began to lose its luster.

The first challenge to the brick maker's growth streak actually arose in 1988, with the expiration of the last of the LEGO Group's patents for its interlocking brick. After that, any company could produce a plastic brick that was compatible with LEGO bricks, so long as it didn't use the LEGO logo. As a result, the LEGO Group's long-standing monopoly on its stud-and-tube brick quickly fractured, giving rise to competitive anarchy. A throng of upstart, low-cost competitors—Mega Bloks from Canada, Cobi SA from Poland, Oxford Bricks from China, and many more—flooded the market with cheap knockoffs of bricks and minifigs that could snap onto LEGO sets. LEGO punched back with a flurry of lawsuits, arguing that although the patent had expired, the design of the LEGO brick was so ubiquitous, any other company's production of it violated trademark law. In every country where LEGO employed the strategy, it ultimately lost.

A second setback was one of the LEGO Group's own making. In 1993, the toy maker's remarkable fifteen-year stretch of double-digit growth had stalled out. The company's capacity to grow sales and expand into new markets with its long-standing portfolio had seemingly run its natural course. LEGO couldn't sustain double-digit sales increases by making incremental improvements to its existing product lineup. To keep climbing, LEGO had to build a new, powerful set of growth engines.

When sales growth stopped, the toy maker responded by going on a development binge, dramatically boosting the number of products in its portfolio. In theory, that was a good thing: experimentation is the prelude to real progress. By launching lots of products, LEGO was bound to come up with a hit. Problem was, the LEGO Group's once-famous discipline eroded as quickly as its products proliferated. From 1994 to 1998, LEGO tripled the number of new toys it produced, introducing an average of five major new product themes each year. The result was a whole lot of busyness but very little good business. Expensive new product lines such as the Primo line for babies; the Znap line with its new, more flexible plastic; the aforementioned Scala line of Barbie-like dolls; and a CyberMaster robotics kit were all outright failures. Production costs soared but sales plateaued, increasing by a measly 5 percent over four years.

The company's most vexing challenge was to catch up with a world that was rapidly leaving it behind. By the late 1990s, interactive games and kid-centered software gained a mesmerizing grip on great swaths of the brick's core consumers. Addictive games such as Sim City and RollerCoaster Tycoon were wildly adept at replicating a building experience in an online world. And digital special effects made the fantasy worlds of movies come alive like never before. Compared to the razzle-dazzle of Game Boy and Xbox, *Jurassic Park* and Nintendo, the humble brick seemed like a relic from a bygone era.

Equally challenging was the fact that the day-to-day lives of

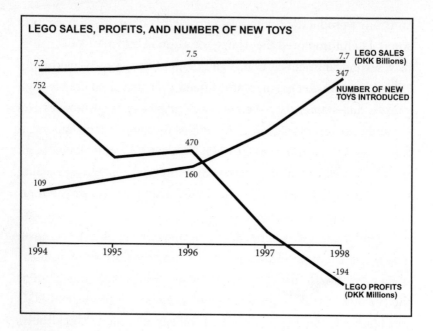

LEGO SALES, PROFITS, AND NUMBER OF NEW TOYS

middle-class children had grown remarkably time-compressed and programmed, leaving far fewer hours for the LEGO style of open-ended, self-guided play. And kids were growing out of traditional toys far faster than they used to. The London *Independent* captured the tenor of the times when it opined in a December 2000 article on LEGO: "Today's instant gratification child does not want to go through the bother of constructing something with several hundred plastic bricks, when a virtual pet comes to life with a stroke of its back."[8]

Those rapidly accelerating forces—a mob of new entrants eager to exploit the LEGO Group's old-guard legacy costs; the revolutionary changes in kids' lives; and an increasingly desperate bid to kick out dozens of new products in the hopes that something, *anything* might goose sales—combined to knock LEGO out of its aerie near the top of the toy industry. In 1998, Billund reported that LEGO had gone $48 million into the red. It was the first loss in the LEGO Group's history, prompting a layoff of more than one thousand people in the first half of 1999, by far the company's largest. Both bitter blows provided further evidence that LEGO was suddenly in a fight for relevance.

LEGO found itself confronting a future-defining challenge: how could its philosophy of free-form, creative play compete in a media-driven entertainment economy where the linear, story-driven experiences of computer games and TV shows reigned supreme?

The LEGO Group's bid to answer that question began with a series of decisive moves. In October 1998, as the losses mounted, Kristiansen brought in Poul Plougmann, a turnaround expert and former chief operating officer of Bang & Olufsen, the Danish maker of high-quality home-electronics equipment, to take over the company's day-to-day management. An avid hunter, art enthusiast, and Francophile who lived with his wife in Paris (he would commute to Billund), Plougmann was a somewhat reclusive executive who shared his thoughts and plans with just a few close confidants. Because he played a lead role in reviving Bang & Olufsen, a Danish national treasure, the Danish press hailed him as a "miracle man" when he arrived at LEGO. In a remarkable concession, Kristiansen stepped aside, though he retained his title as president of the company and renewed his focus on developing toys. In an effort to stanch the bleeding, Plougmann, who was given the title of finance director (he was later promoted to chief operating officer), formulated and initiated the mass layoffs of early 1999. But LEGO was not about to hunker down and retrench. Plougmann was promised a hefty bonus if he doubled the LEGO Group's sales by 2005. He was recruited and incentivized to grow LEGO out of its malaise.

Plougmann joined LEGO at what were arguably among the worst and best moments in its modern history. The company would soon endure its first-ever large-scale downsizing, the discordantly titled Fitness Plan, which resulted in the aforementioned firing of one-tenth of the company's workforce. At the same time, LEGO was just beginning to glimpse the market's lust for LEGO *Star Wars*, whose first year's sales exceeded the company's initial forecast by 500 percent. Emboldened by the stratospheric results of *Star Wars* and the enduring strength of the LEGO brand—which, despite the company's recent travails, was still embraced by more than 70 percent of households with children in Western countries—Plougmann and his team embarked on an ambitious initiative for reigniting growth. The effort was oriented around seven of the business world's most popular strategies for developing new products and services. In fact, they're now so pervasive they've become a kind of gospel: the seven truths of innovation.

Hire diverse and creative people.

Head for blue-ocean markets.

Be customer driven.

Practice disruptive innovation.

Foster open innovation—heed the wisdom of the crowd.

Explore the full spectrum of innovation.

Build an innovation culture.

Many of the business world's best and brightest minds have extolled at least one of these principles for boosting innovation; many of the world's most admired companies have championed them.

- Procter & Gamble *opened up* its innovation efforts through its Connect + Develop initiative, through which it formed more than one thousand successful agreements with top innovators from around the world. At one point, innovators who worked outside P&G's walls contributed to more than half of the company's new product initiatives.

- Quicken and Southwest Airlines redefined their industries largely because they sailed to *blue-ocean markets*, which competitors ignored.

- Canon's digital cameras *disrupted* and all but destroyed the film camera market.

- Apple sustained its chokehold on the MP3 music player market largely because it surrounded the iPod with a *full spectrum of complementary innovations*: the iTunes music service with its game-changing 99¢-per-song business model; its extensive catalog of docks, skins, chargers, and other accessories; and its iconic branding campaign.

Faced with the challenge of doubling the LEGO Group's sales by 2005, Plougmann and his lieutenants refocused the company's developers on the seven truths of innovation and challenged them to surpass such giants as McDonald's and Coca-Cola and become "the world's strongest brand among families with children." Although LEGO never explicitly called these innovation strategies the "seven truths," it pursued them nonetheless.

Here's what LEGO did. In the next chapter, we'll reveal how it all turned out.

Hire diverse and creative people. Modern management strategists have long proclaimed that heterogeneity fuels creativity—company cultures that are marked by a potent mix of varied experiences and work styles yield better ideas, execute those ideas better, and even develop people better. Nicholas Negroponte, founder of the MIT Media Lab, has gone even further, declaring that the surest way to tap into a wellspring of new ideas "is to make sure that each person in your organization is as different as possible from the others. Under these conditions, and only these conditions, will people maintain varied perspectives and demonstrate their knowledge in different ways."[9]

When Plougmann joined LEGO, he found a work culture that was isolated and calcifying—its mostly male, very veteran Danish executives and designers were hamstrung by a lack of urgency and by homogenized thinking. "Product development was in the hands of people who'd been at LEGO for twenty or thirty years," he recalled. "They were so inward looking, they expected that whatever they created would be right for the market." He also concluded the company had hit the limit in terms of the talent it could attract to the LEGO Group's remote, rainy hometown. If LEGO were to reenergize product development and appeal to the world's plethora of ethnic groups and play experiences, it would have to break out of Billund.

In very short order, LEGO lured top talent from beyond Denmark and expanded its links to the outside world. The company purchased Zowie Intertainment, a San Mateo, California–based maker of technology-driven education toys, which gave LEGO a close-up look at new ventures emerging out of Silicon Valley. To build out its gaming and Internet offerings, LEGO hired a development outfit outside London and set up another in New York. It created a toys-for-tots design outpost in Milan. And it strove to scope out new toy trends by establishing a network of LEGO designers located in Tokyo, Barcelona, Munich, and Los Angeles. Instead of trying to bring world-class design talent to Billund, LEGO essentially brought Billund to the talent.

Plougmann injected more fresh thinking into the company's product development group by recruiting a former Bang & Olufsen colleague, an Italian executive named Francesco Ciccolella, to reimagine LEGO toys and remake the LEGO brand. Ciccolella and his brand development team sought nothing less than the total transformation of LEGO from a toy to an idea, declaring that the company "will build businesses wherever our idea can be translated into unique concepts." He also issued the brand statement "Play On," which drew on the English translation of the LEGO name, "play well." No doubt the "Play On" slogan reflected the company's desire to keep kids playing with bricks—and buying bricks—through childhood and beyond. Writing in the new LEGO branding manual, Ciccolella's image makers decreed, "PLAY ON is the ultimate expression of the LEGO brand."

One product line that was not, in Ciccolella's view, an encapsulation of the LEGO brand was DUPLO. In two of the toy maker's largest markets, Germany and the Netherlands, DUPLO was nearly as big a brand as LEGO. But DUPLO was far less of a presence in the United States, where LEGO executives were unnerved by the sudden rise of electronic educational toys from companies such as LeapFrog, which would soon bound past LEGO to (temporarily) become the third-largest toy maker in the toy world's largest market. Recalled veteran DUPLO designer Allan Steen Larsen, "There was a real fear that electronic toys were taking over from physical, traditional toys."

Seeking to build a bigger American beachhead with higher-priced electronic toys, Ciccolella's team played down the DUPLO brand of starter bricks and largely replaced it with a radically different line, dubbed LEGO Explore, which they branded as a "complete discovery system from birth to school age." Featuring creations such as the Explore Music Roller (see insert photo 5), an electronic pull toy that chirped singsongy tunes while a toddler towed it, Ciccolella's design team hid the brick—which would have been unthinkable just a few years earlier—and fashioned a brand of toys whose look and feel were far more akin to Fisher-Price than to LEGO.

The logic behind launching Explore, explained Plougmann, was to "make the single brick less important in the minds of mothers. What mattered was the skill and knowledge that the [Explore] system could bring to their children." Of all the diverse, wide-ranging ideas to come out of the company's new cast of creatives, Explore would prove to be one of the most daring, un-LEGO-like lines that LEGO had ever imagined.

Head for blue-ocean markets. For more than a decade, business thinkers such as W. Chan Kim and Renée Mauborgne, the authors of *Blue Ocean Strategy*, have exhorted companies to push beyond the tactic of making incremental improvements to existing products and instead swim for the open water of untapped market spaces. If red oceans are the crowded, bloodied waters where companies chew each other up for smaller and smaller chunks of market share, blue oceans are vast markets, unsullied by cutthroat competition, where outsize profits await. The LEGO Explore toys were an attempt to discover a blue ocean in the toddler toy market by producing electronic educational toys under the LEGO brand.

In another blue-ocean move, LEGO leaped from toys to education. The company's first foray into the education market actually goes back to 1950, when it created sets of large LEGO bricks for kindergarten classrooms. In the late 1990s, LEGO conceived a strategy of moving from education products to services. The market for after-school education in Japan and South Korea was booming. (A typical South Korean child could attend as many as two or three after-school programs each day.) LEGO bet the market was ripe for an entirely new type of learning experience, with LEGO bricks at its core.

LEGO partnered with a South Korean company, Learning Tool, to develop a series of programs that used bricks and other LEGO elements to teach science, technology, engineering, and math to kids. The idea was to help kids solve problems through hands-on building; one lesson, for example, used LEGO gears to teach ratios. LEGO lent the initiative its brand, helped develop the curriculum, trained personnel, and developed special kits for the LEGO Education Centers. Here was an entirely uncontested market for LEGO. Launched in 2001, the centers got off to a promising start, and within three years South Korea alone featured 140 LEGO Education Centers.

On the product side, LEGO headed for Hollywood. Having hauled in a treasure chest of record sales by licensing *Star Wars* from George Lucas, the LEGO Group's brain trust concluded that another maker of Hollywood blockbusters, Steven Spielberg, could steer it to a new, unbounded blue ocean. But rather than license a hot Spielberg property, LEGO licensed the Spielberg name. It created a product that had never been offered to kids: a buildable "movie studio in a box" for creating LEGO animations. The kit consisted of a collection of minifigs and LEGO pieces for building a movie set; a motion-detecting digital camera in a LEGO casing; and software for editing. Taken together, the awkwardly titled LEGO & Steven Spielberg MovieMaker set (see insert photo 4) gave kids the ability to make movies that captured the play scenes they'd been acting out in their heads.

"There was nothing out there where kids could build their own model and make a movie out of it," asserted John Sahlertz, who led the MovieMaker development team. "It was a completely new category for toys."

In a clever twist on blue-ocean strategy, LEGO aimed not only to stake out uncontested market space with the Spielberg kits but also to entice kids to clamor for more traditional sets such as LEGO Pirates, by using the camera and software from the Spielberg set to make pirate-themed movies. Thus, Spielberg MovieMaker would catalyze sales for LEGO Pirates and other classic lines. If the strategy succeeded, the Spielberg MovieMaker—a category-defining, blue-ocean creation—would clear the water for red-ocean stalwarts such as LEGO Pirates.

Be customer driven. There's hardly a modern business strategist who doesn't contend that successful brand builders are so inquisitive about their customers' lives and so attuned to their desires, they can't help but put the customer's point of view above all else. And LEGO was as good as any company at seeing through the eyes of an inventive seven-year-old boy. But soon after Plougmann's arrival, LEGO sought to grow its sales by appealing to a different customer.

After a team of outside consultants produced surveys showing two-thirds of children in Western households were moving to electronics and discarding traditional toys at an earlier age, Plougmann and his deputies concluded that LEGO should take a decisive turn. Rather than redouble its efforts to become the top toy maker for the smaller slice of kids who loved to build, LEGO opted to pursue the larger population of kids who didn't. The effort's essence would later be captured in Ciccolella's revised brand manual, which shockingly declared that the company's "greatest strength," the LEGO brick, "is our biggest limitation."

As always, LEGO aimed to remain customer driven. But suddenly, an entirely different set of customers—kids who desired a faster form of gratification and were deemed to be less skilled at building with bricks—was doing the driving. "There was a lot of concern that children couldn't build anymore," recalled Niels Milan Pedersen, a longtime LEGO freelance designer. "It was thought that American children, in particular, couldn't build as well as they did in the eighties. We were told the kits had to be very basic."

The LEGO Group's developers knew that simpler sets, by themselves, lacked the magnetism to pull in the media-saturated kids of the late 1990s. But what would? Flush with the success of LEGO *Star Wars*, developers doubled down on the notion that in *Star Wars*, kids were drawn to something that LEGO had never before delivered: a rich, theme-driven world where kids could play out their fantasies. LEGO *Star Wars* and, later, the LEGO Group's line of *Harry Potter*–themed sets put an exclamation point on the notion that in a world where movies, television, and the Internet shape so much of today's play, storytelling matters.

Seeking to combine a compelling narrative with a seamless building experience, a team of LEGO designers set about crafting a character-driven toy line oriented around an easy-to-build action figure. They began by fabricating a set of cube-shaped bricks that could be snapped into a humanoid figure that was 30 percent larger than the minifig. They called their new set Cubic.

"The whole idea was to get it down to where a five-year-old could easily build with it," said Jan Ryan, who led the Cubic design team. "And then we had the idea that he was going to be a kind of hero."

Mindful of the need to create a toy that would kick up a craze among American boys, the Cubic team gave itself a design challenge: what is the LEGO version of a very American toy hero, G.I. Joe? Over many months, they sculpted a set of muscles onto the Cubic figure, outfitted it in a quasi-military flight suit, and gave it a plucky, quintessentially American name, Jack Stone. In this bad-guy-battling boy hero, kids confronted an entirely different kind of LEGO experience—darker and edgier, with a fast-paced story line that had him piloting Res-Q copters and foiling bank robbers. LEGO bet that Jack Stone would attract swarms of new customers who desired kits that were less buildable but more playable. So confident was LEGO of Jack Stone's potential that designers began to suspect the character would do the unthinkable: supplant the iconic minifig.

"They wanted to [replace] the minifig and put in this Jack Stone figure," said Pedersen, who helped design Jack Stone. "We were told from the top that the minifig wasn't considered cool."

The Jack Stone "minifigure" (right) and a classic LEGO minifigure. Unlike the classic minifigure, the Jack Stone figure could not be disassembled.

Practice disruptive innovation. In his book *The Innovator's Dilemma*, Harvard Business School professor Clayton Christensen introduced his theory of disruptive innovation, which he defined as a less pricey product or service, initially designed for less-demanding customers, which catches on and captures its market, displacing the incumbents.[10] Christensen saw how low-quality, low-cost technologies were ramping up faster than ever before. Unburdened by the legacy costs and organizational inertia of more mature competitors, these new technologies quickly replaced established technologies and destroyed the incumbents' core markets. Technologies such as digital photography and computer disk drives started out as low-end alternatives to their pricier counterparts; industry incumbents felt little pressure to respond. But those technologies quickly improved and eventually revolutionized their industries. Believing video game makers such as Nintendo would further roil the markets for traditional toys, LEGO bet that it could do some disrupting of its own with a project called Darwin.

The seeds for Darwin were planted on an autumn day in 1994,

when a Swiss man showed up unexpectedly at the LEGO Group's Billund headquarters and asked to speak to Kjeld Kirk Kristiansen. Clad in knickers, with shoulder-length hair and a beard that flowed down to his chest, the man carried a four-minute video clip featuring computer-generated LEGO spaceships blazing across the heavens. He introduced himself as Dent-de-Lion du Midi, otherwise known as "Dandi" (pronounced "Dondee"). He didn't get to see the LEGO Group's president, but he did talk his way into a meeting with two technicians from the company's audiovisual department.

Dandi showed the two men his clip, whose 3-D modeling far surpassed anything LEGO had in the works. And he presented a plan to transform LEGO bricks into digital bits. He proposed creating a database of high-quality, digitized renderings of the thousands of pieces in the LEGO Group's product portfolio—bricks, wheels, minifigs, rods, gears, and beyond. Once completed, the database would give any LEGO design team the capacity to quickly create digital versions of physical kits, as well as 3-D LEGO cartoons, films, building instructions, television ads, and other marketing collateral. Dandi's presentation was so convincing, he won a meeting with LEGO executives, who concluded that such a database might propel LEGO to the forefront of the market for computer-animated play experiences. In May 1995, Dandi and a small band of software programmers set to work on the Darwin project.

Darwin was a massively ambitious venture that required an enormous start-up investment, both to build the LEGO 3-D database, dubbed L3-D, and develop commercial opportunities for L3-D and digital technology. LEGO recruited alpha software coders and 3-D computer graphics wizards from across Europe and the United States to the Darwin project, which eventually grew to include more than 120 people. And LEGO armed them with the largest installation of Silicon Graphics supercomputers in northern Europe.

Although the task of creating a computerized LEGO construction system was loaded with technological challenges, the Darwin project's risks were somewhat leavened by the fact that software development trends were moving in the LEGO Group's direction. Bjarne Tveskov, who led Darwin's software team, was one among several commentators who noted that the move toward object-oriented programming, where applications could be fashioned out of small, predefined blocks of code, was a lot like building with LEGO. Tveskov recalled how the Darwin team took enormous inspiration from the author Douglas Coupland. In his epistolary novel *Microserfs,* Coupland described LEGO as "a potent three-dimensional modeling tool and a language in itself."[11] Coupland later told a Danish television interviewer that if LEGO played its cards right, it would be the Microsoft of the twenty-first century. (In the 1990s, that was considered a soaring compliment.)

For a time, it seemed as if Coupland's heady prediction had a whiff of truth to it. In 1996, the Darwin team wowed the crowd at SIG-GRAPH, the world's largest computer graphics conference, with a virtual-reality demo of a LEGO-ized version of the gathering's host city, New Orleans. Participants explored a fully immersive, virtual New Orleans made of 3-D LEGO bricks and populated with digitized minifigs. Afterward, an overjoyed group of Darwinites gathered with LEGO execs for dinner. "Kjeld stood up and told us, 'You people are the future of the company,' " remembered Tveskov. "And we totally believed him."

Foster open innovation—heed the wisdom of the crowd. During the first years of the past decade, the heaving growth of massive online communities inspired books such as *Open Innovation, Wikinomics,* and *The Wisdom of Crowds,* which showed how creative companies were harnessing the collective genius of virtual communities to spur innovation and growth. LEGO, a conservative company whose numerous battles over patent infringements had made it hyperprotective of its intellectual property, certainly did not rush into the crowdsourcing craze. But LEGO did take some tentative first steps.

For much of its history, LEGO was a monolith—a massively intractable organization that viewed its fans solely as consumers, never as cocreators. The company's mostly Danish designers believed that when it came to conjuring the next cycle of brick-based construction toys, they were the smartest guys in the room. And who could argue with them? Their creations, from the minifig to battery-powered trains to enduring themes such as Space and Castle, had fueled the LEGO Group's double-digit growth for the better part of two decades.

By the mid-1990s, however, the Internet gave rise to fan-created sites such as LUGNET.com, which let LEGO enthusiasts from around the globe chat, link to one another's personal sites, and even inventory all of the pieces and sets LEGO had ever made. Most tellingly, such sites let fans share online photos and videos of their strikingly clever "MOCs," otherwise known as "My Own Creations," which offered tangible evidence that not even the LEGO Group's most talented designers could consistently outinnovate the millions of LEGO fanatics from across the globe. The creative output of its sprawling, online community of independent brick masters convinced LEGO to give crowdsourcing a modest test.

In mid-2000, LEGO commissioned a software development outfit to begin work on the LEGO Digital Designer, a computer-aided design program that let enthusiasts build their own dream models using virtual 3-D bricks (see insert photo 6). The company's strategy was to let fans use the Designer software (which was based on the Darwin project's technology) to create virtual models and upload them to a LEGO website, which would eventually come to be called LEGO Factory. LEGO would then manufacture the custom-designed, physical sets and ship them to consumers. Thus, LEGO enabled people to create their own kits—designing them, shaping them—according to their own individual desires. If other fans liked the custom-designed sets, they too could order them.

An early exemplar of this strategy was the LEGO Blacksmith Shop, created by a fan named Daniel Siskind. A designer living in Minneapolis, Siskind had launched Brickmania.com, an independent site offering brick-based kits that sometimes featured subjects such as

modern warfare, a popular theme with some fans and decidedly un-
popular back in Billund. But Siskind also created and marketed kits
based on train and castle themes, which very much fell within the
LEGO Group's wheelhouse. Siskind's first kit for Brickmania was a
medieval blacksmith shop; it sold so well that that in 2003, LEGO
took notice and licensed the set from Siskind. Consisting of 622
pieces, set 3739 retailed for $39.99. It was the first fan-designed set
that LEGO launched. With that, LEGO began to open up to its most
creative fans. The monolith had cracked.

Explore the full spectrum of innovation. For more than a decade,
innovation strategists such as Northwestern University business
school professor Mohanbir Sawhney and consultancies such as
Chicago-based Doblin have challenged business leaders to shake off
their myopic pursuit of conventional notions of innovation, which
too often was confined to product development and traditional R&D,
and open their eyes to a far more panoramic view. To reap outsize
profits in highly competitive markets, companies must pursue *all*
opportunities to create new revenue streams by introducing clusters
of complementary innovations. By itself, a new product is easy to
copy. But a full-spectrum approach to innovation, where a family of
complementary products with new pricing plans is offered through
new channels, is hard to beat.[12]

The LEGO Group's embrace of full-spectrum innovation dates
back to 1999. As part of an unrestrained effort to stretch out and
reimagine the LEGO play experience, the company's design leaders
gave a concept development team an almost heretical assignment:
create an entire building system that omits the brick.

After several months of brainstorming ideas, the team came
up with a building system where kids could snap together exotic
plastic parts to create weird fantasy creatures, such as a caterpillar
with webbed feet and an alien's head. The system allowed for a very
LEGO-like, free-form style of play. Kits came without instructions,
harking back to the days of classic LEGO. Parts from one kit could

seamlessly connect with parts from another kit, just like bricks. Except for one thing: there was no LEGO brick. The kit was made up of wholly original, snap-together pieces that eschewed the LEGO stud-and-tube coupling system. The team called the concept LEGO Beings. The idea was too outlandish to be commercialized, but it did give design leads tangible evidence that they could break out of the LEGO System of Play. What's more, LEGO Beings became the genesis of one of the LEGO Group's biggest bets of the new century.

Just when the concept design team was developing LEGO Beings, a new mania for action figures was breaking across Europe and America, led by Hasbro's Action Man, a modern adventurer who battled archenemies. The LEGO Group's toy makers moved to capitalize on the craze by creating an action figure of their own, which took inspiration from LEGO Beings. A newly established product development team compiled a one-hundred-page research report on the action figure category and recruited the former head of action figure development for Hasbro to guide the LEGO Group's foray into the market. After months of experiments, the team conjured a generic, organic building platform—like the one that was created for LEGO Beings—and used it to imagine a cast of kid-magnet characters.

"The driving force behind the action figure category, more than anything, is about triggering boys' imaginations through role-play," said Jacob Kragh, who led the new toy's development effort. "And role-play, more than anything, is about having strong characters."

Kragh's team dubbed the new line Galidor, a cool-sounding, nonsensical word, which they hoped would resonate powerfully with nine-year-olds. Galidor featured archetypal, kid-friendly characters from the sci-fi genre—a pair of teenage heroes, sinister but unscary villains, and a sidekick robot—that consisted of a dozen-something parts that kids could connect via pins and holes instead of studs and tubes. To boost the line's chances of becoming a runaway hit, LEGO followed a marketing script that offered a striking departure from the toy industry status quo. Instead of promoting the toy by tying it to an established TV series, LEGO hired Hollywood producer

Thomas Lynch to create its own TV series, *Galidor: Defenders of the Outer Dimension*, which tied into the toy.

"The idea was to use the TV show to build awareness for [the toy]," said Kragh. "As ratings for the TV show increased, toy sales would follow."

Galidor marked the LEGO Group's most ambitious attempt to explore the full spectrum of innovation. From a new-product perspective, Galidor was an entirely new kind of building system that brought LEGO into a new toy category. From a customer-experience perspective, the TV show, as well as a video game and DVD, paved new avenues for interacting with Galidor. From a value-creation perspective, the TV show and video games let LEGO discover untapped revenue streams and recapture the value the line created. And from a delivery perspective, the company's plan to package Galidor characters in McDonald's Happy Meals was a clever way to connect with American kids (especially those kids who had previously ignored LEGO) as well as open up yet another source of revenue. (Insert photo 7 shows some of these Galidor products.)

"We wanted to make sure we created new growth streams and more adjacent parts to the core product," said Kragh. "And then, when we started to incorporate the ambitions we had on the media side with the TV show, our executive team became incredibly enthusiastic about Galidor."

When it came to taking a 360-degree view of innovation, LEGO didn't bind itself solely to new product themes. As part of the bid to make LEGO "the world's strongest brand among families with children," Plougmann and Kristiansen launched an ambitious drive to expand LEGOLAND theme parks and LEGO-branded stores. The company's original, flagship LEGOLAND in Billund attracted more than a million and a half visitors every year. Its success led the LEGO Group to launch a second LEGOLAND, outside London, in 1996. Hoping to introduce millions more youngsters to the brand and drive even more demand for the brick, Plougmann accelerated the push into theme parks, launching LEGOLAND California near

San Diego in 1999 and LEGOLAND Deutschland outside Munich in 2002 (see insert photo 8).

As for the LEGO store idea, it was not unprecedented. The company had earlier created LEGO Imagination Centers at the Mall of America in Minneapolis and Disney World in Orlando, which connected kids to the brick in an interactive, playful retail atmosphere and promoted the LEGO brand to more than twenty million people a year. With an eye toward creating millions more emotional attachments to the brand, Plougmann promised to launch three hundred additional LEGO stores.

"We couldn't have a dialogue with an American mother if we always forced her to the shelves at Walmart," Plougmann explained. "We needed to bring her into LEGO's world. And that would be through LEGO-branded stores. Along with the LEGOLAND parks, stores would be our brand builders."

Build an innovation culture. In just a few short years, Plougmann and his team put innovation at the top of their management agenda and drove it throughout the company. Having awakened to the toy industry's dramatically accelerating pace of change, they recruited the very best design talents and positioned them in some of the world's most creative hotspots. Having been challenged by the revolutionary transformations in kids' lives, they pushed designers and developers to think beyond LEGO and imagine play experiences that diminished and even eliminated the brick. They cracked the company's insular culture by taking the first steps toward opening up the development process to outside contributors. They put a premium on audacity and nonconformity, daring to scuttle a beloved but tiring brand such as DUPLO and replace it with something entirely new. Again and again, they upended the LEGO status quo.

What's more, the LEGO Group's executive team built a culture within the company that valued and celebrated creativity above all else. Management encouraged people in every part of the organization to think outside the proverbial box and it rewarded those who

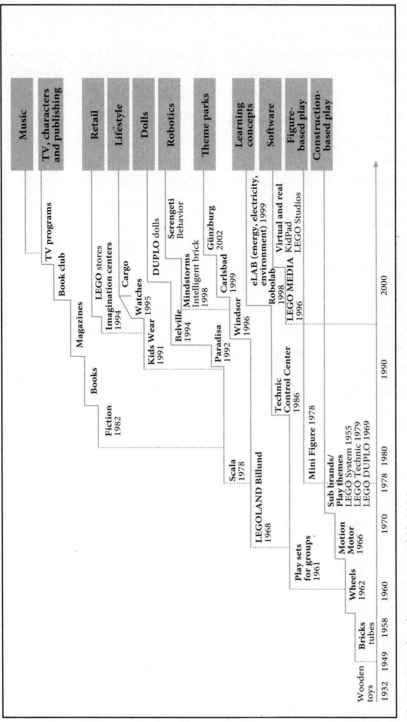

The LEGO product-line structure, 1932–2000.

did. As a result, LEGO became a freewheeling creative machine, spinning off one big idea after another.

From the birth of the brick until the early 1990s, LEGO innovated around two core areas: construction-based play with the LEGO System and figure-based play with the minifig. And then, in the late 1990s and early 2000s, Plougmann and his deputies pushed LEGO from its core into every conceivable new market—just as he was hired to do. LEGO pursued new channels, new customer segments, new businesses, and entirely new categories of products. It ventured into software with Darwin and LEGO MovieMaker. It launched the new generation of theme parks. It moved into retail with LEGO stores. And it entered the publishing arena with its TV series, DVDs, and video games.

LEGO heeded the proclamations of management strategists and adopted the seven truths of innovation. For a time, the strategy worked. Despite the de-scaling effects of digitization and a horde of new, low-cost competitors that fueled the toy industry's volatility, the LEGO Group's sales increased by 17 percent from 2000 to 2002. Looking ahead, senior management remained cautiously optimistic that LEGO would continue to outinnovate its competitors. Kristiansen and Plougmann declared in the company's 2002 annual report that it had been a "good year." As for the next year, they predicted that "thanks to its broad product range," the company could "look forward to a largely unchanged result and turnover in 2003."

As it turned out, that was wishful thinking. For a company that was struggling to catch up with a world that was passing it by, there was an inherent logic in the LEGO Group's pursuit of the seven truths. But LEGO had placed a lot of big bets in just a few short years. The company was trying to expand on so many fronts, it was in danger of losing its focus and discipline. If just a couple of those bets went bad, all of the LEGO Group might come crashing down.

Losing Control

The Scattered Remains of
Runaway Innovation

We are on a burning platform.

—Jørgen Vig Knudstorp, June 2003 memo to
 the LEGO Group's board of directors

IN THE EARLY MONTHS OF 2003, THE LEGO EMPIRE BEGAN TO crack. The previous year had started out strong, with the company on track to realize roughly 10 percent growth, largely due to the jaw-dropping success of the LEGO *Star Wars* and *Harry Potter* themed sets. In fact, some felt the company, for the first time since 1993, would exceed a profit of DKK 1 billion ($150 million). But as 2002 neared its end, the LEGO Group's sales rapidly lost altitude. Christmas sales sank well below the company's internal forecast. By February 2003, behemoth retailers such as Target and Walmart were choking on a backlog of unsold LEGO sets. LEGO inventory had ballooned by 40 percent at some outlets, to more than twice the amount of stock that's considered acceptable.

With the company's fiscal health dramatically deteriorating, its senior management assigned the recently hired Jørgen Vig Knudstorp, then the company's head of strategic development, to diagnose the problem and report back to the board of directors.

With his rumpled hair, Harry Potter glasses, and boyish enthusiasm for all things LEGO, Knudstorp must have seemed, to some LEGO senior managers, even younger than his thirty-three years. Having joined LEGO just eighteen months earlier, he was still very much a newcomer in a place where it's not uncommon to find brick-in-the-blood veterans of two, three, and sometimes even four decades. Despite his brief tenure, he had already become one of the LEGO Group's more networked executives.

Knudstorp, a PhD who spent eighteen months as a trainee kindergarten teacher before switching to a business career, had come to LEGO by way of the Copenhagen branch of the global strategic consulting firm McKinsey & Company. In the late 1990s, hypercompetitive, athletic Danes dominated McKinsey's Copenhagen office. A former colleague remembers Knudstorp as being different from others in the office—a genial, somewhat nerdy fellow who always sported the latest technological gizmo. He proved himself a capable consultant. But the firm's macho, very traditional culture never fully embraced him, and he left after just two and a half years, a relatively short time even by McKinsey standards.

Knudstorp proved a better fit at the LEGO Group. Although he never consulted for LEGO while he was at McKinsey and had never visited the company prior to his arrival in September 2001, Knudstorp had grown up less than an hour's drive from Billund. As a child, Knudstorp had not been allowed any electronic toys and so spent many hours with his LEGO sets. "I was keenly aware of LEGO's heritage, so the call represented a kind of homecoming," he recalled. "But what really made me think about joining LEGO was the company had gone through a rough patch. It seemed like it was back on track but still had some challenges ahead of it. From a professional angle, it was an exciting opportunity."

Once ensconced at LEGO, Knudstorp became a kind of at-large strategist who roved throughout the company, taking on different assignments as new challenges arose: collaborating with the management team of LEGOLAND to improve the theme parks' performance, developing an action plan for building out the company's nascent line of retail stores, deconstructing its global supply chain and recommending improvements. Acting on his belief that "relationships are just as important as results," Knudstorp formed many critical ties across what was then a heavily compartmentalized organization.

Within six months of arriving at LEGO, Knudstorp began reporting directly to the chief operating officer, Poul Plougmann. The theme park and LEGO store projects, in particular, frequently engaged him with Kjeld Kirk Kristiansen, the company's president. As a result, he often delivered reports to the LEGO Group's board of directors. To prepare his state-of-the-company analysis, Knudstorp drew heavily on his McKinsey training, which preaches that fact-finding is the first step toward problem solving. He spent several months sleuthing in every part of the LEGO organization, interviewing senior managers, front-line employees, and major retail customers on what was working and, more critically, what was failing.

The LEGO Group's immediate problems were not so difficult to discern. In fact, they were plainly evident to many of the company's executives. Buoyed by the over-the-top sales of LEGO *Star Wars* and *Harry Potter* kits in 2001 and the first half of 2002, retailers had doubled down on LEGO for the Christmas season. Trouble was, neither a *Star Wars* film nor a *Harry Potter* movie was scheduled for 2003, so kids weren't primed for repeat offerings of LEGO Yoda and Chamber of Secrets sets. (And as we'll see, sales of many other LEGO lines proved lackluster at best.)

Knudstorp believed the company's dilemma was in no way due to a lack of innovation. Even though he was new to the company, he was well aware that LEGO had been delivering novel products for the past three years. But as he dug deeper into the LEGO Group's sales results and its manufacturing, distribution, and advertising costs, he saw there was a shocking lack of *profitable* innovation. LEGO had plumped up its top line, but its bottom line had grown anorexic. All the creativity of the previous few years had generated a wealth of new products, but only a few were actually making money. To make matters worse, the LEGO Group's management organization and systems, shaped by decades of success, were poorly equipped to handle a downturn.

LEGO was trapped in a painful double bind. Instead of pushing the new product lines that the company was advertising in early 2003, retailers were trying to unload their LEGO inventories from Christmas 2002. The result: robust sales of new LEGO sets never materialized, while retailers had to heavily discount their existing LEGO stock and watch their profits evaporate. Not surprisingly, they soon regarded LEGO as extraordinarily unappetizing. Adding to the LEGO Group's misery, the U.S. dollar started to depreciate. Not only did LEGO lose sales in dollars, but it lost income due to the weak dollar. As the year progressed, the decline accelerated. "Our problems couldn't be pinned to one failing product," said Knudstorp. "It was the failing performance of nearly the entire LEGO portfolio."

As Knudstorp dug deeper into the LEGO Group's malaise, he

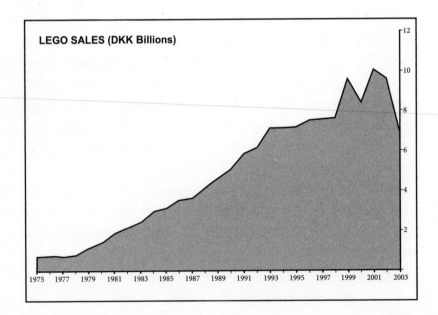

LEGO SALES (DKK Billions)

found the company's problems were far more systemic than a falling U.S. currency and a failed Christmas. First and foremost, the company's management team, which consisted of twelve senior vice presidents who oversaw six market regions as well as such traditional functions as the direct-to-consumer business and the global supply chain, was "highly dysfunctional," recalled Knudstorp. "They didn't work together. They operated in silos."

The chill from the executive suite often frosted the company's retail partners, who regarded LEGO as aloof and largely uncaring. Knudstorp also found the company's designers and developers chronically failed to grasp the business implications of their actions. And too many managers did a poor job of allocating responsibilities and carrying out decisions. Although there were clear lines of authority throughout LEGO, there was far too little accountability.

Equally troubling, the company's ability to track its product inventory and produce a reasonably accurate financial forecast was shockingly poor, largely because the LEGO Group was organized as a loosely linked holding company, with every business unit keeping track of revenues and expenses in its own unique way.

Despite senior management's difficulties in getting a timely sense of the LEGO Group's inventories and cash flow, Knudstorp thoroughly vetted the company's performance over the previous decade. He homed in on economic value added (EVA), where opportunity costs are deducted from revenues. A standard industry metric, EVA measures what the owners of a company could have made if they'd invested in risk-free government bonds instead of the business. Calculating the EVA is something of an academic exercise for companies that are owned by a large swath of shareholders. But for Kjeld Kirk Kristiansen, the leader of the LEGO Group's owners and the guardian of the family fortune, EVA mattered.

Knudstorp's finding was shocking. His analysis revealed that with the exception of 1998, the LEGO Group had steadily produced accounting profits from 1993 to 2002, yet the company had lost some $1.6 billion of economic value over the same period. In other words, the company's owners would have been better off investing in no-risk, low-return government bonds than in LEGO. By backing LEGO, they had depleted their family fortune at the rate of almost half a million dollars per day, every day, for ten years.

Guided by former General Electric CEO Jack Welch's axiom that a leader must "see things as they are, not as [you] wish them to be," Knudstorp's report on the LEGO Group's performance was unflinching. His message to the company's board of directors at its June meeting in Billund was unsparing. He summarized his analysis in a slide titled "What is the price of good management?"

And then he provided some answers. The LEGO Group's immediate future looked even bleaker than its recent past. The company was on track to suffer a 30 percent drop in sales and bleed out $250 million in operating costs. It was running a negative cash flow of more than $160 million. By year's end LEGO would likely default on its outstanding debt of nearly $800 million, and it lacked committed lines of credit. The forecast for 2004 looked every bit as ugly, if not worse, as the company's net loss was expected to double.

"I [told them] we are on a burning platform," recalled Knudstorp. "We need to take action, because the problem is not going away."

As they took in Knudstorp's report, more than a few directors found it difficult to shake off their surprise over the company's predicament. Although they grudgingly accepted Knudstorp's reading of the LEGO Group's challenges for 2003, several directors pushed back forcefully against his forecast for 2004. The skeptics argued that although the losses meant they should strip out between $135 million and $155 million in operating costs, sales would rebound as soon as the U.S. currency crisis cleared and the next *Star Wars* movie hit the street. Exclaimed one director: "I don't know where you're getting this, that 2004 is going to be another difficult year. What are you building this on?" As Knudstorp walked out of the meeting, it occurred to him that he might well lose his job.

"I wasn't deliberately trying to disagree with them," he recalled. "I just felt that I would serve them best by telling them the truth as

I saw it. Of course, they saw things differently. So I did think about whether that was the end of my time at the company."

As the summer progressed, it became more and more apparent that LEGO would not easily reverse its declining fortunes. In an attempt to stabilize the company's balance sheet, Kristiansen and Plougmann recruited Jesper Ovesen, the chief financial officer of Danske Bank, one of the largest banks in Scandinavia, to steer the LEGO Group's financial operations.

Ovesen arrived in Billund on the first of November 2003, took a suite at the LEGOLAND hotel, and began a solitary dive into the company's books. Although he has a boxer's broad shoulders and expansive forehead, Ovesen possesses the mathematically inclined mind of a pencil-necked geek. He's been known to remark, "Behind every product and person there's a number, and that's what I look for." It wasn't long before people at LEGO likened him to the characters in the sci-fi thriller *The Matrix*, who see the world as a vast, ceaselessly scrolling grid of computer code.

Ovesen was taken aback by what he found at LEGO—and what he couldn't find. Since the company's inception, the LEGO Group's leaders had operated on the notion that if they consistently delivered great products for kids, profits would follow—a philosophy that might have served them well during the organization's early years but ultimately left them without an overarching system for monitoring the company's financials. LEGO also lacked a robust, up-to-the-minute accounting system that would alert managers when things went wrong.

"They had no control over their investments," Ovesen later exclaimed, still amazed by the company's lack of fiscal oversight. "They didn't know where they made money. They didn't know if they made money on the product side. They didn't know product profitability. They did know the LEGOLAND parks were a cash drain, but they didn't know why."

Even by late 2003, the LEGO Group's tangled corporate structure, where every country organization ran a separate P&L, continued to plague its performance. The company's newly installed IT system for managing the company's finances let executives see if the United States or Germany, for example, yielded profits. But the company still didn't track which *products* made or lost money. LEGO lacked an activity-based costing system, so it had only a crude view of the costs it incurred to produce individual products and its returns on individual sets. If it had dug deep enough, LEGO could have figured out product profitability, despite its complex corporate structure. But it never felt compelled to do so. LEGO had been so successful for so many years, it never did the work to really understand what different sets cost.

Even so, it didn't take a sophisticated financial analysis for Ovesen to see that in just the third quarter of 2003, the company's total sales had gone into free fall, declining nearly $800 million compared to the previous year's quarter. Toward the end of November, the LEGO Group's board of directors gathered again in Billund. This time it was Ovesen who stood before them. His message was blunt: LEGO was indeed teetering on the edge of a financial abyss. "It was purely a financial disaster," he exclaimed.

Ovesen is widely regarded as one of Europe's most astute CFOs; it would have been exceedingly difficult to discount his assertion that LEGO was close to bankruptcy. Even the skeptics now had to confront what once had been unthinkable: if the company that produced the toy of the century didn't find a way to reinvent itself, Kristiansen and his family might well have to break LEGO into pieces and sell it to save it.

For Knudstorp, Ovesen, and the board of directors, the company's plight was shocking, not least because LEGO had always seemed so strong. The seventy-one-year-old icon of the toy world had endured the Great Depression, a brush with bankruptcy in its early days, the ravages of the Second World War, and the constantly shifting tastes of one of the world's most demanding consumers—the seven-year-old boy. In 2003, the LEGO Group's annual revenues were forecast to exceed $1 billion, making it the fifth-largest toy company in the world and the undisputed king of construction toys. LEGO products, ranging from the DUPLO line for preschoolers to the LEGO Technic line for teenagers, could be found in about 75 percent of American and 80 percent of European households with children. The LEGO brick was almost as ubiquitous as it is today. Yet the company was draining cash and destroying the owners' wealth at an alarming rate. How could one of the world's most beloved brands have been brought down so swiftly and so decisively?

Yes, its businesses were siloed and its designers were too far removed from the market. The LEGO Group's brain trust had for years let climbing production and marketing costs cannibalize the company's profits. And the company had wrongly bet that LEGO *Star Wars* would remain a blockbuster even without the release of a new *Star Wars* movie to help drive sales. But the full explanation for the LEGO Group's steep decline resides in those seven innovation truths. Big, bold moves often come with the risk of a long-term slide, even when the early results are all rosy.

Individually, the seven truths have worked for other companies. Collectively, they almost pushed LEGO into bankruptcy. Following the seven truths boosted sales at LEGO but also led to skyrocketing costs. Because LEGO lacked an effective system for monitoring its innovations and swiftly alerting management when an initiative took a wrong turn, the company was caught off guard and couldn't recover.

To better understand what happened, let's revisit those seven truths.

Hire diverse and creative people. Although LEGO succeeded in recruiting blue-chip talent and deploying satellite offices throughout the world, the rapid expansion proved devilishly difficult to manage. New hires lacked a connection to the company's DNA and an overarching vision of where Plougmann wanted to take LEGO; new designers lacked a feel for creating with the brick and for collaborating with their veteran counterparts in Billund. Consider the effort to develop the LEGO Explore line, which we discussed in Chapter Two. This was marketing chief Francesco Ciccolella's attempt to replace the long-running DUPLO line, whose sales were stagnating, with an entirely new global brand for the preschool set. Through Explore, LEGO aimed to build a bigger presence in the U.S. market, which was clamoring for electronic toys that delivered some educational value.

"Explore was our favorite," Plougmann asserted. "The idea was to regain strength in the toddler category by segmenting it into different themes and ages. The LEGO Explore system—the skill and knowledge it would bring to children—would make the single brick less important in the minds of mothers."

Just as Kristiansen's decision to license *Star Wars* had earlier proved the value of ceding a degree of decision-making autonomy to Peter Eio and his LEGO Americas team, Plougmann believed he'd reap similar gains by letting Ciccolella and his talented team of Milan-based designers take the lead in developing Explore. From the outset, the effort was fraught with a command-and-control management mind-set that hobbled creativity, as well as the near-total inability of the Milan- and Billund-based designers to work together.

In LEGO Explore, the Milan shop fashioned a line of electronic toys, some of which entirely omitted the brick. Although the Milan team created the concepts for the Explore line, a group of Billund-based designers was charged with developing the toys and preparing them for the market. More than a few of those designers were aghast when they received their design briefs.

"The heads of marketing and product development presented Explore in a big meeting, and it was not very well received at all," recalled Allan Steen Larsen, one of the Billund designers who worked on the line. "First they took away the [DUPLO] rabbit logo that meant so much to our core markets. Second, all the values we were taught to communicate in the packaging and the products were completely thrown away." Ciccolella gave the Milan team full design authority and told the Billund team to follow Milan's lead. No dissent was tolerated. Said Larsen: "They told us not to come up with any objections. They didn't exactly threaten to fire us, but that was definitely the message."

Explore's success in part depended on melding the Milan group's creativity and design prowess with the Billund designers' deep understanding of the LEGO play experience. Yet, remarkably, there was no attempt to coordinate the two departments' development efforts. Larsen, who helped create the Explore Music Roller—a very un-LEGO-like concept developed in Milan—couldn't recall a single meeting between his team and his counterparts in Milan. "We felt like we were being amputated" from the development of core preschool toys, he asserted.

If senior managers had defined Explore in such vivid terms that designers knew where they needed to take the line, the Billund and Milan teams might well have meshed and learned to collaborate effectively. But the company's top managers remained divided over the Explore strategy and therefore couldn't deliver a clear sense of direction to the line's developers.

Plougmann and Ciccolella believed that LEGO Explore, because of its capacity to stimulate children's development, held great promise. In the LEGO Group's 2002 annual report, Plougmann declared that switching to Explore was "the right decision and it will prove itself in the long run." But veteran LEGO executives led by Mads Nipper, who then headed up the company's central Europe operations, argued that Explore was too radical a break from classic LEGO. Scuttling a beloved brand such as DUPLO would prove disastrous. An animated, energetic executive who can be strikingly candid, Nipper was not shy about voicing his distress. "DUPLO was the second-strongest toy brand in northern and central Europe after LEGO," he later fumed. "And we in all our wisdom decided to kill it."

On a winter's day in 2002, the infighting boiled over. Nipper and the three other heads of the company's largest markets got a call to report to a suite at the LEGOLAND hotel, a short walk from the company's headquarters in Billund. LEGO staffers called it the "firing room." If you were employed by LEGO and you were summoned there, chances are you'd be unemployed when you left.

For months, Nipper and the three executives had continued to press their case against Explore. Plougmann decided he'd heard enough. He instructed his lieutenants to gather the dissenters and deliver an ultimatum. Recalled Nipper: "All four of us were brought in and told that if we didn't shut up and loyally support Explore, we would leave the company."

Faced with a choice between supporting Explore or losing his job, Nipper relented. Nevertheless, when LEGO presented the Explore line to its key central European retailers, his misgivings resurfaced even more powerfully. The general manager of Idee+Spiel, one of Germany's largest chains of specialty toy stores, was especially unimpressed by Explore. He approached Nipper and asked, "Are you sure you know what you're doing?" Nipper found himself reprising Ciccolella's argument that since DUPLO's sales were stagnating, it was time to make a big break from the past.

"As I was talking," he recalled, "it was just like eating something that you don't like. When the people who knew the market exceptionally well explicitly expressed what I was feeling, I was no longer reasonably sure that we were on a disastrous course. I was 100 percent sure."

In the end, the misgivings of Nipper and other executives proved prescient. LEGO Explore was such a striking departure from the brick-based toys that parents knew from their childhoods, it confused the market and ultimately decimated sales. Even worse was the decision to let Explore supplant DUPLO. Although DUPLO had struggled in recent years, its strong LEGO lineage nevertheless helped make it the second-best-selling toy brand in Europe. Nipper's "very rough" estimate is that over its three-year lifetime, the Explore adventure cost LEGO at least DKK 500 million (about $65 million). "Explore was a smoking disaster," he exclaimed. "Our least fine moment of all time."

The LEGO Group's new wave of designers can't be blamed for

the Explore debacle. Rather, the company's leaders tripped up in three critical areas. First, they failed to ensure that the new hires' skills were in sync with the company's needs. Although LEGO recruited world-class developers who were celebrated for their work with graphics, animation, and 3-D moviemaking, far too few had mastered the craft of using the brick to create compelling play experiences.

Recalled Paal Smith-Meyer, who was one of the new wave of designers hired under Plougmann and now heads up the LEGO New Business Group: "[We all] wanted to be great industrial product designers, the next Philippe Starck"—the French designer famous for his sleek, organic renderings of everyday furniture and household items. "LEGO thought it was cool that we could draw well. But no one ever told us that for the company to make money, you have to be able to build it in LEGO."

The company's second misstep: the near-total lack of coordination between Explore's Billund-based developers and the satellite team in Milan, which was not an isolated event. LEGO likewise never bothered to ensure that the developers at Zowie Intertainment, a company LEGO acquired in 1998, worked well with the Billund design teams.

One of the major products that LEGO planned to develop at Zowie was the KidPad, an electronic toy that allowed kids to play a computer game by moving physical pieces around in front of a camera. LEGO originally forecast that the KidPad would deliver DKK 500 million in first-year sales. In the end, the company failed to sell a single toy, as the KidPad never made it to market. Nor did any other toy concept produced by the Zowie unit. In 2001, three years after acquiring Zowie, LEGO shut the studio down and laid off most of its employees.

The company's third mistake was to refuse to learn from those setbacks and take corrective action to reset its strategy and better deploy its new hires. After LEGO killed the KidPad effort in the fall of 2000, Ciccolella met with Smith-Meyer for a postmortem. "He said he only had a half hour," remembered Smith-Meyer. "And when we finished, we would never talk about the project again. His attitude was, 'Let's move on. There's nothing to see here.' " The result was that LEGO, by failing to learn from its reversals, was far more likely to repeat them.

Plougmann was certainly correct in concluding that to compete on a global stage, the company needed a globally diverse design culture. Diversity fosters creativity; when similar scrapes up against dissimilar, it can generate the creative spark that ignites white-hot innovation. For LEGO, problems arose when it failed to channel the new hires' energy and inspiration. LEGO set off a chain reaction of human creativity but never contained it and managed it. The result was a cascade of runaway innovations that either bombed or imploded.

Head for blue-ocean markets. The urgency with which LEGO pursued uncontested, blue-ocean markets was in large part due to the fact that the brick appeared to be trapped in an increasingly crowded and bloodied red ocean. With the expiration of the last patents for the LEGO brick in the 1980s, sharks such as Tyco Toys and Mega Bloks tore into the LEGO Group's market share with knockoff bricks sold at a steep discount to LEGO sets. At the same time, consultants were advising the company that the brick itself was passé.

"We had all these external experts telling us the LEGO brick is going to die," said Smith-Meyer. "They said the twenty-first century is not about little square plastic blocks. It's digital."

According to the consultants, the LEGO Group's future resided not in the brick but in exploiting the highly trusted, widely beloved LEGO brand. Their advice led to the strategy of pursuing an untapped, blue-ocean market in the digital arena by yoking the LEGO brand to the Spielberg brand. The result, of course, was the LEGO Studios Steven Spielberg MovieMaker.

The LEGO Group first launched its "movie studio in a box" solely in the United States in October 2000. The thrill of creating stop-motion animations with LEGO bricks proved to be a minor hit with American kids, though hardly a blockbuster. Buoyed by the kit's reasonably successful sales of DKK 80 million (about $10 million) in just a three-month span, LEGO gave the Spielberg MovieMaker a splashy global launch in early 2001.

The idea was to leverage the MovieMaker's success in the United States and grow it into a hot property the world over. Such a strategy was fully aligned with the LEGO Group's stated ambition to become the world's strongest brand among families with children by 2005. To achieve that goal, LEGO would have to double its annual sales by 2005. Thus, promising product lines such as MovieMaker had to find their blue ocean and quickly grow into big fish. LEGO, however, made the mistake of trying to grow the MovieMaker too soon and too fast.

Taking a page from the blue-ocean playbook, LEGO pushed to transform the MovieMaker product into a full-blown product line. First there came the MovieMaker kit with its bricks, minifigs, digital camera, and editing software for creating stop-motion animations. LEGO then followed up with nine additional MovieMaker kits that came with bricks for building movie sets but lacked the camera and software. The company's intent was to create a platform that would entice kids to keep adding to their MovieMaker collection, even after they'd bought the more expensive kits with the camera. Trouble was, for those nine cameraless kits to sell well, they would have to deliver a great building experience. They didn't. "Without the camera, they were really nothing special," conceded John Sahlertz, the Movie-Maker design lead.

The MovieMaker's global launch also meant instructions and software had to be translated into thirteen languages. So LEGO went from raising the curtain on one MovieMaker set in the fall of 2000 to spinning off twenty-three different versions in early 2001. Although the MovieMaker performed reasonably well as a niche product in the United States, it was a bust as a worldwide product line. Because the cameraless kits lacked a clear and compelling value proposition, they never caught on. Retailers were forced to discount unsold boxes so as to clear out inventory. As is often the case with toys that hit the discount racks, the shift signaled the product's demise.

Every innovation has its own cadence. Especially with new product concepts, marketers must balance out the inevitable ebb and flow of consumer demand. The MovieMaker line might well have succeeded had LEGO given the original set more time to grow before it rushed out all those add-on sets. But LEGO never got the pacing right. By rapidly ramping up the release of its sundry MovieMaker sets, it flooded the market and diluted the line's value.

Hobbled by the LEGO Group's weighty ambitions, the Movie-Maker couldn't complete its long swim to those wide-open, blue-ocean waters. The line went under in 2002 and never resurfaced. Even the combined power of the LEGO and Spielberg brands couldn't save it from drowning.

As for the company's other attempts to find a blue ocean—LEGO Explore and LEGO Education Centers—the huge losses from Explore greatly outweighed the meager gains from the Education Centers. Almost a quarter of the centers were unprofitable and were shut down in 2004, the same year Explore was shuttered.

Be customer driven. The LEGO Group's ambitious push to pursue an entirely new set of consumers—the two-thirds of kids who told researchers they'd rather plug into an Xbox (and the like) than play with construction toys—led to that all-out effort to think beyond the brick and fan out in entirely new directions, not only with digital toys but also with physical toys that were easier to build with because they had bigger, chunkier pieces. Above all, LEGO set its sights on developing turn-on toys featuring amped-up, good-versus-evil story lines.

"In the design department, the new buzzwords were to make things edgier and darker," said Smith-Meyer. "Boys wanted more aggression, more conflict."

According to Plougmann, much of the pressure for a cool, character-driven product line that was less buildable but more playable came from the LEGO Group's "very demanding" U.S. division. "The American market was becoming dominated by Walmart, Kmart, Toys 'R' Us, and Target," he asserted. "We were told that if we didn't do this stuff, we would lose shelf space."

The result was the aforementioned Jack Stone, who came off as a younger, less threatening mash-up of the action heroes G.I. Joe and Batman. From a theoretical point of view, Jack Stone looked like a winner. Here was a "new kind of hero . . . ready to save the day," as one TV commercial put it, for a toy market that was becoming increasingly dominated by story-driven concepts. And here, too, was a quick, snap-it-together toy for the majority of kids who'd rather put their free time into playing than into creating. But when Jack Stone hit the market in 2001, it proved to be a "terrible product," according to executive vice president Mads Nipper. "To be quite frank about it . . . the [Jack Stone] fire truck is probably my number one disliked product of all time from LEGO."

Jack Stone failed on three fronts. First, it couldn't capture the imaginations of the majority of kids who were indifferent to construction toys. Jack was a wholly fabricated toy hero without any real history or context, so kids didn't care about him. In 2001, U.S. kids sent action-packed toys such as Mattel's Hot Wheels Cars and Fisher-Price's Kawasaki Ninjas to the top of the bestseller lists. Jack Stone never even got an honorable mention. Second, the chunky pieces that made up the Jack Stone toys required expensive new injection molds for manufacturing the parts, making the toy unprofitable even in relatively high volumes. And third, the LEGO Group's new hero alienated the company's core fans. Parents who grew up with the brick couldn't find any of the company's classic play values—the "joy of building, pride of creation"—in that overgrown minifig. And on websites around the world, the influential AFOLs (adult fans of LEGO) bemoaned Jack Stone as further evidence of a damning trend: the "juniorization" of LEGO play themes, where the building experience is so unchallenging, it barely qualifies as LEGO.

The move toward radically simplifying the line was not an accident. Niels Milan Pedersen, the Galidor freelance designer who also worked on Jack Stone, recalled that he and his colleagues were explicitly instructed to prioritize action and play values above all else. "[Managers] told us the building experience wasn't the main purpose any longer."

In theory, Jack Stone should have worked. "All the research, all the rational arguments supported it," said Nipper. "A larger and larger part of the toy market was and still is driven by stories, so we gave them a story context. And if we could make it easier for the boys who didn't particularly fancy to build, why wouldn't we do it?"

Despite the LEGO Group's clean break with its past, poor sales forced the company to pull the Jack Stone line off the market just one year after the toy's 2001 launch. Here was a case where the company's internal compass put it on a course that diverged sharply from the fundamental principles—development, imagination, creativity—that constituted the classic LEGO play experience. Plougmann and his executive team quite rightly tested the outer edge of what kids and their parents would accept from LEGO, but the company clearly crossed a line. Jack Stone not only failed to capture a chunk of the two-thirds of kids who disliked construction toys but also turned off the core group of loyal LEGO consumers who did.

Practice disruptive innovation. By the late 1990s, there was the distinct sense among many in the LEGO community that with the rise of video games and Nintendo's Game Boy—which by 1998 had sold more than sixty-four million units worldwide—digital play experiences were about to overtake the decidedly physical, tangible experience of building with the brick. The Darwin project, by aiming to create a unified database that rendered every LEGO element in high-quality 3-D, was the LEGO Group's boldest bid to jump ahead of the trend and get to the digital future first.

No doubt Kristiansen's enthusiastic backing of Darwin was in part due to his pure love of technology.* After all, he saw to it that LEGO, along with IBM, was the first company to cosponsor MIT's Media Lab. Perhaps the grandson of the LEGO Group's founder believed all those Silicon Graphics supercomputers, upon which the Darwin team was building its massive database, would revolutionize LEGO and help the company disrupt its own business model, just as the plastic injection molding machine had done a half century earlier. At the very least, Darwin promised to digitize LEGO.

To recap, the goal of the Darwin project was not only to create ultra-high-quality virtual versions of physical toys—where the LEGO logo, for example, would be perfectly etched onto each stud on a digital LEGO brick, just as it is on a physical brick—but to become a storehouse of digital LEGO elements that could be used for creating computer-animated building instructions, games, TV ads, cartoons, and even feature films.

Creating a computerized rendering of the entire universe of LEGO parts not only was a massive engineering challenge but also posed some fundamental questions about the nature of the LEGO play experience. Should a digital brick have the same constraints as a plastic brick? How should a minifig act in the digital world? A plastic minifig can't bend its elbow to drink out of a glass—should a digital minifig be able to do so?

The Darwin team made enough progress on both the engineering and the philosophical fronts to underscore the project's potential. Darwin contributed to both LEGO CyberMaster, a toy that merged computer gaming with robotics, and LEGO Island, the company's very first software title. Sales of CyberMaster were mainly limited to Europe and Australia/New Zealand. But Island, which was released in the fall of 1997, went on to sell more than seven million copies

---

* This is the one "truth" that Kristiansen—not Plougmann—pursued. Darwin's failure helped precipitate the 1998 financial loss. By the time Plougmann arrived at LEGO later that year, the stink of Darwin was still so strong there was no appetite for major investments in virtual play experiences.

worldwide and was named Family Game of the Year at the Interactive Achievement Awards in 1998. Despite those successes, in 1999 the LEGO Group shut the project down.

Darwin's undoing was largely a matter of trying to do too much, too soon. It was a daunting mathematical task to begin with—representing complex shapes in three dimensions is extraordinarily difficult. That challenge was compounded by a lack of focus. Darwin tried to do everything for everybody, from creating digitized versions of specific toy lines to rendering the thousands of LEGO elements in 3-D. In the end, the Darwin team chose the wrong data model for reproducing the shapes of LEGO pieces, and the company was later forced to scrap all of Darwin's work.

Darwin's collapse was as much a management failure as it was a technological failure. Darwin was not widely loved, partly because the team enjoyed a separate-but-unequal status compared to the rest of the LEGO Group. Because the team worked in its own building on the outskirts of Billund, it was never integrated into the rest of the organization. The project's founder drove a Porsche, a car that's not often seen on Billund's back roads. Rumors soon swirled that LEGO was lavishing luxury cars on Darwin's hot-shot technologists to entice them to leave Boston and Silicon Valley for the company's dreary hometown. Even if the rumors were untrue, the outward appearance of favoritism was all too real.

"Whatever we asked for in terms of money and people, we were given," said Bjarne Tveskov, the leader of Darwin's software operations. "It was just like, 'Here's another check.' "

But Darwin never got the two things it needed most from top management: a clear sense of direction and useful critiques that would keep the project on the right track. Darwin was home to Scandinavia's largest computer graphics studio; its designers could don virtual-reality goggles and "play with the data" in a highly advanced, virtually collaborative workspace. But they never delivered the digital tools that other LEGO departments could utilize. Hence, the project enlisted few allies from other LEGO departments to its cause. Darwin was in need of a serious midflight correction, but it never got one.

"We didn't have the proper feedback loops to get that reality check as we went along," Tveskov asserted. "To be frank, there weren't any software experts in top management, or anyone with a deep knowledge of digital technology. It's hard to give qualified feedback if you don't know it."

In the end, Darwin lost out to a competing division, LEGO Media, which was set up in London in 1996. Christian Majgaard, who oversaw LEGO Media, took a very different approach to developing computer games and other online play experiences. Instead of doing all the technological heavy lifting in-house, Majgaard believed in collaborating with the best outside experts when the opportunity warranted it. That strategy proved to be more efficient and, for a time, more sustainable than Darwin's go-it-alone approach. And so, in 1999, the LEGO Group quietly pulled the plug on Darwin. Its immodest bid to push back against the video game publishers and unleash some creative destruction on conventional toy companies instead hit an evolutionary dead end.

Foster open innovation—heed the wisdom of the crowd. In the first years of the past decade, the LEGO Group's new-business mavens watched as a generation of Web 2.0 companies—YouTube, Facebook, Flickr—tapped into a seemingly bottomless reservoir of creativity by encouraging the masses to contribute to an online product or service. LEGO was far too cautious to open up its design studios to a crowd of outsiders, but it did make some modest moves toward harvesting the genius of its burgeoning fan community. Essentially, LEGO combined the technology of the crowdsourcing craze with the ethos of the design-it-yourself movement.

As we saw in Chapter Two, LEGO developed a computer-aided design program, dubbed LEGO Digital Designer, which let fans imagine and create their own LEGO kits using virtual 3-D bricks. They could then upload their dream models to the website of LEGO

Factory, and LEGO workers would assemble the physical sets and ship them to their citizen designers. If other fans liked the designs, they, too, could order the bespoke sets from LEGO Factory. Here, then, was a case of mass customization on an individual basis.

LEGO originally conceived Factory as a DIY site for adult fans, who by some estimates accounted for 20 percent of the company's sales. But after surveying users, LEGO marketers discovered Factory was also popular with the nine- and ten-year-old set. They rebranded Factory with a self-explanatory name, LEGO Design byMe, and watched as the service gave LEGO a far more personal connection with its legions of fans by letting them create one-of-a-kind kits. Design byMe could also be seen as an outgrowth of one of the company's founding principles: authenticity. Rather than make only sets that conform to the company's image of its consumers, LEGO had found a way to let people create sets that conform to their image of themselves. Design byMe let them invent sets that reflected who they were and who they aspired to be.

Although Design byMe let LEGO forge a more personal, more genuine bond with its fans, as a business, it failed to take off. At its peak, Design byMe had a conversion rate of less than 0.5 percent—for every two hundred visits to the site, less than one purchase was made. That rate was certainly weighed down by the service's price tag. Although the design feature was free, the price for the custom sets was significantly higher than store-bought LEGO sets, as the bricks were costlier and LEGO had tacked on a $10 service fee for producing the custom-designed box and instructions.

Increasingly, the DIY effect gave the LEGO Group's brain trust a migraine. LEGO fans, eager to show off their creations, might upload a LEGO Homer Simpson set and offer it for sale, exposing LEGO to lawsuits from Twentieth Century Fox, the owner of *The Simpsons* intellectual property. Another group of malicious fans tried to upload inappropriate content, such as detailed reconstructions of parts of the male anatomy.

Design byMe's performance oscillated for many years, but the site never made money. Certainly it did not materially fuel the LEGO Group's fall. But while Design byMe was a modest attempt to build a business by sourcing the crowd, the crowd never really responded, and the service was finally shut down in January 2012.

Explore the full spectrum of innovation. The LEGO Group's effort to stretch into every genre of innovation—by conceiving decidedly un-LEGO-like products, as well as summoning new consumer experiences and services—should have advanced the company's goal of doubling its annual sales by 2005. But as it turned out, the strategy very nearly dragged LEGO over a cliff.

On the product innovation side there was Galidor, the line of sci-fi action figures that dramatically broke from the classic LEGO building experience. To recap, Galidor featured its own building system, which entirely omitted the brick. And rather than spin Galidor off from a world-beating movie franchise, as it had done with *Star Wars*, LEGO opted to develop its own TV series to propagate the toy. A hot sci-fi show, combined with an utterly atypical character-driven theme from LEGO, just might capture some of the action figure craze that was sweeping the toy world.

Plougmann and Kristiansen were well aware that Galidor represented a significant risk. After all, just one in five action figure toys is a commercial success. But coming out of 2001, LEGO was reaping eye-popping sales from its *Star Wars* line. LEGO had also just released Bionicle, a best-selling line of buildable action figures based on an original work of science fiction, just like Galidor. Given the triumphs of *Star Wars* and Bionicle, LEGO bet that it could beat the odds with Galidor. "We had such a belief in ourselves," recalled Jacob Kragh, Galidor's development lead. "We thought we could walk on water."

Kragh and his team ran the Galidor toy and its story line through numerous kid-centered focus groups; the boys' enthusiasm for the concept led LEGO to conclude the line would triumph. What was unknown was whether the TV series would captivate kids. Hollywood producer Thomas Lynch, the series' creator, had scored so many hit children's programs that the *New York Times* dubbed him the "David E. Kelley of tween TV." But *Galidor: Defenders of the Outer Dimension*, which aired on Fox Kids for two seasons, was an unmitigated mess, amounting to little more than a half-hour pitch for the toy line. "We were gobsmacked with disgust when we saw the first episode," recalled Niels Milan Pedersen, one of Galidor's designers. "It was terrible."

Meanwhile, Andrew Black, who was then head of LEGO Americas, was so high on Galidor, he instructed his sales team to dramatically ratchet up the line's forecast and front-load their sales channels with inventory. It was then that Kragh began to fear that he and his team had gotten the LEGO Group's leaders a little *too* excited about Galidor's potential. "We were very uncomfortable with the [increased forecasts]," he confessed. "We talked quite a bit about it [with upper management]. But we weren't really heard. Besides, there was really no turning back at that point. The entire portfolio was built around Galidor being the first priority."

When the TV series flatlined, Galidor lost its platform. Retailers couldn't clear the toy from their shelves, and it quickly hit the discount bin. Just a year after its launch, Galidor was a goner. LEGO later called Galidor its "worst-selling" theme of all time. Mused Plougmann, reflecting on his decision to green-light the line: "I still don't understand why we didn't burn that project."

In fact, there were very good reasons to launch Galidor. LEGO couldn't catch up with the rapidly changing toy industry if it simply continued to churn out classic play themes such as Space and Castle. Repeating past successes would never help LEGO get ahead of competitors that were ramping up new businesses faster than ever. To get to the future first, LEGO had to outinvent the competition. And given that Bionicle—the first LEGO toy to be based on a work of fiction created by LEGO itself—was a world-beater in just its first year, why couldn't another fictional, buildable action figure prove just as successful?

Aside from the *Galidor* TV series debacle, the LEGO Group's big mistake was that it didn't properly pace its innovations. Instead of allowing designers to spend more time developing, focus-testing, and getting Galidor right, LEGO pushed the line out into the market as soon as it saw that Bionicle was an unequivocal success. Kids wouldn't gravitate to Galidor when they were already clamoring for Bionicle. "Had we done Galidor a few years later, that would not have been stupid," Nipper asserted. "What was stupid was doing Bionicle and Galidor in parallel."

The LEGO Group's attempt to innovate new consumer experiences and services through its LEGOLAND theme parks and LEGO branded stores likewise had the perverse effect of bleeding its balance sheet. Plougmann bet that unveiling a new park every two to three years and rolling out three hundred stores would help rocket the LEGO brand to the top of the toy world. But former LEGO executives such as Peter Eio argued that, once again, poor pacing doomed both initiatives.

"The success of *Star Wars* gave [Plougmann] a kind of euphoria, that this was the time to really expand into a lot of areas," noted Eio. "But instead of researching them and tackling them one at a time, there was a flurry to do as much as possible. It was all intended to build the brand, but there were a lot of negative factors that had to be overcome."

Among the toughest challenges was surmounting the fear among the LEGO Group's retail partners that LEGO stores would cannibalize their businesses. Eio recalled that soon after he launched the first store, the LEGO Imagination Center at the Mall of America, he was summoned to a meeting with Charles Lazarus, the founder of Toys "R" Us. "You're making stores to compete with me," Lazarus snapped. In fact, Eio demonstrated that one year after the LEGO Imagination Center opened its doors, sales at the nearest Toys "R" Us store, in Bloomington, Minnesota, jumped by 25 percent. Clearly, the Imagination Center had a halo effect on Toys "R" Us. At that point, Lazarus "seemed quite comfortable that we weren't going to take away his business," said Eio.

But for retailers, the notion of LEGO launching *hundreds* of stores raised the threat level from guarded to severe. Even within the LEGO Group, the plan was greeted with great skepticism. "The stores had, so far, not been very successful and also had been considered a very expensive adventure," said Knudstorp, whose first assignment as the company's strategist was to review the entire store enterprise. "Most important, they were threatening to the retail trade."

As for the theme parks, LEGO lacked both the management know-how and the deep pockets to ensure their success. Although the Billund LEGOLAND was profitable, the newly launched parks in California and Germany quickly plunged into the red. Each cost DKK 1.5 billion to build and each sustained operating losses of DKK 300 million in their first year. "The parks were draining cash and still they wanted to build more," recalled an incredulous Jesper Ovesen, the CFO who joined LEGO in late 2003. "It was completely crazy."

Crazy or not, LEGO did explore the full spectrum of innovation. But the company was too myopic to spot the ominous warnings that it was dangerous to bet a priority product on an untested TV show and delusional to think that managers could master the retail and theme park businesses all at the same time. LEGO forgot that when it comes to igniting a range of ambitious innovations, you reduce the risks by taking a stepwise, learn-as-you-go approach.

Build an innovation culture. By almost any standard, the LEGO Group's new regime created a fertile culture for sowing the seeds of innovation, out of which germinated a dazzling array of ambitious ventures. But from an innovation management perspective, Plougmann and his executive team were too content with half measures. They never supported all of those sundry innovations in a way that would yield a rich harvest. Just consider:

- In recognizing they couldn't always bring top design talent to Billund, they essentially brought Billund to the talent by launching small project teams throughout the world. But they never truly connected those far-flung design teams with the company's core product development units. The result was that the outposts ended up as orphanages, filled with ventures for which the Billund-based teams bore too little responsibility.

- Although the LEGO Group's leaders encouraged, even insisted, on risk taking, they had little tolerance for the too-frequent outcome: failure. As we saw with Ciccolella's refusal to discuss the KidPad misadventure, rather than learn from setbacks, LEGO often preferred to sweep them aside.

- To borrow a phrase from Apple's overused argot, Plougmann and his lieutenants challenged people to "think different" and deviate from the norm. Kids wanted to play, not build. The brick was out; cool and edgy was in. "New and different" was better than "more of the same." But when people pushed back and questioned, say, whether it was smart to kick over a beloved subbrand such as DUPLO, the company's leaders ordered the skeptics to fall into line. In so doing, they reneged on a core tenet of every truly innovative culture: the right to honestly dissent.

Poul Plougmann and his team were hardly the first executives in the history of business to slap back internal skeptics. No doubt it sometimes required a heavy hand to push a change agenda through the LEGO Group's insular culture. Much to his credit, Plougmann dared to think big and act boldly. And some of the company's innovations might well have worked had they been given sufficient direction and focus:

- The impulse behind LEGO Explore—to nurture preschoolers' creativity—might or might not have been spot-on, but management's inability to graphically define the brand's value proposition and coordinate the efforts of its Milan and Billund designers ultimately doomed the line.

- There was a clear and compelling need for LEGO to convert its physical bricks into digital bits, but the company's leaders likewise failed to ring-fence Darwin's copious initiatives and better integrate them into the rest of the organization.

- LEGO quite rightly sought out untapped markets, but it lacked both the feedback mechanisms to know whether to kill a flawed project before it hit the market (Jack Stone) and sufficient oversight to course-correct troubled but still promising product lines (Galidor).

- Above all, LEGO never nailed down the right sequencing and pacing of its myriad innovations. A new LEGOLAND theme park every two to three years, three hundred new LEGO stores by 2005—the all-out race to launch these and other expensive forays severely taxed the company's management machinery and its balance sheet.

In the end, the LEGO Group's poor execution of the seven truths of innovation brought it to the brink of bankruptcy. The company's leaders welcomed an influx of talented new designers but never melded their contributions with the business's real needs. They promoted creativity but never sufficiently channeled it. And they brazenly pushed into new markets but never instilled sufficient focus to ensure that its innovations harvested outsize rewards. The result: runaway innovation, which soon proved a curse.

By late 2003, the LEGO Group's leaders finally began to concede that the glowing success of LEGO *Star Wars*, as one executive put it, was ultimately a "thick, fat layer of cosmetics" hiding the raw blemishes of a sickly core business. By November of that year, it was apparent that all the rouge and mascara had melted away. Without a *Star Wars* movie, LEGO couldn't reprise the line's explosive growth, and sales rapidly lost altitude.

Of course, LEGO knew there wouldn't be a new *Star Wars* movie until 2005 and anticipated a drop-off in the interim. But executives believed that the company's big-bet product lines—Galidor, Jack Stone, and Explore—would pick up the slack. Their collective and expensive failure threw even more accelerant onto the fire that was consuming LEGO. To make matters worse, the company's inability to master the many ambitious ventures it had undertaken—the television shows, the video games, its own retail stores, and, not least, the theme park business—made the flames burn even hotter.

As the year drew to a close, Plougmann admitted in a November bulletin to the LEGO Group's employees that 2003 would be "much worse" than originally forecast. He pleaded with staffers to "put in that extra effort" and insisted, "A final year-end push can improve our result." It's doubtful many believed him. As LEGO headed into the all-important Christmas season, a grim mood permeated its Billund headquarters. "It's hard to describe how bad things were," recalled designer Niels Milan Pedersen. "There was this feeling that LEGO wouldn't exist in another year."

Behind the scenes, Kristiansen and a few trusted lieutenants launched a make-or-break bid to save the company. Two weeks before Christmas, Knudstorp was summoned to a meeting with Kristiansen, CFO Jesper Ovesen, and the chairman of the LEGO Group, Mads Øvlisen. The LEGO Group's owner asked Knudstorp and Ovesen to formulate a rescue plan and recommend a management team that would pull the company out of the fire. Plougmann and Ciccolella were out. (Their firing was announced in early January 2004.) Kristiansen was back as chief executive. But in an arrangement that was not made public, the grandson of the LEGO Group's founder tapped Jørgen Vig Knudstorp to take over the company's day-to-day operations. It was an unconventional, perhaps even desperate gamble. The future of the LEGO Group, which had just embarked on its eighth decade, was in the hands of an untested ex-consultant who'd been with the company for barely two years.

LEGO was beset with so many challenges that for more than a year, a turnaround strategy eluded Knudstorp. Even so, he knew from the outset that unless they quickly learned to master at least two of the seven truths—"build an innovation culture" and "be cus-tomer driven"—LEGO wouldn't stand a chance of getting back in the black.

The company's anything-goes work culture, where developers were encouraged to think far beyond the brick and managers were expected to pursue market opportunities that were only remotely connected with the brand, had very nearly sunk LEGO. As a result, Knudstorp and other leaders would have to shape a performance-based culture where people's passion and creativity were balanced with discipline and focus. Only then could a higher percentage of people's ideas be channeled into developing profit-generating products.

Under Plougmann, LEGO had hotly pursued the vast numbers of kids who were indifferent to the brick but turned on by electronic games and action-oriented toys. The results were disastrous. To sur-vive, LEGO would have to move its focus back onto the kids who loved to create with construction blocks. But that wasn't enough. LEGO needed to discover new ways to delve into the lives of LEGO kids and learn to see the world through their eyes. If LEGO didn't reorient itself around its core customers, it would be far harder to reanimate its core products.

LEGO had badly botched its first attempt at mastering the truths of innovation. This time, with its future hanging in the balance, LEGO would have to get them right. It wouldn't get another chance.

Part Two

Mastering the
Seven Truths of
Innovation and
Transforming LEGO

Building an Innovation Culture

The Return to Core Values

We wanted to break the back of the culture.

—Jørgen Vig Knudstorp, CEO, the LEGO Group

ALTHOUGH KNUDSTORP, IN HIS PRESENTATIONS TO THE LEGO Group's board of directors, was prescient in predicting the company's near collapse, the first few months of 2004 found him struggling to diagnose why the company had fallen so far so fast. He knew he couldn't return LEGO to profitable growth if he first didn't understand the root causes of how such a creative powerhouse had so decisively lost its way.

The conundrum gnawed at him as he boarded an overnight flight from New York to Amsterdam. On the plane he happened to sit next to Chris Zook, a partner at the strategy consultancy Bain & Company and the author of *Profit from the Core*. In his book, Zook argued that sustained, profitable growth comes when companies focus on core products for a clearly defined segment of customers. He warned that companies must exercise careful planning and great care when they expand into related or "adjacent" areas, such as significantly new channels, value chains, technologies, or product lines. If they diversify too much in too short a span, the results probably will be ugly.

As Zook explained his thesis, Knudstorp reflected on the kaleidoscopic array of new businesses that LEGO had taken on in just the past decade: software (computer games and LEGO MovieMaker), learning concepts (LEGO Education), lifestyle products (LEGO kids' wear), girls' toys (LEGO dolls), media (books, magazines, television), three more theme parks, and the goal of three hundred more retail stores. Despite all of that effort, expansion, and experimentation, far too many of those ventures ended up in the red. In fact, the rate at which the LEGO Group dove into new markets roughly corresponded to the rate at which it racked up losses.

Thinking back on the company's many disparate ventures, it occurred to Knudstorp that the root cause of the LEGO Group's problems resided in the simple fact that its approach to creating distinctive, desirable offerings was far too aggressive. "Chris said his research showed that if a company has a strong core business, it can move into one adjacency every five years," Knudstorp recalled. "As he was saying this, I was thinking we read the book the other way around. We did five adjacencies every year. Suddenly we had to manage a lot of businesses that we just didn't understand. We didn't have the capabilities and we couldn't keep up the pace.

"It's fine to experiment and diversify," he continued. "But behind the scenes, there's a management system that needs to keep its integrity. And there was no overall guidance of the innovation process."

Knudstorp knew that if LEGO was to pull back from the abyss, the company's culture—its goals, beliefs, habits, and ways of working—would have to value discipline and focus as much as creativity. Only then could the company consistently invent something new while keeping it LEGO. The goal was to foster a culture where developers and marketers were highly empowered to reimagine what was possible for LEGO but also highly accountable for the results—where they'd have both the flexibility to do the right thing for kids and the stimulus to do the right thing for profits.

At least in the near term, rebuilding a company culture where profitable, sustained innovation flourished would be an exceedingly difficult challenge. For starters, an unwieldy triumvirate consisting of Kristiansen, Knudstorp, and Jesper Ovesen would lead LEGO in its all-or-nothing effort to get back in the black. In January 2004, under the terse headline "Plougmann and Ciccolella Are Leaving the Company," the LEGO Group announced sweeping changes at the top of the organization. In its press release, the company stated, "As a consequence of the LEGO Company's expected deficit in the order of DKK 1.4 billion" ($225 million), Kjeld Kirk Kristiansen would resume day-to-day responsibilities for managing the organization, "assisted" by Knudstorp and Ovesen. If LEGO had been rudderless during the Plougmann era, with innovation efforts spiraling out in every direction, it was difficult to see how the company would once again rebuild its culture when there'd be three different hands at the helm.

Surprisingly, even though LEGO was in a death spiral, many staffers greeted the leadership shake-up with unmitigated joy.

Poul Plougmann was less than loved at the time of his departure. Unfairly or not, his Nordic complexion and shock of white hair, along with his having axed one thousand employees in 1998, had led some LEGO staffers to bequeath him the sobriquet "Mr. Death." The grandson of the LEGO Group's founder, on the other hand, was hailed as the company's savior. Upon hearing news of the changes, an elated designer Photoshopped an image of Kristiansen's face onto a poster for the movie *The Lord of the Rings: The Return of the King*. Within a few hours of the announcement, copies of the doctored poster were plastered all over the hallways of the LEGO Group's headquarters. At a town hall meeting later that day, staffers cheered Kristiansen's homecoming. But although the king had reclaimed his throne, his court was nevertheless riddled with angst over the company's benighted future. People's apprehension sprang out of three questions that reside at the epicenter of almost every turnaround effort: Would the company make it? Who was really in charge? And what was the strategy?

The new management team's real-world answers to those questions were honest and direct.

Would the company make it? As 2003 wound down and the bleeding accelerated, Plougmann described the company's predicament, in an interview with the Danish newspaper *Boersen*, as "unexpectedly bad, nearly catastrophic."[13] If anything, the LEGO Group's plight was even worse than Plougmann admitted. The company was in the midst of a meltdown.

By the end of 2003, the LEGO Group's sales had plunged by 30 percent compared to the previous year and it had lost its leadership position atop all of its core markets. LEGO was running a negative cash flow of DKK 1 billion ($160 million) and had racked up debt of DKK 5 billion ($800 million). Although 2003 brought the biggest deficit in the LEGO Group's history, 2004 was forecast to be even worse, as the company's net loss was expected to double to DKK 1.9 billion (about $300 million).

At least over the short term, there was no possibility that LEGO might grow its way out of the debacle. In early 2004, an internal survey of the company's entire product portfolio revealed that 94 percent of LEGO sets were unprofitable. Only *Star Wars* and Bionicle kits were making money. Not only had LEGO sustained the largest losses, on a percentage basis, among toy makers, but it was by far the industry's least profitable brand.

As news of the brick maker's crash spread beyond Billund, analysts predicted that with toy industry heavyweights and private equity firms closing in, LEGO would probably be broken up and sold off in pieces. The *Financial Times* reported the LEGO Group's "financial independence" was at stake. The British newspaper the *In-*

dependent cited "growing speculation that LEGO cannot survive alone." In a headline, the London *Telegraph* flatly declared, "Family Likely to Lose Control of the LEGO Set."

Kristiansen was determined to keep LEGO in the family, but the headlines weren't just hype. The company's financial health was so dire, Ovesen had at least one discussion with Mattel about acquiring LEGO, just in case the turnaround foundered. His blunt assessment of the company's dilemma: "We didn't know if we would make it through the year."

Who was really in charge? Although the message to both the LEGO organization and the outside world was that Kristiansen was back in the driver's seat, he was not about to steer the company's day-to-day operations. Having led LEGO for the better part of a quarter century, Kristiansen believed the challenge of reinventing the company required a new chief. But who?

Ovesen had the acumen and the throw weight to take on the financial restructuring, but he was a CFO lifer who had no desire to become CEO. Knudstorp had the right long-term vision for LEGO, as well as impressive people skills, but the board of directors fretted that he was too inexperienced to shepherd the organization at such a decisive moment. The board wanted to recruit a turnaround expert from some other organization, but Kristiansen concluded that after Plougmann's volatile tenure, another outsider would be too great a shock to the LEGO Group's system.

In the end, the board decided the best way forward was to settle for the aforementioned triumvirate, with Kristiansen as the face of the organization, Ovesen as the financial overseer, and Knudstorp as the master strategist and CEO-in-waiting. Although there was a certain "make our weakness our strength" logic to the arrangement, it hardly inspired confidence. Because Knudstorp wasn't the company's officially designated leader, he lacked a clear mandate to make big changes.

"It was not a super construction, because the company was in a real critical situation," he conceded. "I just didn't have enough formal authority. We needed to make decisions at a pretty high pace. When you're running a turnaround, you don't want confusion."

What was the strategy? Having been assigned the knotty task of devising a turnaround strategy, Knudstorp found that clarity proved elusive. Any instinct he might have had for choosing the best way forward was consumed by a swirl of confusing choices.

In announcing Plougmann's firing, the LEGO Group's press release declared that the company's future strategy would put renewed emphasis on its "core products." Kristiansen told the *Telegraph* that new product lines "did not give the expected results. We will now focus on profitability, especially the attractive potential of our core products."[14] In an interview with the *Financial Times*, he opined that the LEGO Group's fall was the result of chasing too many fads and neglecting the construction toys that had once made it great. "We have simply not had enough focus on our core products," he averred. "Too much of our growth has been generated by licensed products."[15] Again and again, the word *core* figured prominently in nearly every account of the company's plan for reviving growth.

At first glance, the road to growth seemed remarkably straightforward: go back to making and selling millions of LEGO bricks and let kids' imaginations take over. Trouble was, that strategy had flatlined in the mid-1990s as simple plastic building blocks lost their luster and more kids shifted to video games and electronic toys. Plougmann had been brought in precisely because LEGO needed to shake up its complacent, inward-looking culture, break out of its rapidly narrowing niche, and seek new pathways to growth. And that was exactly what he had done.

When LEGO tied into the *Harry Potter* and *Star Wars* franchises and those deals yielded blockbuster sales, few complained that the Danish family firm had abandoned its core. Had the company shunned *Star Wars* and thereby let Hasbro grab the deal—at the time, a very real possibility—LEGO would have been roundly criticized for relying overmuch on its aging, brick-based product lines and missing out on a promising growth opportunity to a more innovative rival. If, five years later, *Star Wars* wasn't "core" to LEGO, as Kristiansen implied in the *Financial Times* piece, it certainly was core to the brick maker's balance sheet.

And what of some of those other big growth initiatives? Were amusement parks and retail stores really so very far removed from the company's roots? Disney had made parks spectacularly successful for its businesses, as Apple had done with stores. Why shouldn't LEGO?

With Plougmann out and his reinvention strategy having been deemed a failure, Knudstorp was expected to reverse course once again and take LEGO back to basics. But which core pathway should he follow? Bricks and minifigs, by themselves, couldn't put LEGO ahead of its competitors. As for licensed lines, LEGO was already overly reliant on them. And with the exception of LEGOLAND Billund, it was losing millions on its parks and most of its stores; at least over the near term, using those vehicles to exploit the power of the brand was not a viable option. Try as he might to discover the one true avenue that was rooted in the past and yet would deliver LEGO to a bright, shiny future, Knudstorp found himself running down one dead end after another.

Night after night, the former McKinsey consultant would meet with the seasoned CFO for dinner at the LEGOLAND Hotel, where he focus-tested his strategies for improving the business. "I had something like eight proposals on what to do about operations, seven proposals on what to do about innovation, and probably another seven proposals for market actions and so forth," exclaimed Knudstorp. "In all, I must have proposed fifty or sixty actions. And Jesper just looked at me and said, 'The way you describe the company and the way I understand the situation, your plan is too complex. It's never going to happen.'"

Ovesen's advice was as direct as it was taut: Forget strategy. The company needed an action plan for its survival.

In cutting through Knudstorp's strategic scenarios and homing in on a plan for survival, Ovesen sought to give people a window into what needed to happen next. A survival plan comes with a list of priorities that aim to restore the organization's fiscal health and competitiveness. When management communicates and follows up on those actions—when it says what it's going to do and then does it—its credibility starts to grow and people begin to move along with the new leadership. "Jesper's clarity was just what I needed," said Knudstorp. "But it was also just what the organization needed."

Putting a survival plan ahead of a growth plan was challenging, given that people were clamoring for *the* strategy—a road map for reviving profits and returning LEGO to the top of the toy industry. At a gathering of the company's sixty top executives, one of them stood up and said what many were thinking: "We need to get clear on the strategy and the mission." But Knudstorp deliberately refused to deliver one. "Right now, our mission is just to survive," he told the group. "To cut costs, sell businesses, and restore our competitiveness."

Knudstorp and Ovesen's decision not to spell out a big, over-arching strategy served a dual purpose. First, they needed to fully focus people's energy, experience, and talent on the treacherous task that lay before them. If they didn't raise cash, secure new lines of credit, and stop selling money-losing products, LEGO wouldn't get to launch a grand strategy because it wouldn't survive 2004 as an independent organization. Second, they were determined to remake the company's mind-set, which in their view was far too compla-cent. Knudstorp recalled how Ovesen couldn't get over the fact that his previous employer, Danske Bank, was among the most success-ful financial institutions in Scandinavia, "and yet everyone came to work grumpy and angry. Then Jesper arrives at LEGO, and he tells me, 'I have never seen so much shit in my life. Everything is broken. You're not making any money. You can't even forecast your sales, and people are so happy—I can't believe it.' "

To Remake the Company's Culture, Begin by Breaking It

All throughout the late 1990s, when LEGO was destroying economic value on a daily basis, Danish business executives had voted it the most admired company in Denmark. And, of course, in 2000 both *Fortune* and the British Association of Toy Retailers had proclaimed the LEGO brick the twentieth century's greatest toy. Although the LEGO Group's steep decline had alarmed some staffers, there remained a bright residue of optimism that ran through the organization—a sanguine belief among too many managers and associates that the storm would pass and better days would soon return. Knudstorp and Ovesen concluded that before LEGO could even begin to reignite a sense of what was possible for LEGO, they first had to persuade people that decades of unfettered growth offered no assurance that the company would ever get its groove back. So rather than follow the example of most leaders in a turnaround, which is to fabricate an inspiring plan that would rally people to a better and brighter future, Knudstorp and Ovesen instead decided to begin by stamping out the last vestiges of overconfidence and deliver a dose of hard realism.

"We wanted to break the back of the culture," said Knudstorp. "We had to go through a one-year, painful process of beating ourselves up and saying, 'You know what? There's no reason to be so enthusiastic. We're not such a world-class brand, as we go around telling ourselves. We say we do a lot for child development, but we're not selling a lot, so how can we be?'

"This was a company that was always very enthusiastic about grand strategies and nurturing the child of all ages," he continued. "Our message was, 'forget [for now] about the visionary, child-development stuff. Let's get more operational and execution oriented. Let's get stuff done.' "

Remaking the LEGO culture—altering people's behaviors and beliefs so that they focused less on grandiose ideas and strategies and more on "getting stuff done"—was really a matter of reconnecting with the bedrock values that had sustained LEGO since its inception.

An organization's values signal what its leaders and associates care about and what they stand for. Values not only serve to bind people to a set of shared assumptions about where the business can and should be going. They also define what's possible for associates, customers, and partners. By reanimating its values, the LEGO Group's leaders stood a better chance of giving people a shared sense of purpose, one that would once again set the company apart from much of the me-too thinking that dominates the toy industry.

Caught up as he was with trying to wrangle the whirlwind of events that engulfed LEGO during 2004, Knudstorp had little time to reflect on how he might map out a return to the values that had guided LEGO for so many decades. Acting mostly on instinct, he concluded that for LEGO to get back to making core products (whatever they turned out to be) for core customers, it had to revive the core set of founding principles that Ole and Godtfred Kirk Christiansen had established so many years ago: that the LEGO play experience is founded not on products but on the brick and the building system, that tightening designers' focus leads to more profitable innovation, that LEGO must return to acting authentically, and that the road to profitability starts with the retailers. Taken together, those essential values, established more than half a century earlier, stood the best chance of preparing LEGO for an increasingly challenging future.

To build a culture where sustained value creation thrived once again, Knudstorp's overriding challenge was to remake the LEGO Group's core values in a contemporary way. As the author and Copenhagen Business School professor Majken Schultz later told Knudstorp, he "used LEGO's history to create a new cultural identity." Knudstorp agreed, although his way of putting it was decidedly unvarnished: "It was not something we were very deliberate about," he mused. "But essentially, we stole from our past to interpret our future."

Here's what they did.

First the Stores, Then the Kids

Although the LEGO Group's mission is to "inspire and develop the builders of tomorrow," its leaders long understood that to nurture kids, it had to forge tight, profitable partnerships with retailers. But those alliances deteriorated badly during the Plougmann era, when chains such as Walmart and Toys "R" Us were whipsawed by such rash LEGO moves as dumping DUPLO and failing to forecast the fall-off in sales of *Star Wars* kits in a year without a new movie. Seeking to repair the damage, Kristiansen and Knudstorp, soon after they took over from Plougmann, took a lap around the world and met with key partners. It was a brutal trip, as the recent years' frustrations with the LEGO Group's mismanagement of its key account relationships finally erupted.

In a February 2004 stop at New York's Toy Fair, the year's largest gathering of North America's biggest toy sellers, Kristiansen and Knudstorp sat down with a disgruntled team of senior buyers from Toys "R" Us. The Toys "R" Us team delivered a blistering brief on the LEGO Group's performance. "They told us, 'We love and understand the LEGO brand better than you guys do,'" Knudstorp recalled. "It was a shocking statement, especially coming from a retailer." Howard Roffman, Lucasfilm's licensing chief and the point man for LEGO *Star Wars*, tendered an unsettlingly similar appraisal, telling Kristiansen: "You've lost your grip on the business. You're not on top of your game."

From the partners' perspective, the LEGO Group's sins were numerous. The company's leaders had lost sight of the deep-seated DNA that had made the brand great, and they were clueless about how to keep it vibrant in a rapidly changing world. Its marketers were aloof and slow to respond to retailers' needs. Worst of all, LEGO had grown stunningly inept at forecasting demand and managing its supply chain. It had overwhelmed retailers' inventory with lackluster kits. At the same time, in the United States, there was an unforgivable lapse: LEGO had failed to deliver sufficient quantities of its two best-selling Bionicle products in the run-up to Christmas. At a time when LEGO had suffered the worst loss in its history, it had created robust demand for Bionicle and then couldn't fulfill it.

Those forthright conversations drove home the notion that senior management must restore not only the LEGO Group's profitability but *retailers'* profitability as well. Upon his return to Billund, Knudstorp pushed to once again put the retailer ahead of the customer, as LEGO had throughout its most successful decades. But that notion proved anathema to some of the company's executives.

"The company's mission statement was to nurture the child of all ages, and I spent the next nine months debating with people in top management whether we were now neglecting the children," he said. "We literally told people to forget about the children for now, because if we don't serve the retailer, we'll never reach the child.

"It just goes to show how incredibly hard it is to change habits and cultures," Knudstorp continued. "Some of those top people had spent so much of their careers dedicating themselves to another strategic direction. In the end, you can only change by letting some of them go."

After a seminar at the Swiss business school IMD (where Kristiansen had received his MBA), the management team identified a set of "must-win battles" for 2004—immediate, do-or-die efforts that aimed to return LEGO to a safe harbor. Chief among those battles was the declaration that LEGO would "restore competitiveness by focusing on our retail customers." That meant working to improve retailers' margins, delivering to store shelves the right kits in the right volumes at the right time, and creating a "balanced" (read: not overly dependent on one hit toy) product portfolio that tapped into kids' desires.

If people are going to follow a leader into the future, they need to know precisely whom they're trying to please. By firing managers who wouldn't change and asserting unequivocally that improving retailers' LEGO sales was crucial for the company's survival, Knudstorp made clear that retailers would be the ultimate judges of the LEGO Group's performance. That might not have been enough to change the hearts of those LEGO staffers who still believed the company should put kids before retailers. So be it. By spotlighting which constituency LEGO must serve, Knudstorp stood a better chance of changing more minds. Such clarity began to infuse staffers with enough confidence to face the future.

Tighter Focus Leads to Profitable Innovation

In the 1950s, when the son of the LEGO Group's founder decided to bet entirely on the plastic brick and cease production of wooden toys, he demonstrated that channeling people's creativity into one specific area could generate an outpouring of profitable products. In the decades that followed, even as LEGO spun out new product lines such as DUPLO for preschoolers and Technic for advanced builders, each of those platforms was rooted in the LEGO building system. By consistently doing more of what it had done before, LEGO improved its chances of making successful products.

But the company lost much of its focus and discipline while pursuing every conceivable adjacency—to use Zook's term—in its bid to become the world's strongest brand among families with children by 2005. Francesco Ciccolella, in his rebranding of the brick, had proclaimed that LEGO was "an idea-based—not a category-based—business." The notion that LEGO was not a toy but an idea—and an undefined idea at that—was so opaque, it opened the way for designers to create products that were far removed from the very real qualities that had defined LEGO in the minds of customers. And his declaration that "the LEGO idea [will] transcend traditional category boundaries" ensured that LEGO would venture into such uncharted terrain as lifestyle products, branded stores, theme parks, and beyond.

Knudstorp understood the logic behind Plougmann's decision

to rapidly expand the LEGO Group's product portfolio, pursue untapped markets, and diversify the ranks of its designers and developers. Problem was, the company's zealous desire to boost innovation had taken it in so many directions, it couldn't manage all of its many initiatives. Ovesen had come to the same conclusion. Citing Apple and its legendary perfectionism, secrecy, and attention to detail, he argued that "the world's most innovative companies are also the most disciplined. You have to have great control over all the basics; only then can you start to be truly innovative."

As they huddled over dinner during the first nights of 2004, Knudstorp and Ovesen began to map out how they'd wage another must-win battle for the company's survival: "Set a crisp and clear direction and change the way we do business." Above all, that meant getting a better grasp on where LEGO was making money and putting people's efforts behind those products that showed the most promise. By jettisoning the businesses that were bleeding money, Knudstorp and Ovesen began to reveal the profitable product lines that were truly core to LEGO.

They were an unlikely but complementary pairing: the mathematically minded CFO who "saw a number behind every person" and the young, humanistic CEO-in-waiting who "saw a person behind every number." But the combination proved effective.

Ovesen plunged into every LEGO business unit and delivered triage reports that made the case for eliminating product lines that were deep in the red, restructuring lines that showed signs of life, and expanding the few that were profitable. The pair's reports back to Kristiansen and the board led to the decision to cut out 30 percent of the product portfolio, curtail the LEGO stores initiative, and jettison the company's theme parks and computer games businesses. The moves were not without controversy. LEGO video games held great promise, but after the Darwin debacle, it was felt the company lacked the resources and the management know-how to successfully commercialize the effort. The theme parks were even more problematic. Because his father had launched LEGOLAND Billund, Kristiansen was deeply reluctant to sell off the business. It would be another year before he rendered his decision.

In the meantime, Knudstorp and Ovesen's most significant move was to immediately halt production of LEGO Explore and revive DUPLO. Restoring DUPLO's primacy signaled to the designers of preschool toys that the line would be a core part of the company's future. "There was a lot of cheering when we got the [DUPLO logo] red rabbit back," recalled Allan Steen Larsen, one of the designers who had worked on Explore. "We felt we were back on the right track."

Following quickly on the DUPLO rebirth was a refocus on other tried-and-true product lines that had sustained LEGO since the brick's earliest days. The World City line, which consisted of futuristic buildings and flying cars, was quickly restructured to realistically reflect the world that kids saw all around them, just as the LEGO town sets of the 1950s had done. The Jack Stone and fanciful Orient Express lines were replaced with updated themes from the 1970s and '80s, such as a Pirates line and Knights of the Kingdom, both of which were reboots of previously successful play themes.

Ovesen also inaugurated a near-term, measurable goal that consisted solely of a number: 13½ percent. He established a financial tracking system dubbed Consumer Product Profitability (CPP), which measured the return on sales of individual products and markets. CPP gave LEGO an unimpeded view into where it was losing and making money. To survive, any existing or proposed product should demonstrate that its return on sales would meet or surpass that 13½ percent benchmark, which was based on the company's analysis of its competitors' earnings and its expectation of what a premium toy brand should deliver.

Of course, most of the toys in the LEGO Group's 2004 portfolio would fail to clear that bar; some product lines were given a temporary reprieve and allowed to slip under it, with 6 percent set as an absolute minimum. But 13½ percent gave managers, when they were considering the prospects of products that were still in development, a vivid reality check. No matter how passionate designers were about a toy in the making, if they couldn't convincingly forecast a 13½ percent return, the product would never see the market. The new standard also communicated to everyone in the organization that, moving forward, they should focus solely on innovations that would yield real profits.

"In town hall meetings, emails, on the factory floors—13½ percent was talked about everywhere, all the time," said senior vice president Poul Schou, who oversees most of the company's product development. "It was a huge ambition in those days to make a number like that, but it gave us something to aim for. When I sat down with my product lines and looked out over all of my markets, we always had to ask the question, 'Where do we hit 13½ percent?' It was an incredibly clear way to set priorities."

Not a Product but a System

All throughout 2004, Knudstorp had extensive conversations with Kristiansen about the nature and continuing relevance of the LEGO System of Play. Knudstorp was reminded that LEGO owed its decades of unbroken success to Godtfred Kirk Christiansen's insight that if every LEGO piece clicked with every other piece—and every LEGO kit was an integral part of a larger LEGO universe—LEGO could offer kids more possibilities for continuous play. And with continuous play came (nearly) limitless sales.

For children and their parents, the benefits of a play system were obvious: combining bricks in almost any way they wanted fired kids' creativity and imagination and delivered a singularly unique building experience. But for Knudstorp, his eureka moment came when he realized the LEGO System is not just a play system, it's also a *business* system. After all, it had been a retailer who suggested to Godtfred, on that ferry trip to England, that instead of following the industry norm of striving to come up with one-hit wonders, LEGO should create a coherent, expandable universe of toys. A LEGO system of toys, the retailer reasoned, would build familiarity and a sense of community around LEGO and thereby would generate repeat sales.

"The system grew out of a retailer's request," Knudstorp recalled. "And it proved to be of real advantage to retailers."

More than anything, the LEGO System's greatest value resided in its benefit to manufacturing, for it shielded LEGO from much of the rapid shifts in kids' tastes. The toy industry was and continues to be enormously fickle—even certified phenomena, such as Beanie Babies and Tickle Me Elmo in the 1990s, eventually ran their course and were replaced by the next hot property. Thus, toy companies have had to constantly scramble to conceive and produce this year's "must-have," knowing that next year they'll most likely have to retrofit their factories for something different.

Thanks to the LEGO System, however, the company's forecasters understood that no matter what kits kids lusted for—LEGO City, *Star Wars*, or something entirely new—it could still produce bricks, minifigs, wheels, windows, and thousands of other components, every day of every year, just as it had done for decades. The sets and themes would change, but many of the components remained the same. Because most components were compatible across so many different kits, LEGO could reap enormous cost savings by not having to dramatically change its manufacturing operations from year to year. Knudstorp knew this intuitively, but his conversations with Kristiansen brought into sharper focus the notion that the LEGO System is an all-encompassing business system.

"Near the end of 2004, I started to understand that we have a customer base, a retailer base, and a manufacturing base that loves the System," he recalled. "I realized that our job was to take what made the LEGO System so successful in the 1970s and 1980s and remake it for the twenty-first century."

As a first step in making the System a centerpiece of the company's survival plan, Knudstorp accelerated an effort that had begun in the summer of 2002: restore the Design Lab's authority. From the System of Play's earliest days, no new LEGO color or piece, whether it be a brighter shade of yellow or a fire engine's windshield, could see the light of day without Godtfred's personal approval. In the years following Godtfred's retirement, the Design Lab continued to impose his strict, authoritarian rule over the universe of LEGO components.

Comprising some of the company's most experienced designers and developers, the Design Lab functioned as an unyielding final arbiter whose foremost goal was to tightly corral the LEGO color palette and tamp down the total number of LEGO elements in the company's inventory, especially one-of-a-kind elements, such as an *Indiana Jones* whip, that worked in just one particular set.

Until the early 1990s, the Lab had been a critical force for driving down costs. But then the Lab lost its sway. As LEGO launched a bevy of wildly divergent products in the hopes that something, *anything*, might capture the malleable minds of its young customers, designers began to openly circumvent the Lab. They conjured models requiring whole new phalanxes of components—variations of arms, boats, cones, doors, and much, much more, in colors that ranged from aqua to speckled silver. They even immortalized themselves in the models

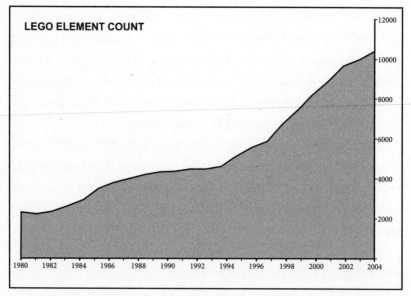

The total number of different elements that LEGO produced each year (measured at the end of each year). The number peaked at 14,200 in 2004.

they built, replicating their own faces on minifigs. They were, quite literally, out of control.

In just seven years, from 1997 to 2004, the number of elements in the company's inventory exploded, ascending from slightly more than 6,000 to more than 14,200. So did its range of colors, which climbed from the original six (red, yellow, blue, green, black, and white) to more than fifty. As the number of components and colors mounted, soaring supply and production costs plundered the company's bottom line. Here's why.

A standard brick with two rows of four studs delivers a profit to LEGO that is orders of magnitude greater than any specialized element, all because the brick is what LEGO calls a "universal" or "evergreen" element that can be used in so many different sets. A one-of-a-kind, specialized piece, however, generally works in just one or a few sets. Moreover, the cost of molding a standard brick is orders of magnitude cheaper than producing a specialized piece.

A mold for a standard LEGO piece costs anywhere from $50,000 to $80,000; over its lifetime, it will spit out some sixty million bricks. The cost of making the mold, spread out over all those bricks, is essentially zero. But when designers concoct a specialized piece and LEGO manufactures just fifty thousand of them, the molding cost rises to as high as $1 per piece. Including just a few of these specialized pieces, as LEGO did with unrelenting frequency during the Plougmann era, can potentially kill a LEGO set's profit potential.

This is not to suggest that specialized pieces are bad. Far from it. LEGO *Indiana Jones* would never feel real without Indy's whip; LEGO Board Games would never spring to life without their unique dice. But there's no denying that specialized pieces are costly to produce, and their proliferation was a prime reason why the LEGO Group's profits plummeted through much of the 1990s, despite steady sales.*

---

* Our back-of-the-envelope analysis found that DKK 1 million of sales per element is a magic number for LEGO. If sales fall or element counts rise—and the ratio between the two drops below one million—LEGO slides into a loss. As the ratio rises, however, profits increase exponentially.

A LEGO brick mold.

Having launched a painstaking review of each of those 14,200 pieces in the LEGO universe, the Design Lab found that 90 percent of new elements were developed and used just once. And many components were duplicates. Among the dupes were eight minifig police officers and six minifig chefs, with barely decipherable differences between them. The Lab dealt with the redundancies by slashing the total number of components by more than 50 percent. When it reduced the product portfolio's minifig chef population from six to one, designers protested and longtime fans howled. To calm the fans, LEGO tried humor: it held a mock online memorial service for the "dead chefs."

Redundant police and chef minifigs symbolized the out-of-control, outside-the-box innovation efforts that had almost put LEGO out of business. So in 2004, the company's new management team responded by restarting a practice that LEGO had once abandoned: putting strict cost limits around its products.

Beginning in the late 1980s, every LEGO development team, when it began work on a new project, was assigned a full manufacturing cost (FMC) for producing the set. The FMC totaled the entire spectrum of the set's costs—acquiring the raw materials, molding the bricks and other pieces, producing building instructions, packing and packaging the assortment of pieces, even the injection molding machine's depreciation. No development team was permitted to exceed its FMC; if it had, it would have eaten into the company's margins.*

In the go-go years of the late 1990s, however, the LEGO Group's management allowed developers to untether themselves from the FMC's limits. The consequences were disastrous. Freed from the FMC's constraints, designers concocted more and more of those specialized pieces. Designers didn't simply decide to go wild. They were spurred by management's insistence that they devise increasingly esoteric models, such as Galidor, Jack Stone, and LEGO Explore, which required radically different components. Although there might have been good reasons to justify the creation of individual specialized pieces, their cumulative effect was to make the LEGO Group's operations increasingly complex. The costs of purchasing new molds to produce each of those specialized pieces rapidly compounded; so did the costs associated with managing the manufacture and packaging of those specialized components. The ironic result was that LEGO, by dramatically ramping up its pace of innovation, plundered its profits.

Beginning in 2004, while marketing managers were pushed to reach the 13½ percent profit targets, development teams were given equally challenging FMC cost targets. A LEGO City team that was designing a new police station would be assigned a specific cost; failing to meet that target would come back to haunt the designers at their annual review. "You had to stay within your FMC model," said Henrik Weis Aalbaek, who helped champion the framework's return. "Otherwise, you were dead."

---

* FMC is the cost part of the CPP system we discussed earlier. FMC cost numbers are combined with sales revenues to give the profitability numbers in the CPP system.

At the same time, designers had free rein to create, so long as they kept within the FMC's parameters. In a very real sense, they were forced to innovate *inside* the box. It was expected that designers would devise pieces that required new molds, since those elements would make, say, a LEGO City police station fresh and exciting. But such specialized pieces had to be *really* special—something that would light up the entire set. At the same time, the FMC frame ensured that designers would tamp down the desire to create lots of cool-for-cool's-sake pieces and instead find creative ways to make more out of universal pieces. As a result, on average, at least 70 percent of every LEGO set, whether it's a LEGO City box or a new play theme such as Ninjago, is now made up of standard, universal bricks. Or to put it another way, 70 percent of the bricks in a City line are used in radically different sets such as Ninjago, and vice versa. This allows LEGO to reap enormous cost savings by not having to produce more molds for "uncommon" elements.

As for the designers, they gradually discovered they were more creative with a smaller inventory. Though the idea runs counter to the notion that great design requires maximum freedom, LEGO designers found that the tighter range of components gave them even more definition and sufficient direction to come up with successful ideas. Apple's designers made a similar discovery when Steve Jobs insisted that the iPhone needed only a single, minimalist control button. Jobs' obsession with simplicity forced his designers to overcome complexity and innovate with less, which resulted in one of the past decade's most iconic designs.

Concluded Knudstorp: "Innovation flourishes when the space available for it is limited. Less is more."

Ultimately, the FMC framework, by putting distinctive cost constraints in place, delivered a sharper sense of direction to designers. "When designers chose a color or a certain element, they could see the costs of their decisions," said Aalbaek. Such knowledge, in turn, increased the odds that they'd create money-making toys.

Make It Authentic

From the 1930s to the early 1990s, authenticity was one of the core strands of the LEGO Group's DNA. Recall that with kits such as LEGO City, kids could re-create the streetscapes, fire stations, and ambulances of their real-world lives. Even a fantasy theme such as LEGO Castle included telling details, such as the knights' movable visors and armor breastplates, that helped make the medieval era as "real as real" for kids.

Over the years, as the company's universe of product lines expanded, the brand's legions of fans came to recognize the essential features that were authentic to LEGO itself: the brick, the System, and the building experience. But as we've seen, those qualities began to bleed out of LEGO during the Plougmann era. Fearing that the brick was passé, LEGO diluted the building experience and frequently violated the System's integrity. As a result, the newer kits didn't feel like they were authentically, classically LEGO.

In 2004, as Knudstorp and Ovesen swiftly moved to shut down money-losing product lines, they also began to strip away much of what was pseudo-LEGO. In killing off Explore, Galidor, and Jack Stone and elevating such foundational LEGO play experiences as DUPLO and City, the pair began to make LEGO a little less ersätz for those true-believing fans who loved to build. At the same time, Knudstorp understood that it wasn't enough to make the LEGO *play* experience more authentic. He had to do the same with the LEGO *work* experience.

Authenticity is really about integrity. It comes to leaders who do what they say they're going to do. When the story that leaders tell through their actions aligns with the story they tell through their communications, people sense that the story is true, and authenticity sets in. Knudstorp knew that words weren't enough to truly instill the company's culture with a renewed sense of discipline, focus, and accountability. Authentic leadership requires action. Borrowing a line from Millard Fuller, the founder of Habitat for Humanity, Knudstorp argued that for LEGO to reset its compass and authentically return to its core, "you don't think yourself into a new way of acting, you act yourself into a new way of thinking."

"As McKinsey consultants, we believed that thinking is paramount—that thought turns into action," he reasoned. "But it's actually the opposite. When you act your way into a new habit, the habit becomes your opinion about how you should do things, and that opinion becomes your character as a person or as an organization. So we started to take some actions that would make us change our behavior."

To build a culture of ownership and accountability, Knudstorp set out to track the company's progress. He created a war room to monitor the supply chain and measure product quality and delivery performance. He also built key performance indicators, or KPIs, into people's performance reviews, to ensure they were helping to fuel the company's return to the core. An essential KPI for some senior managers, for example, set goals for cutting the number of LEGO elements.

At every step, Knudstorp changed many of the artifacts—facilities, offices, tangible awards, and recognition—that together constituted the most visible aspects of the company's cultural fabric. That meant creating physical changes that held people accountable for their results and the organization's performance. After a first round of layoffs in 2004, he shuttered offices and moved the remaining associates into far tighter quarters. His reasoning: half-empty office space gave people a sense of abundance. At a time when LEGO was bleeding losses and starving for resources, he wanted people to have a sense of scarcity. To that end, he also sold off the LEGO Group's head office in Billund, with its posh executive suites, and moved himself and other senior managers to a building that also housed the packing plant. And he eschewed the kind of luxe wheels that most European executives drive, such as a BMW 7 Series, and instead took to commuting to Billund in a far humbler 2001 Citroën C5, a car similar to the Volkswagen Passat or Ford Mondeo.

Knudstorp also changed some of the company's rituals. Instead of managers holding sway over minions, colleagues held colleagues accountable for their results. At the war room meetings, where executives ran through weekly sales results, he insisted that the heads of product lines post their numbers on a whiteboard. "We could have done it in SAP or some other IT system, but the point was to do it personally," he explained. "Here's a group of eight leaders. You step up. 'Sorry, guys, I didn't make it this week. Here's the corrective action I'm taking.' " The idea was to use peer pressure, rather than pressure from some corporate overlord, to change behavior.

Looking back at the events that transpired during 2004, Knudstorp recalled that a significant part of his job that year was to "break down the confidence of the organization, because we had been overconfident and we needed to come back to reality." His constant reminders that LEGO was resting on a "burning platform" and his insistence that the company needed a survival plan instead of a strategy certainly deflated people's sense of entitlement. So did the blizzard of pink slips that befell the LEGO Group. The *Financial Times* later reported that during the restructuring, Knudstorp and Ovesen ran LEGO "like a ruthless private equity firm," and that's about right. The pair cut twelve hundred jobs, nearly a third of the company's workforce at the time. By shuttering costly factories and unprofitable product lines and selling off real estate, they cut the LEGO Group's cost base by $600 million over two years. "When we announced the layoffs and sell-offs and cost-cutting and all the rest of it, you can imagine the mood in the organization was not exactly optimistic," Knudstorp concluded drily. Nevertheless, he had gotten people's attention.

Knudstorp had also begun to position people for success. By

restoring the company's fundamental values, he laid the foundation for an innovation culture that put the retailer first; that focused designers as well as managers on creating only those toys that stood an odds-on chance of generating substantial profits; that revived the enduring LEGO product lines that appealed to kids who loved to build; that championed inside-the-box creativity; that challenged people to do more with less; and that pushed people to act authentically by showing instead of telling. Even so, it would take at least a year before any of those actions would reap real rewards.

On a sun-splashed day in June 2004, Knudstorp stepped before a gathering in Billund's LEGOLAND Hotel of sixty of the LEGO Group's top managers. Although it had not yet been made official, this was his coming-out as the company's new chief.

Knudstorp's first words had nothing to do with the LEGO Group's dire financial predicament, nor even with LEGO itself. Instead, he spoke about his love for the Scandinavian summer. By revealing his "passion for this place we're in, this culture," he hoped to summon the sense of unity and shared purpose they would need to face the difficult challenges confronting LEGO, of which there remained many: limited cash, increasing price pressure, high fixed costs, the shift away from traditional play, dreadfully few products that were actually profitable.

After Knudstorp was finished with his remarks, there was a smattering of applause. Though it was plain that Kristiansen had tapped Knudstorp as his heir apparent, more than a few executives might well have wondered whether he was the man for the job. The company had survived the year and staffers were beginning to brace themselves for a difficult future. But a return to profitability still seemed like a pipe dream, and Knudstorp had yet to reveal a long-range strategy for turning the company around. In fact, it's safe to assume that some in that room believed *they* should have been given the CEO job. After dinner that night, just one executive called to congratulate him.

Four months later, after forecasting the company's record loss for 2004, Kristiansen announced he was stepping aside. Knudstorp would be just the second outsider to head LEGO since its founding. In Billund, some wondered how long Knudstorp would last. At the supermarket and other gathering places, conventional wisdom held that the new chief would never be the LEGO Group's real leader until he convinced Kristiansen to divest the company of the LEGOLAND parks. And so far that hadn't happened. It was still very much an open-ended question whether seventy-two-year-old LEGO would keep its independence intact, and whether its thirty-four-year-old CEO would keep his job.

5

Becoming Customer Driven

The Rebirth of LEGO City

*Children and drunks are the last honest people
left on the face of the Earth. And children
will never buy a product that isn't fun.*

—Mads Nipper, executive vice president for
  markets and products, the LEGO Group

IN EARLY 2004, WHEN THE LEGO GROUP WAS STILL DEEPLY
mired in its financial crisis, Mads Nipper got a video
conference call from Kristiansen. Recall that Nipper, who was based in Munich, where he oversaw the company's
all-important central Europe markets, was not at all shy about prodding Billund to kill off LEGO Explore and swiftly revive DUPLO. He had directly relayed to Kristiansen himself the frustrations that were welling up from Germany's largest retailers, who were alarmed by the company's hot pursuit of distinctly un-LEGO-like play themes such as Galidor and Jack Stone.

Kristiansen might well have been tempted to banish the bearer of such relentlessly negative news. Instead, he offered Nipper a promotion: return to Billund and head up the company's marketing and product development. Kristiansen and Knudstorp had concluded that LEGO had lost its way in part because it had lost touch with retailers and customers. As Knudstorp later put it, LEGO suffered from a "lack of realism. There was no dialogue with the world outside LEGO, which is one of the most dangerous signs that the corporate culture is not working." In their view, no other LEGO executive had tighter ties with retailers—or a better capacity to see the world through the eyes of the brick's core customers—than Mads Nipper.

Having joined LEGO in 1990, Nipper first headed up the company's trade marketing department for Europe, where he worked closely with retailers to improve in-store marketing and sales. He then went on to make the first case for creating a direct-to-consumer business; as a result, he led the creation of LEGO.com. Soon thereafter, as the chief of the company's toy business for nine- to sixteen-year-olds, he oversaw a vital core business, LEGO Technic, as well as the launch of two of the company's greatest successes, Bionicle and the Mindstorms robotics set. From his perch in Munich, he had witnessed firsthand, during the first years of the previous decade, the collapse of LEGO lines targeted for kids ages five to nine, which he called "the rock-solid core of our business since the 1970s."

Nipper believed that LEGO had to become far more adept at letting customers help the company determine what the market wanted, instead of relying on executives such as Plougmann and Ciccolella to decide what customers should want. As the year unfolded, he and other leaders would go on to unleash an array of initiatives—from engaging directly with customers at fan events to working with representatives from the global network of LEGO user groups to testing concepts with kids—all of which aimed to translate customer insights into growth opportunities.

But all Nipper knew when he took the call from Kristiansen was that he was about to shoulder a weighty responsibility. As the overseer of all of the LEGO Group's product lines, he would be the point man for resetting the company's direction. He believed that if the company was to rediscover what was authentically "core," LEGO had to reengage with its legions of passionate fans. But setting up a process for brainstorming with adult fans and testing toy concepts with kids would take time. Until that happened, Nipper and a handful of other empathetic, customer-centric managers would have to act as surrogate fans and try to divine what twenty-first-century kids really desired from LEGO.

Nipper's many years of working with retailers, engaging with customers, and overseeing designers and marketers told him that despite all the research showing that children had fallen under the thrall of video games and had far less time for the open-ended play that LEGO stood for, there still remained a great swath of kids who loved to build. The key to attracting those children, he believed, was to revive the classic look and feel of iconic LEGO and yet still find a way to make the toys contemporary and, above all, fun.

Nipper was convinced that the path to those core LEGO customers led out of the confines of Billund. Having worked and lived in Germany, the company's most enthusiastic and loyal market, he saw how isolated the company had become and how much its developers and marketers could learn by forging a deeper, more insightful understanding of those kids who find joy in building.

"Children and drunks are the last honest people left on the face of the Earth," he quipped. "And children will never buy a product that isn't fun."

Because of its financial crisis, LEGO lacked the time and the resources for launching an extended program of field research and product testing. Until they could get such a program up and running, Nipper would have to stand in for the prototypical LEGO kid and forcefully demonstrate to designers how they might create compelling new lines out of what amounted to a contradictory brief: make it new, but keep it classic. It was a back-to-the-future moment. Nipper wanted parents who came across a new LEGO City kit to recognize a fresh version of the toys they remembered from their childhood. At the same time, Nipper knew his developers had to make City modern enough so six-year-olds would sense that LEGO reflected the police stations, hospitals, cement mixers, and garbage trucks that they saw every day.

It was a supremely knotty design challenge. How could Nipper push his veteran designers to create more brick-based models without simply repeating past successes? How could he help his new-to-LEGO designers discover what was quintessentially LEGO? And how could he meld those two seemingly antithetical directions?

An answer began to emerge in late February, during a design review for LEGO City. The City line had long been a robust moneymaker for LEGO, accounting for more than one-eighth of the company's sales in 1999. But during the Plougmann era, the Jack Stone line had largely pushed City aside. Looking for a way to spark City's revival, Nipper spotted a prototype for a fire truck fashioned by a designer named Henrik Andersen. Inspired by the 1980s City fire trucks that he had built in his youth, Andersen had given the two-decade-old truck a modern yet classic makeover. The kid in him told Nipper that Andersen's truck was a winner. "When I saw that fire truck, I knew it would be the icon for the entire City turn-

The LEGO fire truck from 1997.

around," he exclaimed. A couple of days later, he used Andersen's truck as the centerpiece of a town hall meeting that aimed to point the way back to the brick.

That March, in two separate sessions, Nipper called his six hundred developers and marketers together to reset the design teams' direction. He kicked off his talk by underlining the stomach-churning fact that LEGO was in a deep financial crisis; its ability to survive as an independent company was very much at stake. The first, most immediate objective was to achieve stable annual growth of 3 to 5 percent by returning to the classic construction play themes that had long defined LEGO. To viscerally illustrate what was core, he showed them photos of three LEGO City fire trucks.

First, Nipper put up a slide of a chunky, somewhat stale 1997 truck from LEGO City. "This is where we forgot to innovate," he announced. "Even though it's an iconic product, not having newness and freshness in a classic toy is a deadly sin."

He next flashed an image of a 2001 fire truck from Jack Stone, the futuristic, theme-based line that had supplanted City. With its bubble cockpit, oversize tires, and blocky rear section, the Jack Stone creation "looks like a spaceship, not a fire truck," Nipper asserted.

The Jack Stone fire truck from 2001.

Henrik Andersen's 2004 fire truck.

He then put up a slide of Andersen's newly reinvented truck, which would soon launch under the revived City brand. Like the best LEGO toys, the truck was strikingly realistic, with more than enough detailing to hold a savvy seven-year-old in its sway. Yet it was also classic LEGO, with the studs prominently protruding from the top of the truck. "This is what a fire truck should look like," Nipper announced. And then, pointing to the Jack Stone toy, he added, "We will never again make a fire truck like that one."

Nipper's declaration resonated powerfully with the company's staffers, especially with the developers and marketers for LEGO City, who had been neglected and unloved during the Plougmann era. Nipper's explicit message to them was, "You guys are back. Development teams that make products that sell with little to no advertising support are this company's real heroes."

Nipper believed that returning to such fundamental touchstones as the brick and buildable, creative play experiences might give designers enough focus and freedom to breathe new life into venerable lines such as City and thereby begin to revive the company's sales. But despite Nipper's explicit, direction-setting entreaty to his developers and marketers, there remained a tough snarl of skepticism over whether gut instinct and this back-to-the-future path were enough to return LEGO to the black. So many veteran designers had been swept out during the 1998 layoffs that LEGO had lost a good bit of the institutional memory of what was authentically core. As for the younger designers who remained, they couldn't be expected to roust that classic LEGO look by simply riffing off Andersen's fire truck.

"There were so many people who hadn't been around when the core was building with LEGO bricks," recalled Paal Smith-Meyer, who heads the company's new business group. "They didn't know who the core consumer was and they didn't understand the core business logic. It was very, very hard."

Nevertheless, resetting the company's direction around classic play experiences such as LEGO City proved both clarifying and liberating. The hot air had leaked out of the previous management regime's overinflated declaration that LEGO would be the world's strongest brand among families with children. Now it was time to make a virtue out of necessity. "In essence, we saw ourselves as a unique niche player in the toy industry," recalled Knudstorp. Echoing the founder's motto, he continued: "We would never be the biggest, but being the best was good enough."

Although Knudstorp had thus far refused to formulate a long-range strategy for sustained growth—opting instead to keep people focused on rescuing the company—the implications of striving to be the best were clear. Any future strategy would be founded on a quest for continuous excellence, which LEGO would achieve in part by forging a deeper affiliation with its legions of fans and by collaborating with enterprises that possessed expertise and technologies that LEGO lacked. Going it alone was no longer an option.

"If you're going to be a global player operating in a niche, you need to be a networked player," said Knudstorp. "You need to leverage partnerships." Thus the newly minted CEO and other senior leaders began a series of initiatives that aimed to help developers migrate to ever-deeper collaborations with customers and even enlist them to help define the brand's future.

Face-to-Face with Customers

As LEGO began to revitalize its core product lines, Knudstorp realized that managers and associates needed to clarify and agree on what the brand really stood for. As he put it, they had to "rediscover what LEGO was all about." LEGO had launched so many new initiatives that Knudstorp believed it had forsaken a "crisp sense of identity"; the end result was a "loss of confidence" in the company's direction and its capacity to execute. It was one thing to get back to the brick and reconnect with five- to nine-year-old boys. It was quite another to dig deeper and try to discover the company's unshakeable, inviolable core.

The new CEO tapped Tormod Askildsen, a veteran manager, to lead a team that would define the attributes that made LEGO unique. The team posed a set of fundamental questions—"Why does LEGO exist? What would the world miss if LEGO went away?"—which aimed to prompt people to define what mattered most for LEGO. Remarkably, for an organization famous for its insularity, Askildsen extended those conversations to some of the brand's most loyal adult enthusiasts, whose numbers were rapidly expanding.

Since the brick's inception, many kids outgrew LEGO when they hit their teens and never returned. But beginning in the late 1990s, a sizable number of adults (mostly men) were once again beckoned by the brick. Two developments lured these prodigal LEGO fans. One was the launch of LEGO *Star Wars*—which appealed to adults' nostalgia for the movie classic—as well as the release of Mindstorms, a LEGO robotics kit that tapped into grown-ups' inner geek. Second, the Internet allowed adult LEGO aficionados from across the globe to come out of the closet and connect as never before.

In 1996, eight years before Flickr flamed to life, adult fans created Brickshelf.com, which today features upward of two million LEGO images—including scans of instructions for countless LEGO kits—all of them posted by fans. Another fan-created site, Bricklink.com, offered a vast online shopping mall for more than 2.5 million LEGO pieces. With the rollout of the aforementioned MOCpages.com, droves of fans found a vast virtual stage for showcasing their most distinctive LEGO models. As those user-created sites took off, so did online clans of fans. In 1999, there were eleven LEGO user groups; by 2006, that number had swelled to more than sixty.*

Askildsen, who was troubled by the company's turn away from classic LEGO play themes during the Plougmann era, had already begun connecting with adult LEGO enthusiasts online and attending fan-sponsored LEGO events. There he had face-to-face meetings with many AFOLs, those adult, hard-core LEGO customers. A good percentage of those fans, he recalled, were mighty unhappy. Many resented the "juniorization" of so many LEGO sets; in their view, easy-to-build kits diluted the creative experience. And parents complained about the dreaded "LEGO bins." These were boxes of disassembled LEGO models, invariably found at the back of a nine-year-old's closet, which were filled with one-of-a-kind LEGO pieces that couldn't connect with pieces from other LEGO kits. The bins signaled a gross violation of the LEGO System, which required that LEGO components should be compatible with other LEGO components. Because the pieces worked only with one model, they failed to live up to that core LEGO promise of "unlimited play."

Above all, there was the sense among the brick's most loyal enthusiasts that they and LEGO had always been on the same wavelength. But in recent years, the connection had broken—and the developers in Billund were too blinkered to notice.

Among the unflattering (and not atypical) comments Askildsen took in was this one, from an adult enthusiast who was still fuming over the Galidor debacle: "What good is Galidor to LEGO fans? Galidor appeals to kids who don't like construction toys. The LEGO name on a nonconstruction toy is a contradiction in terms to a casual consumer and outright blasphemy to AFOLs."

---

* As of February 2012, there were more than 150 LEGO user groups with more than 100,000 active adult fans worldwide.

In August 2005, Askildsen convinced Kristiansen and Knudstorp to attend BrickFest, a fan-organized event that was held at George Mason University near Washington, D.C. That in itself marked a change in the company's culture. In previous years, when Askildsen had tried to convey the adult fans' criticisms to senior managers, he had been rebuffed, as many LEGO veterans believed adult fans were few in number and not worth listening to. LEGO even actively discouraged direct contact with adult fans, adopting the mantra "We don't accept unsolicited ideas."

"We were walled off from the fan community," recalled Jake McKee, formerly the company's global community-relations specialist. "LEGO really didn't recognize the outside world."[16]

But following the launch of LEGO *Star Wars* and Mindstorms, the outside world was far more difficult to avoid. Although the growing AFOL community accounted for about 5 percent of the company's total market by the early 2000s, the average adult fan outspent the average family with kids by a margin of roughly twenty to one. These black-belt LEGO hobbyists also were a potent marketing machine for LEGO. It was not at all unusual for four or five AFOLs to show up at a LEGO fan event and build a jaw-dropping creation, such as a nine-foot-tall replica of Chicago's Sears Tower, which would draw upward of twenty-five thousand kids and their parents, as well as local media. To Askildsen's way of thinking, if LEGO was to find its true core, it had to connect with its most hard-core fans. The grandson of the LEGO Group's founder and the new CEO agreed with him.

At the LEGO jamboree that was BrickFest, Kristiansen and Knudstorp engaged in a three-hour question-and-answer session with five hundred AFOLs. Knudstorp later called it a "crucial meeting," his first face-to-face encounter with the adult fan community. In his conversation with the group, Knudstorp revealed how his understanding of the company's future direction had begun to crystallize. He cited research demonstrating that kids were spending more time with video games and TV and growing up faster, but he shrugged it off, declaring, "We must remain true to who we are and not what others want us to be." Of course, many companies that clung to their core were left behind because they ignored changing consumer tastes—Kodak and its film-based camera business comes to mind, as does Research in Motion, the maker of the no-longer-loved Black-Berry. But LEGO had only recently endured the losses that came from chasing kids who were in thrall to digital toys and indifferent to the brick. He promised LEGO would "navigate across those trends," and he bluntly asserted the brick "is not a toy for everyone. It is a toy about the LEGO way of playing, of being creative." In the months and years to come, he wanted LEGO to conceive toys that felt fresh and new, "yet fit completely within the LEGO System."

The conversations resurfaced the notion that LEGO creativity, at its core, is all about the brick. At first glance, it seems remarkable that the company needed to embark on a series of wide-ranging conversations with customers to rediscover that the System and the brick are the essential features of the LEGO play experience. But in almost any business crisis, the first casualty is clarity. The LEGO Group's former leaders had heard from so many consultants that the brick was passé, and they were so stunned by the financial meltdown and the forfeiture of their leadership positions in all of their most critical markets, they had largely lost sight of the fact that the brick was beloved the world over. If LEGO went away, what the world would miss most wasn't the brand or the trademark, the theme parks or the retail stores. They'd yearn for the brick.

Those talks with fans convinced Knudstorp that Nipper's instinct to get back to the brick was the right course of action. Moreover, the fans' critiques of recent LEGO offerings helped give the rookie CEO the courage and the ammunition he needed to face down internal skeptics who doubted that going back to the future with the brick and the System would sustain the company over the long run.

"We debated whether we should lower the quality of our products" so as to also lower the price, Knudstorp recalled. "We debated whether creativity was still a key word for LEGO. We asked the

[fans], and they were very clear. 'Creativity is what sets you uniquely apart. And if you lower the quality, we'll leave this brand.' "

The dialogues at BrickFest and other venues left Knudstorp with an insight that continues to resonate: "Your most valued customers will tell you what can be done with the brand."

Keep the Conversations Going

In his talk at BrickFest, Knudstorp underlined the notion that working with fans would prove beneficial for LEGO. "We think innovation will come from a dialogue with the fan community," he told the gathering. And he made good on his declaration, as LEGO took its first tentative steps toward directly engaging with customers. Within a matter of months, LEGO unveiled three initiatives that sought to solicit ideas for potential products from adult users and gather feedback from kids on products that were under development.[17]

- To engage directly with fans, in 2005 the company introduced a new crowdsourced line of toys, to be marketed under the aforementioned LEGO Factory brand. Søren Lund, who was then a LEGO marketing director, recruited ten AFOLs to create enticing models that would inspire kids to give Factory a whirl. LEGO challenged the ten fans to create LEGO models for a theme, code-named Micro City, "the biggest little LEGO city in the world." The adult fan team leader set up a secure Web forum, where the expert amateurs could critique and improve one another's designs. In a matter of weeks, the volunteer developers devised scores of dazzling microscale models of cityscapes. "I was overwhelmed by the quality," said Lund. In 2005, the best of the designs—an airport, an amusement park, and a cluster of office buildings—hit the market. The project team's professionalism and creativity, Lund added, "sent shockwaves through our development organization."[18]

Although the Micro City experiment ultimately failed to grow into a thriving business, it delivered irrefutable evidence that LEGO could successfully open up to its fans.

- As more senior managers such as Lund began to see the potential in soliciting ideas and feedback from customers, LEGO sought to fashion tighter ties with the fan community by launching its Ambassador Program. Comprised of scores of representatives drawn from more than thirty user groups spanning the globe, the program gave voice to the worldwide community of LEGO fans. Ambassadors relayed questions and requests from the community directly to LEGO managers. And LEGO managers, in turn, tapped ambassadors to cast about for ideas or solicit feedback from user groups on projects that were under development. Moreover, the program gave LEGO managers a vast window into the amazing creations that were always bubbling up from the fan community.

- The LEGO Group's outreach wasn't limited to adult fans only. To better understand the lives and interests of children who loved the brick, LEGO dreamed up Kids Inner Circle, a kid-centered test panel for toys. LEGO enlisted two thousand children from across the globe. With their parents' permission, the kids logged on to a Web forum where they commented on photographs of designers' concepts for future toys and critiqued kits that were headed for the market. They also filled out questionnaires about their own purchasing patterns, as well as their wish lists for toys. When LEGO developers wanted unfettered feedback on an early-stage prototype, they'd simply post their renderings to the Inner Circle forum, where the kid testers would issue their verdicts within twenty-four hours.

Taken together, these first-step efforts at gleaning the experiences, desires, and opinions of fans who were kids and fans who were kids at heart began to signal a far more inclusive attitude at LEGO. The company that had refused to accept ideas from the outside was finally going out of its way to solicit them.

Back Up Customer Dialogues with Customer Data

In parallel with its fan dialogues, LEGO conducted one of its most sweeping customer research studies. In March 2005, Askildsen launched a project dubbed Core Gravity, which aimed to identify the brick's biggest fans, especially those kids who exuded enough enthusiasm—or, to put it another way, magnetism—to spread the gospel of LEGO and pull other kids into the brand's orbit. This psychographic exploration of "buzzworthy" kids gleaned fifty-six thousand responses through online surveys, which were then followed up with market tests and kid focus groups.

The study centered on two crucial, direction-setting areas for LEGO. First, it identified and described the "MVCs," or most valuable customers—kids who not only loved LEGO but were viewed by their peers as opinion leaders who unabashedly advocated for the brick. Second, the project aimed to rediscover what, from the true fans' perspective, was the essence of the LEGO play experience. Though it took a year to complete the project, Askildsen produced an interim report in August, right around the time that Kristiansen and Knudstorp were meeting with adult fans at BrickFest.

One of the study's most critical takeaways was that core LEGO kids were "normal." They watched slightly more TV and read a few more books, but in other significant ways they were just like other kids. They played sports and video games; they listened to music and hung out with friends. Another insight kicked over a big assumption from the Plougmann years: for LEGO kids, video games and bricks *weren't* mutually exclusive. Just because a kid loved to power away on Xbox, it didn't mean he wouldn't dig into LEGO *Star Wars*.

Most important, even though LEGO kids played with little plastic blocks, they weren't social pariahs. The study suggested that LEGO kids were smart and often well regarded by their peers. That sounds like stating the obvious, given that LEGO is loved the world over. But back at Billund, more than a few folks felt—after years of hearing that the brick had lost its allure—that LEGO was at best a solitary play experience. "The study took away the fear that LEGO kids were nerdish and didn't have any friends," said Askildsen. "That was a very important finding, which told us we shouldn't be afraid of focusing on them."

Core Gravity also revealed a key differentiator for LEGO. Although they expressed it in different ways, core LEGO parents and kids loved to build, and with LEGO they could build anything they wanted. Their message: LEGO is a catalyst for creativity and imagination precisely because it delivers a *buildable* play experience, an insight that adult fans at BrickFest shared repeatedly with Kristiansen and Knudstorp.

Finally, the study showed that while LEGO was competing in a niche market, it was a sizable niche, with a LEGO-connected community of more than two million households. And the market for creative, buildable play experiences was by no means waning, as LEGO had feared during the late 1990s. As Knudstorp asserted at BrickFest, it wasn't unreasonable to expect that the outer circle of the LEGO fan base could easily be two, five, even ten times as large as those two million registered customers. Additionally, the study underlined the notion that LEGO should compete in just the high end of the toy market. By putting a high level of quality into everything it did, there was an opportunity for LEGO to attract customers who found tremendous value in its products and were willing to pay premium prices.

The notion that LEGO would compete only in the premium part of the toy market by delivering high-quality, buildable play experiences was both narrowing and liberating. "By defining LEGO as niche, Jørgen provided focus," said Askildsen. "We'd focus on kids

who loved to build and we'd build a premium brand. Anything outside those boundaries, we didn't need to worry about."

If the first victim of the LEGO Group's crisis had been clarity,
the second had been confidence. The company's overexpansion and
loss of focus, which sparked the 2003 meltdown, had badly shaken
its spirit and spunk. By helping to define the brick's most impas-
sioned customers and declaring there was a big opportunity to turn
many more casual users into acolytes, the Core Gravity study began
to brighten staffers' sense that LEGO had a future.

Reduce the World to Those Customers Who Matter Most

Buttressed by the Core Gravity's findings, Nipper and his team shut
out all the chatter about the majority of kids who disliked construction toys and instead eyed the smaller but profitable group of kids
who still were drawn to the brick. Executives defined the company's
defend-at-all-costs markets, those where LEGO still was king—
Germany and Scandinavia (back then, the United States was more
of a growth opportunity)—and tamped down any design initiatives
that wouldn't immediately appeal to those regions. At times, they re-
sorted to a blunt but effective shorthand for the prototypical LEGO
customer profile: five- to nine-year-old German boys who loved
construction toys. As a result, they narrowed the product lines that
LEGO "would do more of" to a very short list of four: LEGO Technic
sets for older, more experienced builders; the Mindstorms robotics
kits; DUPLO themes for preschoolers; and a relaunch of City.

"We needed to edit down the world we operated in," Nipper asserted. "We edited everything down to something that was manageable, overseeable, and relatively easy to act on. Of course, we knew
the future of the LEGO Group could not only be Germany. But unless
we were successful in those markets, we would never have a future."

The result was a dramatic change from the previous era. Designers could no longer go off in any direction they pleased. Instead, they had to focus on developing a specific toy, such as a LEGO City fire truck, for a clearly delineated market—five- to nine-year-old German boys who were enthralled with LEGO and wanted more. For veteran designers such as Henrik Andersen, who'd been shunted aside for years because he preferred replicating real-life buildings and vehicles, the return to creating brick-based building experiences "was like a pat on the back."

Direction from the Top

Mads Nipper knew that under ideal circumstances, it shouldn't be solely up to him and a few other executives to select the look and feel of the next round of LEGO City products; that was best left to designers and marketers who could base their decisions on insights gleaned from deep ethnographic research and extensive focus testing with kids. It's a hoary adage, but still true: before you can earn, you've first got to learn. But in the crisis years of 2004 to 2005, there simply wasn't sufficient time to dig into kids' lives and work with them to discover toys that would propel LEGO into a robust future.

At the conclusion of his "fire truck" talk, Nipper put up an unsubtle slide predicting that people would react to his call to rally around the core in one of two ways: some would "stop working until all details are clarified and complain that top management will probably also miss the point this time," and others would "trust that what we're doing now is right for the company . . . The choice is yours."

Nipper's intent was to inject a sense of urgency into the organization and spur people to "fight harder than ever to help the LEGO Company survive." But in challenging people to "trust" that those perched at the top of the company's leadership pyramid had settled on the right strategy, he was implicitly declaring that until the crisis abated, LEGO would depend on a command-and-control approach to innovation. Forget about grassroots innovation or inventions that would work their way up from the design ranks. Instead of freeing people to pursue their passions and develop creative play themes that would define a "new" LEGO, innovating for survival meant that the company's leaders would set clear, action-oriented goals. It was up to the company's developers and designers to follow through on those targets and, as Knudstorp had earlier put it, "get stuff done."

Such a hierarchical approach to managing innovation, where an authoritarian group at the top sets targets and hands them down to product-focused business units, runs counter to the popular notion that innovation thrives when it functions like a democracy, where everyone has a vote. But Knudstorp and Nipper concluded that for LEGO to return to profitability, their first priority was to restore discipline and direction. And that would come only from a series of goals passed down through a chain of command.

Knudstorp formed an Executive Innovation Committee, comprising the heads of all the product development groups, the market heads from the different regions, and a representative from manufacturing and supply chain operations. The group's brief was to oversee and coordinate innovation efforts across the entire company. The committee decided on the mix of innovation projects that LEGO took on, allocated resources, assigned clear lines of accountability, and monitored the development process. Recalling the mind-set that characterized LEGO during 2004, Knudstorp called it "only one truth and black-and-white thinking."

Cocreate with Kids

One of the catalysts of the LEGO Group's financial crisis was its remarkably high mortality rate for toys that were under development. All through the Plougmann years, developers were encouraged to follow their muse and pursue revolutionary designs that would take LEGO far beyond the brick. But freedom carried a price. Designers worked tirelessly to evolve concepts for newfangled LEGO models, only to see management kill most of them off.

"If a designer worked on ten ideas, only one or two made it to market, because we were experimenting a lot, exploring new things," recalled Per Hjuler, senior vice president of consumer marketing and innovation. "Most ideas seemed to go nowhere."

The cascade of constant setbacks took a toll on designers' morale, as well as the company's returns on its R&D expenditures. The fact that it required, on average, three years to develop a concept and bring it to market only added to the sense of futility. It was not unusual for designers to spend months or even years developing LEGO kits that would never find their way into a child's hands.

Seeking to improve the hit rate for toy concepts, in 2005 Hjuler and his team led an overhaul of the LEGO Development Process (LDP). Conceived in 1995, the LDP consisted of a step-by-step series of management reviews of developers' prototypes, wherein executives decided which ideas LEGO would actually cultivate and launch. But in the decade since the LDP's inception, each product group had adopted its own version of the process.

For example, the group that targeted five- to nine-year-olds had created an LDP that worked well at first but eventually grew overly bureaucratic. "It got too dense," recalled Hjuler. "Each step of the way, people had to fill out multiple forms and checklists."

The product group for nine- to sixteen-year-olds, on the other hand, ran with more of a freewheeling LDP, with fewer check-ins but far more elaborate mock-ups of concepts. Their logic: by devising extravagant presentations, developers hoped to sell executives on their designs. Regardless of the approach, under the old system less than 20 percent of developers' ideas made it to launch. As for those ideas that evolved into finished products, growing numbers of them—such as Galidor, the Spielberg MovieMaker, and the Jack Stone and Explore lines—ultimately flopped.

The company's solution was to create one universal development process that every product group would adhere to. The new LDP was built around four stages: product teams would brainstorm ideas, select concepts for further development, test business plans for each proposed product, and ultimately allocate resources and lock in the design and business strategies for those toys that LEGO would take to market. Because each stage lasted just a few months, the new process slashed the average development time for a new product from three years to eighteen months.

The core of the new development process consisted of constant, empathetic contact with customers. At every stage, teams met with small groups of children and showed them their ideas for new toys, watched them engage with the prototypes, and looked for play themes that really resonated with kids. No idea could progress to the next stage without a big thumbs-up from kid testers.

To be sure, there are wildly successful innovators who've cast a skeptical eye on focus testing. Henry Ford famously quipped, "If I had asked people what they wanted, they would have said faster horses." Steve Jobs was equally disdainful. "It's really hard to design products by focus groups," he once told *BusinessWeek*. "A lot of times, people don't know what they want until you show it to them."[19]

LEGO, however, took an inside-out approach to testing. Instead of asking kids what they wanted, developers would show kids illustrations or prototypes of what they *might* want, such as a space theme or a Mars Mission Crystal Reaper, and then gauge their reactions. The goal was to trigger a child's imagination. If the Reaper, with its "spinning harvester blades" and detachable spaceship, inspired kids to dream up battle scenes, tell stories, and play with the set for an extended period, the team knew it had a winner. But if the kids' storytelling fizzled out after a few moments, it was time to push on to the next option. Such an approach meant that designers still bore the responsibility for imagining what would turn kids on. But working with kids helped them identify, develop, and refine the ideas that stood the best chance of succeeding in the marketplace.

The LEGO City design team was one of the first groups to embrace the new approach. Although Henrik Andersen's fire truck and the rest of the 2004 City line were mostly designed in-house, the team began venturing out in search of inspiration and ideas for ever more realistic play experiences. The team took firefighter training, rode in police cars, and got locked in jail cells, and they brought their insights from those experiences to the look and feel of City toys.

The 2005 City edition of construction and police sets, which were developed with children's input, more than tripled the line's revenue, to DKK 350 million ($60 million). As the line continued to expand, revenues doubled and doubled again, reaching DKK 1.5 billion ($275 million) in 2007. The City team's morale also got a boost. What had been a beaten-down group that was relegated to the company's back bench was now the new star.

The insight sessions with kids, combined with the revamped development process, resulted in a radically improved hit rate for toy concepts. The wide-ranging exploration of the 1990s resulted in a low hit rate, with only 10 to 20 percent of designers' ideas developed into toys that found their way onto store shelves. Now, according to Hjuler, "if a designer works on ten ideas, about nine will make it to market."

While some designers chafed under the new restrictions and ultimately left LEGO, others reveled in their newfound productivity. No longer did most of their ideas and prototypes end up in a circular file, never to see the light of day. Under the new system, if they could show that kid testers loved the concept and they could present a persuasive business case for the idea, they could be reasonably certain that they'd see their creation on toy-store shelves throughout the world.

Other teams followed City's lead. The team charged with bringing back the DUPLO brand saw the new approach's power when it redesigned the Intelli-Train Gift Set, which came out in 2002 as part of the Explore line. Priced at $99.99, the original train was "stuffed with electronics," the designer Allan Steen Larsen recalled. "People didn't understand what they were getting." The set, which LEGO had never bothered to pretest with customers, was a spectacular flameout that cost LEGO 13 percent of its train business in its core markets.

In 2005, Larsen was a member of the team that gave the Explore train an overhaul. Under the revised LDP, this time the team tested with kids. Among its other discoveries, the team found there was no point in including gear mechanisms for reversing the train. When the preschoolers wanted the train to reverse course, they simply picked it up and turned it around. "That's the logic of a three-year-old," said Larsen. Such head-slapping observations let LEGO halve the production cost of the new train. The Train Starter Set, which was relaunched under the revived DUPLO brand, sold so well that it remained a mainstay of DUPLO's offerings for more than seven years.

Some Lessons

What should we take away from the LEGO Group's bid to become a truly customer-first company? Let us suggest four essential lessons.

In a crisis, act first; then plan. Before it could get the new LEGO Development Process up and running, the company relied on deeply experienced and engaged executives such as Mads Nipper to point the way. Until they developed an approach to testing with kids, designers essentially tested their ideas on Nipper and other veteran managers. Their ready-fire-aim review sessions were far from ideal, but they were good enough.

Mix it up. LEGO didn't attempt to find one "right" solution. It launched a wide array of ventures to reconnect with customers—from small, no-risk efforts such as the Ambassador program to experimental approaches such as tapping adult fans for LEGO Factory and big structural initiatives such as remaking the LDP. As time went by, managers culled what didn't work, even as they sought new ways of engaging customers.

Let customers walk in your shoes. LEGO grew adept at finding creative ways to use the Web to connect with kids and adult fans. But the most far-reaching changes came out of its face-to-face interactions with customers at events such as BrickFest and at testing sessions with kids. LEGO found that it's not enough to walk in customers' shoes. Sometimes you have to let them walk in *your* shoes, by letting them create stories, characters, and building experiences out of ideas that you show them.

Set the course; then get out of the way. As the LDP took shape, the company's leaders began to take less of a top-down approach to innovation. Managers still decided what customers they wanted to target. And they still allocated resources, enforced processes, and set priorities. But when the development teams started engaging with kids, the execs let the teams take on far more decision-making authority. (We'll delve into this point in Chapter Ten.) The teams and the kids, not the managers, ultimately predicted what the market wanted.

A Shared Vision

By the summer of 2005, right around the time he was meeting with fans at BrickFest and getting his first look at the Core Gravity research results, Knudstorp was deep into drafting a document that would spell out the direction in which the LEGO Group was moving and how the company would achieve its goals. It was time to shift from identifying must-win battles to mapping out the bigger journey that lay ahead.

LEGO was still very much in its survival phase, but it was close to turning a corner. By the end of 2005, it would boost its sales by 15 percent. Of course, that increase is less impressive than the number suggests, given that LEGO was coming off the worst year in its history. Moreover, the company had used up many of the "structural options" for cutting costs and generating cash—selling off assets, pink-slipping employees, jettisoning unprofitable product lines, and reviving core lines such as LEGO City—and would soon need a set of guiding principles for the far harder work of restarting growth. Thus Knudstorp was under pressure from other senior executives, and especially the board of directors, to deliver a long-term innovation strategy, as opposed to the past year's tactical initiatives.

"Kjeld said the board was very depressed with me—they thought I wasn't optimistic about the future, and at that point, I probably wasn't," he admitted. "They felt like I was short-term focused and didn't have a vision."

In fact, Knudstorp did have a strategy for transforming LEGO, which he captured in a document that came to be called "Shared Vision." Its intent was to identify a common identity among the LEGO Group's owners, leadership, and employees, and from there build a platform for putting the company back on a growth path.

"Shared Vision" was born out of several workshops that Knudstorp held with his network of veteran LEGO associates, which included executives as well as front-line folks. Just as Askildsen had done with the AFOLs and internal gatherings of LEGO staffers, Knudstorp put a big, philosophical question to the group: what is the company's shared identity? He got a range of answers, each a variation on what was really vital to LEGO. One answer was that it was about profiting from the core; another was the understanding that LEGO needs a premium positioning. For one executive, it was Nipper's slide of the fire trucks. At first, people worried that they'd all come up with disparate definitions. But to Knudstorp's ear, they were saying the same thing in slightly different ways, and that was encouraging.

"You want to make sure the company's direction can be expressed by everybody," he explained. "It's not about using exactly the same words. Because if people are really going to share this [direction], they have to be able to state it their own way."

The immediate purpose of "Shared Vision" was to align on where to look for growth. But it was also an ideology; a philosophical piece that aimed, in principle, to give LEGO a robust sense of identity that would guide it for many years to come. And that meant reconnecting with one of the LEGO Group's most animating values, Ole Kirk's dictum that "only the best is good enough." In recent years, LEGO staffers had grown to disparage the motto, believing it had significantly slowed the development process by encouraging designers to dither over products, overcomplicating and overdesigning them. Perfecting had gotten in the way of acting. But Knudstorp revived the motto and gave it more of a direct translation from the Danish: "even the best is not good enough."

Knudstorp's reinterpretation worked on several levels. It signaled that at the center of the LEGO Group's core was a shared vision of excellence: no matter what the company accomplished in the future, it would ceaselessly strive to do better. Additionally, the revision was another reminder that LEGO had reset its direction and now aimed to be the best, not the biggest. But the revision also tapped into the company's heritage, so as to create a tough-minded cultural identity. Having "broken the culture's back" during its survival phase, Knudstorp called people's attention to the fact that the company's values would guide their pursuit of the long-term goal: to build a sustainable business.

Knudstorp believed that to transform LEGO into an organization that was as resilient as the brick itself, he and his team would have to seize on those "assets and capabilities" that had sustained the company for so many decades. His notion of what was truly core to LEGO wasn't limited to products, customers, and markets. As outlined in the "Shared Vision" strategy, the company's core also resided in its chief assets, which Knudstorp and his team defined as the LEGO brick and the building system, the brand, and the company's unique relationship with its stakeholders (read: owners, retailers, business partners, and customers). The company's core capabilities consisted of its capacity to use the LEGO System to innovate products, its molding and manufacturing expertise, and its direct dialogues with customers, which ranged from conversations with fans at events such as BrickFest to cocreating with kids and enlisting skilled LEGO hobbyists to improve offerings such as LEGO Factory.

By focusing managers and associates on the company's prime assets and capabilities, Knudstorp signaled that returning to the core was really a matter of "becoming more of what we already are." According to "Shared Vision," that process would unfold in three stages over a seven-year period.

In the first phase, "fight for survival," Knudstorp and Ovesen had aligned the company around the must-win battles of setting a clear direction, restoring competitiveness by refocusing on retailers, and concentrating only on those product lines that showed a good chance of turning a profit. The key to winning those battles lay in mastering two of the seven truths. LEGO had to create a culture that was truly innovative—one where developers focused on cost and profitability as much as creativity, where people championed operational excellence and "getting stuff done." And LEGO had to reach out, connect

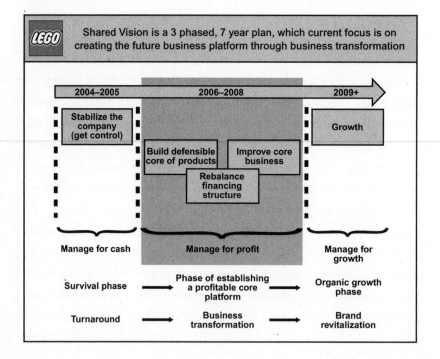

with its core fans, and become authentically customer driven. By engaging with five- to nine-year-old boys who loved to build and the adult fans who were returning to the brick, LEGO stood a far better chance of getting control of its future.

By 2006, Knudstorp anticipated that LEGO would commence with the second stage outlined in "Shared Vision," which was to build a "defensible core" of profitable products. To make the most of its core business, LEGO would have to master two more truths. First, it had to explore the full spectrum of innovation. LEGO couldn't substantially improve its margins solely through product innovation. It had to develop a broad range of complementary innovations, pioneer new channels to market, conceive new business models, and restructure the way it worked internally and with outside partners. Second, LEGO would have to open up its innovation processes through crowdsourcing. Because the company was still stretched for resources but nevertheless was blessed with legions of hard-driving, hyperskilled fans, LEGO had both the need and the means to seek out new ways to work with its most creative customers to invent new play experiences.

If LEGO managed to achieve a healthy balance sheet and a profitable core business, by 2008 it could roll out the final phase set out in "Shared Vision," which called for discovering entirely new growth drivers. To achieve organic growth—that is, growth (not just profits) from its core business instead of through acquisitions—LEGO would have to unleash the final set of truths: head for blue-ocean markets and practice disruptive innovation. Once the company began generating profits and growing again, it would have to learn how to harness the skills of its diverse and creative people.

Knudstorp summarized the "Shared Vision" strategy in a single slide. When he unveiled the plan in 2005, it gave people a sense of direction and a plausible notion of how the future would unfold (assuming all went according to plan). Like Plougmann, Knudstorp also sought to make LEGO a great global brand. But through conversations with people such as the strategist and author Chris Zook and

LEGO CFO Jesper Ovesen, the new CEO concluded that continuous innovation required a certain sequencing and cadence. Before they could renew the brand, they first had to turn around the business. If LEGO didn't restore its balance sheet and restructure its operations, contended Knudstorp, the brand would never again shine.

———————

By the summer of 2005, people had begun to believe in Knudstorp. Tellingly, he finally succeeded in convincing Kristiansen to sell the four LEGOLAND theme parks to a British operator of amusement parks, Merlin Entertainments Group, a move that silenced some of the doubters within LEGO and the chatter in Billund. (LEGO retained a 30 percent stake in the new venture.) A photo caption of the owner and new CEO at BrickFest dubbed the pair "master and apprentice." Kristiansen would always retain his mastery of the LEGO experience. But with Knudstorp's ascent, now there was a new man in charge.

Even so, many challenges remained. The LEGO Group's leaders still had to return the company to profitability and restart sales growth. They still had to transform LEGO into a faster, nimbler, and more cost-conscious innovator. All this had to be done at a time when the toy market was contracting, big retailers were increasing their bargaining power, kids were "getting older faster," and the company's return on sales, as it closed out 2005, was still an anemic 7 percent, far short of the 13½ percent target that had been set the year before. LEGO was on the verge of winning its first big battle. But the war was far from over.

6

Exploring the Full Spectrum of Innovation

The Bionicle Chronicle

Bionicle is the toy that saved LEGO.

—Jørgen Vig Knudstorp, CEO, the LEGO Group

BY 2005, HAVING RECONNECTED LEGO WITH ITS CORE consumers and markets, Knudstorp, Nipper, and other leaders concluded they couldn't put the company on a long-term growth curve simply by refreshing LEGO City police cars and fire stations. To generate enough profits to propel LEGO into a healthy future, they'd also have to pursue a variety of innovations that create new markets. To figure out a way forward, the management team took a look back at the company's recent past.

When the company's senior managers delved into the past decade's three most successful LEGO toys—LEGO *Star Wars*, LEGO *Harry Potter*, and Bionicle—they saw that the lines had one thing in common: each drew on a full spectrum of innovations to complement the core LEGO sets. The rich story line, compelling characters, and licensed merchandise of a property such as *Star Wars* brought in new revenue streams and helped boost sales of the kits beyond Billund's most optimistic forecasts. The one drawback with *Star Wars*, from the LEGO Group's point of view, was that a sizable percentage of the line's profits went back to Lucasfilm, as specified by the licensing agreement.

Like *Star Wars*, the wildly successful Bionicle line also featured a wide variety of complementary innovations. Bionicle, launched in 2001, was built around a new business model, pioneered new sales channels and markets, and was founded on a magnetic story line that played out over many years—and thereby augured many years of robust revenue. Best of all, because Bionicle had been invented in Billund, the majority of its licensing profits flowed back to LEGO. So when Knudstorp and his team began to roll out the second phase detailed in "Shared Vision"—manage for profit and prepare for

Gorast, a Bionicle from the 2008 Mistika line. According to lego.com, "Makuta Gorast is known throughout the universe for her raw power and violent rage."

growth—the team that had created the toy called Bionicle provided a road map for moving LEGO into the future.

The Bionicle story actually arcs back to the summer of 1999, when a development team from LEGO visited the offices of Advance, a Copenhagen-based advertising agency, with a concept for a decidedly different line of LEGO toys. Initially titled Voodoo Heads, the line of exotic action figures was to be targeted at what industry insiders call the "craze category": flash-in-the-pan toys that strike it hot for a season and then flame out. The plan was to package Voodoo Heads in plastic canisters and sell them for less than $10. LEGO asked the Advance team, which included an art director named Christian Faber, to help create background visuals for the Voodoo Heads advertisements.

As he tucked into his new assignment, Faber, who earlier had worked on the LEGO *Star Wars* line, thought back to how the movie's spellbinding narrative and riveting characters drove the LEGO Group's sales to record heights. Voodoo Heads showed a glimmer of that same *Star Wars* mojo. Inspired by the talismans of voodoo practitioners, the Voodoo Heads characters—freaky, skeletal figurines—were unlike anything else that had come out of Billund. Faber was captivated by the opportunity they presented. Instead of drawing static backgrounds for ads, he decided to push beyond the Voodoo Heads characters and instead illustrate an epic, multipart adventure such as *Star Wars*, which would amp up his client's revenues for many years to come.

For Faber, the inspiration for this new, illustrated narrative came from his recently diagnosed brain tumor. The tumor was benign, but it would spread if he didn't take a daily injection of medication.* Reflecting on the illness that fired his imagination, Faber "had the thought that when I took these injections, I was sending a little group of soldiers into my body, fighting on my behalf to rebuild my system. Then it all just came together."

---

* Thankfully, Faber's medicine worked, and he was able to tell us his story ten years later.

Faber imagined the toy canisters as vials of medicine drifting toward the head of a giant, comatose robot that was infected with a virus. The medicine's active ingredient was an army of nano-size creatures that arrived in pill-shaped capsules, entered the titan's body, and fought to liberate it from the virus. The story played out in a microscopic world, but for its "part-organic, part-machine" inhabitants, the scale was sweepingly vast. Faber provided visual depictions of the island and its inhabitants and also suggested to his colleagues at LEGO a name for the new toy: Bionicle, a combination of the words *biological* and *chronicle*. (Insert photo 12 shows two of Faber's early concept sketches for the toy. Insert photo 13 shows the pill-shaped canisters that were the packaging for the 2001 launch of Bionicle.)

Scripted by a LEGO story team, the inaugural Bionicle narrative kicked off with six hulking heroes, the Toa Mata, arriving on a tropical island called Mata Nui. They venture into a strange world of massive domes, swamps, and underwater caves, where they encounter Rahi, Bohrok, and Piraka—savage beasts controlled by a supervillain, Makuta Teridax. The Bionicle creatures, which resembled mechanized gladiators, were as exotic as the plot—and, as it turned out, they were a powerful kid magnet.

With its sinister look and feel and a roiling story featuring dozens of characters doing battle, LEGO Bionicle was a sensation for Poul Plougmann and his team—the only unmitigated success, besides LEGO *Star Wars* and LEGO *Harry Potter*, to come out of Billund during the early 2000s. Bionicle artfully melded the LEGO building experience with the storytelling and adventure of an action figure saga. And it employed a full arsenal of innovations, with a constantly unfolding narrative delivered through the Web, a book series, direct-to-video movies, licensed apparel, and comic books. Bionicle was a worldwide hit that almost single-handedly sustained LEGO through the depths of its fiscal crisis.

In 2001, its inaugural year, Bionicle's sales exceeded $160 million and the Toy Industry Association declared it the year's "Most Innovative Toy." In 2003—the year the rest of LEGO came crashing down—Bionicle's soaring sales accounted for approximately 25 percent of the company's total revenue and more than 100 percent of its profit (as the rest of the company was tumbling to a net loss), making it a financial anchor in turbulent times. By mid-2004, while Knudstorp and Ovesen were busy closing down unprofitable lines and selling off assets, the LEGO Bionicle website averaged one million page views per month and the toy spawned a host of fan-generated sites. That year, retailers sold a Bionicle set every 1.4 seconds. By the end of the toy's nine-year run, LEGO would sell some 190 million Bionicle figures, more than the combined populations of France, the United Kingdom, and Italy; 85 percent of American boys ages six to twelve would know the Bionicle brand, and 45 percent would own at least one Bionicle toy. The Bionicle book series, numbering forty-six books, regularly topped the sales lists for young adult fiction. At one point in 2003, the DC Comics Bionicle books, with a circulation of 1.5 to 2 million copies every other month, were the world's most widely read comics.

With its vibrant story line and rich universe of characters, Bionicle was also the company's first successful, internally developed intellectual property, or IP.* In a very real sense, Bionicle was the LEGO Group's own, homegrown *Star Wars*, and it let LEGO take on the role of licensor and put the brand's imprimatur on a plethora of products. Bionicle-crazed boys could snag a simple Bionicle toy with a Happy Meal (from McDonald's), kick around in Bionicle sneakers (Nike), retrieve a Bionicle video game from a box of Honey Nut Cheerios (General Mills), show off their favorite brand with Bionicle lunchboxes (DNC), amp up their cool factor with Bionicle T-shirts, sneakers, and backpacks (Qubic Tripod), and dream their Bionicle

---

* We use "IP" as shorthand for a company's intellectual property, which can include patents, trademarks, and copyrights. These properties can become some of a company's most valuable assets. Although LEGO had to send a portion of the profits from its licensed *Star Wars* toys to Lucasfilm, it could keep *all* of the profits from its Bionicle toys, since it owned the Bionicle IP.

dreams while tucked into Bionicle-themed bedding (Dryen). Because LEGO invented the Bionicle IP, all the royalties from the sales of all that merchandise flowed back to the company's coffers.

When Knudstorp looked back to the birth of Bionicle, he saw more than the emergence of a supremely successful moneymaker for LEGO. The line demonstrated the value-creating potential that came from pursuing a wide array of interconnected innovations. Back when the rest of LEGO was running off the rails, the Bionicle team not only invented a new toy category, the buildable action figure, but also created new business models, forged diverse partnerships, pioneered markets, concocted a streamlined product development process, and delivered to customers an immersive play experience. Thus Bionicle presented a rough prototype for developing and bringing to market a full spectrum of complementary innovations. At the close of 2005, as Knudstorp looked for a way to coordinate the company's disparate innovation efforts, he found a model in the process that gave birth to Bionicle.

In all, the Bionicle team launched eight complementary innovations, which helped usher in a new era of profitable creativity at LEGO.

A New Building Platform

Full-spectrum innovation begins with a product platform that's sturdy enough to support a broad range of complementary innovations. In 2005, Knudstorp had two very different models to learn from: Bionicle and Galidor. Both themes attempted to create complex story lines, rich play experiences, and a broad array of revenue streams. While Galidor, with its limited building experience and underwhelming story, was an expensive failure, the Bionicle platform was entirely different.

More than a few veteran LEGO executives believed Bionicle was *too* different. In the traditionalists' view, Bionicle breached the sacred LEGO principle of open-ended play. After all, it was the Bionicle story, not the brick, that invested the toy with meaning. A boy could build a Toa Mata model, but when he was done, he wouldn't understand what he'd created—unless he knew the story. There was also the vexing matter of some distinctly creepy play themes that dwelled within Bionicle. Take, for example, the Bohrok, a race of insectoid creatures controlled by brain-eating parasites called Krana (see insert photo 14). With characters such as Krana and the Bohrok, Bionicle was more akin to the sci-fi horror film *Alien* than to the family-friendly LEGO sets that Godtfred Kirk Christiansen had long ago imagined.

Knudstorp, however, disagreed with the toy's critics. In Bionicle, he saw a team that was competing from an original innovation playbook that nevertheless summoned the company's DNA.

Although Bionicle was distinctly different from any previous LEGO toy, it was rooted in the company's foundational touchstones. The characters still must be assembled, just as with LEGO. Bionicle incorporated LEGO Technic pins and gears, which meant the components from one Bionicle model were interchangeable with other Bionicle models, in the same way that components from other LEGO kits were interchangeable. And Bionicle hewed to the fundamental LEGO play experience, "joy of creation," even as it introduced a new LEGO building platform.

The core of the Bionicle building platform, and a defining characteristic of the toy, was the newly created ball-and-socket connector. With this mechanism, a character's leg was topped off with a ball-shaped joint, which could be inserted into the hollow socket of the character's hip. The leg could then be easily rotated. For the first time, boys could build LEGO figures that featured fully articulated heads and limbs, which added a degree of realism that couldn't be found in more static plastic beings such as the minifig. This multibillion-dollar breakthrough put the "action" into this buildable action figure and ushered in a swarm of knockoffs from the likes of Mega Bloks and Hasbro. Thus the Bionicle building platform took the System of Play in a new direction while at the same time remaining faithful to it.

Bionicle was far from an overnight success. It took nearly five

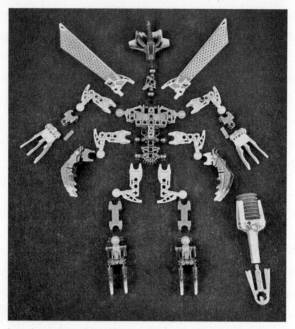

The ball-and-socket joint, which allows a character's arms and legs to rotate, was developed specifically for Bionicle. The pins that connect the hands to the upper arms were borrowed from the Technic line.

years and many trial-and-error experiments to bring the line to life. The toy evolved from an idea to a real-world product largely because its development team was tenacious enough to keep grinding away at a challenging problem: how to keep kids who had outgrown LEGO System sets (such as City) from abandoning the LEGO brand before they were old enough and skilled enough to take on the more challenging LEGO Technic line of products. But perseverance didn't come at the expense of prudence. LEGO management didn't bet on Bionicle until the development team had launched two earlier products, Slizer and RoboRiders, and learned through real-world experience what worked and what didn't. Although Slizer was a minor hit and RoboRiders an outright failure, creating those toys pushed the team to test the market and learn from its mistakes.

The earliest concepts for the toy that became Bionicle date back to the mid-1990s, when LEGO mapped out a strategic brief that charged the development team with creating introductory sets of

LEGO Technic models. The goal was to drive multiple purchases by conjuring models that were so enthralling—or, to use Christian Faber's term, so crazed—boys would collect multiple sets.

From the very start, different functional groups within the development team, which was drawn from the Technic design group, contributed breakthrough ideas.

- The design team came up with the notion that the LEGO models should be inspired by manga, visually dynamic Japanese comics featuring robots, space travel, and heroic action-adventure themes.

- The engineering team invented the ball-and-socket connectors, which let boys build character-based models featuring an unparalleled range of motion.

- Meanwhile, someone from marketing suggested that the toy could be sold through nontraditional (for LEGO) retailers, such as gas stations and convenience stores.

Based on those insights and innovations, the team identified the cornerstones of the customer experience: the toys would be collectible; they'd feature memorable characters; they'd be priced for pocket money, so kids (as opposed to only parents) could buy them; and they'd be sold through everyday outlets that kids visited on a weekly or monthly basis. No previous LEGO product line had ever combined those four traits.

Not only did the development team break down the walls between corporate departments and cross-collaborate—with engineers, marketers, and designers for the first time working side by side—the team also stretched the notion of what constituted a LEGO play experience. "We really wanted to rock this world," said Søren Holm, formerly the team's design chief. "We had a mantra: concepts with an attitude. There was a lot of internal competition [between different LEGO development teams] at that time. Who was the best? Who dared the most? We dared. We dared big-time."

The initial result of their daring was Slizer (see insert photo 9), one of the first lines in the company's history to be based on characters that LEGO itself had developed.* The line consisted of eight robots from different planets that warred with one another for territory. (In North America, the toy was dubbed Throwbots, a name that referenced the robots' capacity to sling small, collectible discs, which were inspired by the Tazo discs found in packets of Frito-Lay chips). Looking like mechanical men made out of winches and helicopter parts, Slizer was so alien to anything LEGO had ever created, management couldn't agree on how to brand the line.

"Was it Slizer from LEGO? Was it LEGO Technic Slizer or LEGO Slizer from Technic? They were so afraid of destroying what we came from and going into this new world," recalled Holm. "It was really an uphill launch. They didn't think it would work."

Despite management's skepticism, Slizer was founded on a compelling market opportunity. It presented an original concept: the toy market's first buildable action figure. And unlike the vast majority of LEGO sets, whose sales were mostly generated during the make-or-break Christmas season, Slizer was priced and promoted to create sales throughout the year. Thus it produced uninterrupted, year-round revenue. Launched in early 1999, Slizer generated sales in excess of DKK 600 million (about $100 million). To management's surprise, LEGO had a hit on its hands.

A New Channel to Market

After Slizer, LEGO managed to pull defeat from the jaws of victory. The company's strategy was to phase out Slizer after one year and replace it with another short-term, collectible product line. By the

* In 1979 LEGO introduced a set of toys around a theme called Fabuland, with characters, stories, and comic books accompanying the toys. The line never really caught on and was discontinued.

time RoboRiders (shown in insert photo 10), a line of six vehiclelike creations with special powers, roared into the market in December 1999, it was too late for management to reverse course and extend Slizer's run. The company's leaders could only hope that Slizer's success would fuel RoboRiders' performance.

Like Slizer, RoboRiders had a backstory: the six motorcycle-style vehicles battled a viral force that was attacking their worlds. And like Slizer, RoboRiders aimed to be a collectible, less-expensive toy that kids could purchase in supermarkets and other nontraditional outlets. RoboRiders also introduced one of the company's most unconventional innovations in packaging. The design team fabricated a clear, soda-can-style canister to package the toy, based on the notion that RoboRiders characters might be sold in vending machines.

Although full-spectrum innovation starts with creating a market-defining product, it also encompasses the critical moment when the product meets the customer. Delivering RoboRiders via vending machines amounted to a novel sales channel for LEGO. Whereas all of its other lines were sold through big-box retailers in the United States and the smaller toy shops that were so abundant in Europe, RoboRiders opened a new front: gas station stores and other purveyors of inexpensive impulse items. The team, having learned its lesson from Slizer, began planning for a multiyear run of the toy if it proved successful.

But RoboRiders never took off, largely because the line lacked the vivid personalities and compelling characteristics that would draw kids in. Sales were lackluster, and the company pulled it off the shelves after little more than a year.

Despite the setback with RoboRiders, the development team continued to believe it had found a winning formula. Feedback from the market—in the form of sales results, field reports from LEGO salespeople, and a cold-eyed analysis of what had worked and what had failed—helped the team reset its strategy for the toy that became Bionicle.

An Epic Story

Slizer proved that a story-driven, character-based line could deliver repeat purchases and year-round revenue. RoboRiders demonstrated that a toy delivered at a low price to nontraditional outlets held promise, but the characters couldn't be too abstract. To hold kids' interest, character-based toys should be founded on an episodic story line with plenty of teasers hinting at new adventures to come. Taken together, Slizer and RoboRiders also delivered a painful lesson: the development team couldn't sustain the relentless pace required to turn out an entirely new product line every year. A better tack was to aim for a story that could be told over many chapters, like a serialized movie. Such an innovation would open up a revenue stream that could flow for years. Based on those insights, the team repositioned the concept for its next buildable action figure: Voodoo Heads, which would morph into Bionicle during the summer of 1999, when Christian Faber and his Advance colleagues were brought into the project.* (Insert photo 11 shows two early concept sketches for Voodoo Heads.)

With Voodoo Heads, the team retained the foundational cornerstones of the Slizer consumer experience—the concept would still be collectible, character-based, highly affordable, and sold through everyday outlets. The team also incorporated the most promising innovations from RoboRiders, such as the canister-style packaging and the notion that the line should be launched through a Web-based promotion, which was still a relatively fresh concept for the toy industry of the late 1990s. What the new concept would most need, though, was an epic, movielike narrative that would sustain interest and sales for many years to come.

Among the significant breakthroughs that helped Voodoo Heads

---

* The concept went through many iterations and was also called Voodoo Bots and Bone Heads.

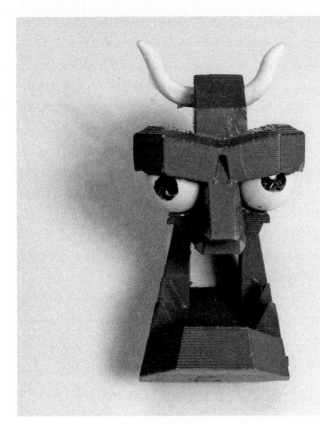

An early Voodoo Heads prototype.

evolve into the Bionicle story, three stand out. First, there was Faber's rich depiction of the Bionicle universe, with its tropical island topped by a massive volcano. "For me, every fantasy story starts not with the characters but with the location," he recalled. "You've got to give kids a compelling place to play."

The next breakthrough came when Bob Thompson, the leader of the Bionicle story team, used Faber's visuals to recast the characters. Taking inspiration from Maori culture, Thompson changed the names of the six main protagonists from the pedestrian-sounding Axe, Blade, Flame, Kick, Hook, and Claw to the more evocative Lewa, Kopaka, Tahu, Phoatu, Gali, and Onua. The words were nonsensical, but they resonated with kids by conjuring an exotic land.

The final missing element came when the development team, working with Bionicle's writers, invented the Kanohi Masks of Life, which released great power to those characters who possessed them. The protagonists' search for the Kanohi Masks catalyzed the story and gave it a narrative thrust. Bionicle was not only about a battle between good and evil forces but also about a quest for a "hidden object of power." Moreover, the masks became the most prominent of the franchise's collectible elements. Just like the Bionicle characters, kids gained power among their peers when they acquired a Kanohi Mask.

"Erik Kramer, who was a product manager for Bionicle, literally interrupted a meeting to show me the [original] mask," recalled Nipper. "He was saying, 'We've got it now. The mask is going to make all the difference.' And he was right. Until then, we'd had a very bumpy ride with Bionicle. We really weren't sure just how good an idea it was. But after the mask was born, the communication, story, packaging—everything just flowed like a river."

The Kanohi Mask of Life.

A New Way of Connecting with Customers

A full spectrum of innovations creates value not only via new products and services for customers but also from changes to a company's business model, internal processes, and even its culture. And for LEGO, inventing Bionicle was very much a culture-altering event. The challenge of creating a new play experience pushed the Bionicle development team to solicit feedback from the outside world, which in the 1990s represented a dramatic break from standard LEGO practice. From the birth of the brick to the last years of the past century, designers were so secure in their knowledge of what kids wanted that they rarely ventured beyond Billund to glean insights into children's lives and apply what they learned to their next creations. To the extent that LEGO designers ever listened to kids and adult fans, those consultations almost always took the form of a kind of reluctant due diligence. Except on the rare occasions when a focus group unanimously disparaged a toy, consumers were brought in simply to fine-tune and validate products that were inevitably destined for the market.

Because Bionicle, as well as the Slizer and RoboRiders toys that preceded it, sought to introduce boys to a story-driven fantasy world, the "designers know best" mind-set had to change. Starting with the assignment that led to the creation of Slizer, the design team sought to acquire a far deeper understanding of its potential consumers and use that knowledge to better position its toy concepts and guide their development.

The effort began when the Slizer team, working from published research on boys' behavior and especially their play lives, created detailed profiles of four different consumers, each with an alliterative name. There was Agent Anthony, who loved action movies and adventure stories. Systematic Siegfried was fascinated with technology. Artistic Arthur would probably grow up to be a craftsman. And then there was Bully Bob, easily distracted and the loudest kid in the room— hardly the typical LEGO consumer and one whom the company had never seriously pursued.* Each of the archetypes informed Slizer and helped shape Bionicle, but none more so than Bully Bob.

"With the Bully Bob character, the model's functions and look and feel had to be very different," said Holm. "We started to give life to concepts that had many more competitive twists to them. There was also a social aspect, which got us thinking about how boys might play in groups, rather than alone. When we gave birth to those types of concepts, the whole world opened up. It felt like we were on to something."

The team's outreach to kids led to a crucial insight early in the development of the toy. When it tested Voodoo Heads, the team worried about the conflict that came with the concept. Part of the play experience involved one character punching the other, causing its head to pop off. The team thought that kids from the United States, with their greater exposure to baleful movies and bloody TV shows, would go bonkers for decapitated characters. To its surprise, the team found just the opposite. Violence was a turnoff, because the American kids personalized the experience. There was also a practical consideration: the boys told testers they were afraid they'd lose the collectible heads if they blew off too easily. Having heard the customers' verdict, the developers went back to their bricks.

As the concepts evolved from Slizer to RoboRiders to Voodoo Heads to Bionicle, Bully Bob morphed into Bionicle Boy, a dynamic trendsetter with a short attention span, a kid who likes to multitask and desires instant gratification. For the designers, Bully Bob and, later, Bionicle Boy were vital signposts for navigating the journey to develop the Bionicle line. When designers began to lose their way they referred back to the archetype, which reminded them, as Holm put it, to "always be a bit more daring." Thus they pushed the features that would make the toy unique: vivid storytelling and richly drawn characters that wouldn't bust a kid's allowance, delivered a

---

* Recall that Bionicle was developed under Poul Plougmann, who wanted LEGO to appeal to the larger market of boys who were indifferent to the brick. Most of those efforts failed. Bionicle was the one shining success.

hefty dose of street cred, appealed to boys' collecting instinct, and, above all, were cool.

Two years after Bionicle hit the U.S. market in the summer of 2001, the development team began working with kids and adult fans to help guide the evolving story line. The effort began by accident. In 2003, right around the time that the news media began reporting on the LEGO Group's financial troubles, a rumor started circulating among LEGO user groups that the company was going to drop the line. Greg Farshtey, who had taken over as the lead writer of Bionicle books and comics, joined one of the toy's fan sites, BZPower, to refute the rumor. Almost immediately, he began exchanging fifty to a hundred daily emails with kids. He soon found fans were an invaluable resource for testing ideas and gauging the story's performance.

"A lot of what I wrote for the [Bionicle] books and website was in response to what kids told me they wanted to see," said Farshtey. "If kids were saying they didn't understand a certain part of a book, I knew we had a problem that needed to be fixed in the next book. I'd also poll kids with questions like, 'What characters from the past eight years would you want to see on a team?' I'd then use their choices to build the team. Interacting with kids gave us an instant read on everything we did."

In the years following Bionicle's launch, other LEGO development teams would go to far greater lengths to elicit feedback from beyond the company's design studios. But more than any other product line, it was Bionicle that helped LEGO take its first tentative steps toward building bridges with kids and adult fans.

A New Development Process

In addition to changing the LEGO Group's design culture, by demonstrating the value in seeking customers' feedback Bionicle also left its imprint on the company's development process. Because Bionicle was based on an episodic story line and new releases came out semi-annually, in the off-season months of August and January, the team took a different approach to managing the clock. Back in the late 1990s, other LEGO creative teams used as much time as they needed to conceive a new toy concept and then presented it to management when it was ready for review. But the Bionicle team didn't have that luxury. It set aggressive, six-month delivery windows and changed the models' range and complexity to fit that schedule. This "time boxing" of the toy's development, a common industry practice where managers set strict deadlines and adjust the scope of the project to fit those deadlines, was new to LEGO and later became a key feature of the revamped LEGO Development Process, in which new-product projects would be divided into three-month stages.

Equally important, the Bionicle team's ability to kick out, every six months, a new story with a new set of characters proved to Knudstorp that LEGO could slash the time it took to develop new products, which in 2004 still averaged a very leisurely three years. Soon after he was elevated to the chief executive slot, Knudstorp launched the High Speed Project, which aimed to transform LEGO into a fast company that could nimbly respond to emerging market opportunities. When skeptics voiced doubts that LEGO could cut its product development time in half, Knudstorp had only to point to Bionicle to prove that it could.

Postlaunch, the Bionicle team managed the development effort very differently than the rest of LEGO did. The LEGO product development process in the late 1990s was a bureaucratic mess, with rigidly defined process steps, multiple review points, mounds of paperwork, and sign-offs at every turn. The Bionicle team did away with that approach and instead focused on the key information that management needed, so it could better determine if the team was on target. Some of that data came directly from customers. At a time when other LEGO teams often pushed products onto retail shelves with little input from customers, the Bionicle group's deep investigations into what boys wanted in a buildable action figure gave managers a far better sense of what would sell. The line's spectacular success encouraged the new management team, when it took over in 2004, to make consumer insight research and product testing with kids key features of the revamped LEGO Development Process.

The Bionicle team kept its efforts on track through regular review sessions with upper management, where executives critiqued model prototypes as well as the business case for the next iteration of Bionicle characters. Because LEGO had never before developed a story-driven product, the design team went to elaborate lengths to bring executives into the concept's science-fantasy world. For its 2000 presentation of the Voodoo Heads concept (which was later renamed Bone Heads), the development team used big blocks of foam board to fashion a strangely wondrous island, eight feet high, replete with cliffs and caves inhabited by the skeletal creatures. The team's working name for the proposed line read like the title of a B movie from the 1950s: Bone Heads of Voodoo Island. As Holm remembers it, Kristiansen and Plougmann were somewhat taken aback by the presentation's scale and over-the-top setting. But the expressiveness of the Bone Heads characters, which evinced some of the ghoulish humor of Day of the Dead figurines, elicited the go-ahead to keep developing the concept.

Prior to the toy's launch in 2001, no other LEGO development team had encountered quite as many hurdles as the team that created Bionicle. Not only did the Bionicle design crew have to meet the challenge of conjuring an entirely new kind of toy, but the writers had to compose the Bionicle narrative, the Web team had to conceive new digital content, the marketing team had to create a movielike campaign, the packaging team had to fashion the soda-can-style Bionicle canisters, and the licensing group had to coordinate with a multitude of companies that wanted a piece of the Bionicle brand. And then, to keep the story fresh and keep priming demand, everyone had to generate an entirely new story line, new characters, and new sets every six months.

Time and again, the development team could have lost its way. But for the nine years of the Bionicle franchise's lifetime, the team kept to its path, largely because it found a different way to organize itself.

Before the rise of Bionicle, the LEGO Group's product teams were siloed from one another and toys were for the most part developed sequentially: designers mocked up the models and then threw their creations over a metaphorical wall to the engineers, who prepared the prototypes for manufacture and then kicked them over to the marketers, and so on down the line. Rarely would one team venture onto another team's turf to offer a suggestion or ask for feedback. If all went well, the team's product would hit the market in two or three years.

The Bionicle team's six-month deadlines forced a different way of working, one that was less sequential than parallel, and highly collaborative. Once the outline for the next chapter of the Bionicle saga was roughed out, the different functional groups would work side by side in real time, swapping ideas, critiquing models, and always pushing to simultaneously nail the deadline and build a better Bionicle.

"We had a massive project team," recalled Farshtey. "It wasn't just the creative people; it was also people from Advance and from marketing, sales, events, PR—all different parts of the company, all helping to steer the franchise."

Because the marketing group worked directly with designers, Bionicle's advertising campaign felt connected to the product. Promotional posters for Bionicle's first-year run had the look and feel of movie posters, precisely because the toy featured the powerful visuals and narrative sweep of an epic film. "We wanted more communication in the product and more product in the communication," said Faber. "That meant the marketing group needed to be involved at the very start of product development, so the story flowed out through the product. We wanted the product almost to tell the story by itself.

"We had a kind of triangle, where the marketing, the story, and the product had to move ahead together," he continued. "None of those could be the spearhead. Each needed to support and inspire the other."

The problem with a more linear approach to product development is that if, say, the marketing group isn't engaged early on in the process, it might not spot a communication flaw until the problem becomes pervasive and therefore expensive to fix. With the Bionicle team, however, the tight linkage between design, marketing, engineering, and the other groups meant that little problems didn't compound into big problems before the team could take corrective action. Moreover, because each functional group was invested in the entire project, as opposed to protecting its turf, everyone had a stake in driving the business forward. This made for an operationally resilient team and contributed to Bionicle's nine-year run.

A New Way of Working with Partners

Team Bionicle's leveraging of a full spectrum of innovations resulted in a new toy category, a new sales channel, a revamped development process, and a first attempt at soliciting ideas from customers. It also proved that breaking out of Billund's insular culture and collaborating with partners could pump up the company's bottom line. Just as no other LEGO development team was ever pushed to work as fast as the Bionicle group, no other marketing team was ever required to coordinate with so many external partners as the Bionicle group. The wide array of Bionicle backpacks, T-shirts, pajamas, and toys fueled the line's profitability by delivering fat royalties, low operating expenses, and almost no risk. Moreover, licensed media products such as the Bionicle book series (published by Scholastic Books), comic books (DC Comics), video games (TT Games), and direct-to-video movies (Miramax) were the primary platforms for extending the franchise's reach. Keeping pace with each initiative meant the Bionicle team had to ensure that every six months, when the product line's next iteration hit the market, all those Bionicle books, backpacks, bedspreads, and the rest reflected the new toy's look, story, and LEGO values.

To help all those different companies work with LEGO, the company set up an independent Licensing Group. The group, which reported to a different senior vice president than the Bionicle team, was responsible for ensuring that every partner's product augmented the Bionicle brand and reflected the LEGO DNA. Through product review sessions, seasoned LEGO managers reviewed every licensee's business plans, product concepts, and production samples. And the Licensing Group closely tracked each external partner's progress in preparing its Bionicle-branded product for the market. The group's progress reports served to alert LEGO when, say, the next Bionicle video game was straying from the toy's story line or a T-shirt featured the wrong color scheme. Taken together, the critiques and reports helped ensure that the Bionicle team, through eighteen product launches, marched in tight formation with more than a dozen different partners.

Because each new version of Bionicle had a short shelf life, the team couldn't afford to wait until after the toy's launch to correct a partner's mistake. The team learned this lesson the hard way. During Bionicle's inaugural year, LEGO took too long to approve the final design of many licensed products, which meant the products weren't launched until the new Bionicle line was nearing the end of its six-month life cycle, a painful delay that crippled sales. Realizing the need for speed, the team developed the Bionicle Style Guide, which helped accelerate and coordinate every external stakeholder's product development effort.

Encompassing nearly fifty pages, the Style Guide, which outlined Bionicle's rapidly evolving strategy, story line, and design, was delivered to licensing partners months in advance of a toy's rollout. The 2006 edition of the guide, for example, delivered a sweeping overview of Bionicle's three-year story strategy, along with visual and written profiles of upcoming characters such as Zaktan, aka "the Snake" ("100% animal, 0% pet"), and Toa Jaller (a "fearless lava surfer"). The guide also dug into Bionicle minutiae, with strict instructions on such granular details as typography ("trademark headlines are always all caps") and Bionicle logo renderings ("always placed on the top of the layout").

Taken together, the 2006 guide gave Bionicle's partners a visceral depiction of the new lineup's color palette, key visual backgrounds, packaging, design elements, and more. As a result, the richly detailed guide let partners align with the brand's strategic blueprint. In 2008, when LEGO executives reviewed the company's strategy for licensing, Bionicle was deemed the best at coordinating with partners, surpassing such iconic properties as LEGO City and the minifig.

A New Road Map for Guiding Innovation

Throughout 2005, as Knudstorp and his team wrestled with the challenge of igniting profits by pursuing the full spectrum of innovation, their foremost goal was to set targets, define initiatives, and establish a sequence for getting things done. Here again, Knudstorp looked to the Bionicle team to point the way.

After many months of digging into the challenge of creating a cohesive model for full-spectrum innovation, a working group came up with a practical if unlovely vision for the entire company: innovation is the "focused introduction of a new idea . . . that improves the product, experience, communication, business, and process." By expanding the definition of innovation beyond the "bright" parts of the organization that create new toy sets, the new definition expressly challenged every part of LEGO—sales, finance, manufacturing, and all the rest—to come up with game-changing ways to amplify the company's performance.

LEGO managers identified four categories of innovation that mattered, with three types of innovation in each.

- *Product innovations* were new toys and platforms. Four years earlier, with Bionicle's launch, the toy's development team had already innovated in both of those categories. It had invented an industry first, the buildable action figure. In creating sub-sequent generations of Bionicle characters, the team was adept at making modest but highly profitable improvements to the line. And with its ball-and-socket connector, Bionicle also represented a new building platform for LEGO.

- *Communication innovations* included novel ways of marketing and also connecting to customers. Greg Farshtey's outreach to customers via Bionicle fan sites, which he and his colleagues used to improve Bionicle's story line, offered a proof-of-concept model for leveraging feedback from fans. (LEGO subsequently expanded on Farshtey's example and uses it extensively today.)

- *Business innovations* consisted of new business models (such as new pricing methods or subscription plans) and new channels to market. Since its debut in 2001, Bionicle had already delivered minor but noteworthy innovations in both areas. With launches in the off-peak months of January and August, and a price tag that required just a few weeks of a boy's allowance, Bionicle filled both a seasonal and a demographic gap in the LEGO brand's market. Although the attempt to sell the toy through vending machines never panned out, Bionicle freed marketers to seek out unconventional ways of pushing beyond such conventional intermediaries as Walmart and Toys "R" Us. Perhaps most significant, the range of licensed products that Bionicle Boys snapped up delivered a healthy stream of royalties back to Billund. As a result, other product teams emulated the Bionicle model of partnering around LEGO-developed properties to boost sales and profits.

- *Process innovations* were core processes (where money changes hands) or enabling processes (such as new-product development). Here again, Bionicle suggested new innovation pathways for LEGO. The Bionicle team's compressed development cycles and customer insight research became staples of the revamped LEGO Development Process. Bionicle proved it was indeed possible to cut development time in half, which resulted in substantial cost savings for LEGO. And it showed that customer research could improve the odds of delivering toys that kids fervently desired. That, of course, augmented the company's sales.

Having defined the different areas of innovation that LEGO would pursue, the working group also recognized that "innovation" doesn't necessarily mean "radical"—that, in fact, different opportunities require varying degrees of innovativeness. The new model spotlighted three different approaches to marshaling the kinds of change that would help LEGO advance its goals. The first, simplest type of innovation was to *adjust* existing toys—that is, to freshen up an evergreen line so that it attracts news waves of kids without adding significantly more development and manufacturing costs. After the first launch of Bionicle, each subsequent release was an exercise in making incremental improvements. Adding new features, new story lines, and (later) vehicles for the Bionicle characters were small but very profitable innovations. Senior vice president Per Hjuler captured the attitude of many LEGO managers when he asserted, "I am continually humbled by the power of the little idea."

The next, more challenging innovation was to *reconfigure*—to change existing building systems or platforms to provide a new customer experience. LEGO had a blockbuster with its *Star Wars* toys and a minor but promising success with Slizer. Combining the two concepts to produce a set of buildable action figures with a rich, episodic story line meant that LEGO had to blaze a new path to profits, but it was starting from a familiar place. The result was a hit series of toys that generated significant sales for almost a decade. Reconfiguring innovations change the terms of competition in an existing market.

The most difficult and unpredictable innovation is the kind that *redefines* a category. Case in point: the 1998 Mindstorms RCX kits, the company's first foray into robotics. (The second version of Mindstorms, released in 2006, was a reconfigure innovation for LEGO.) Another example was LEGO Universe, an online game where kids from all across the planet could connect and play. In the next two chapters, we cover each of these radical attempts at redefining LEGO play.

The LEGO Group's senior management put all these definitions onto a single page—an innovation matrix—that it used to map the kinds of innovations it would pursue. In the first year following the crisis, the company focused most of its efforts on the adjusting kind of innovations—the lowest-risk, surest-reward section of the matrix. Later, when LEGO gained momentum and began generating profits, it took on the more ambitious innovations, reconfiguring and redefining. But LEGO always made sure it continued to seek out the everyday innovations that simply enhanced an already profitable line. So long as it innovated around its customers, sales channels, business processes, and the rest, LEGO wouldn't always have to churn out a

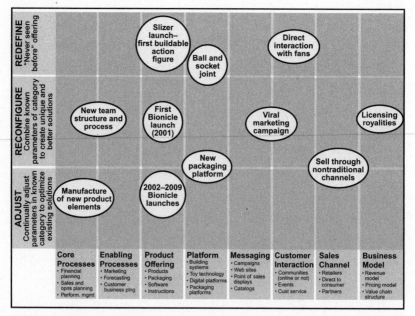

The LEGO innovation matrix, with some of the major innovations from the development of Slizer, RoboRiders, and Bionicle.

Bionicle-size blockbuster every year. Sometimes a simple makeover of an already successful line would suffice.

As it turned out, Bionicle racked up its peak sales in 2002 and then began a long but very profitable return to earth. By the time the line was phased out in 2009, the Bionicle business was much like the sleeping giant Mata Nui—still a force, but considerably diminished. And yet, while many factors beyond Bionicle have shaped the LEGO Group's approach to guiding innovation, the team that created the toy has left an indelible mark on the way LEGO works. Thanks to Bionicle, what once was considered heresy at LEGO is now a kind of orthodoxy.

Bionicle proved it was possible to roll out a new product every six months instead of taking three years. By developing detailed profiles of different consumer segments, the Bionicle team took the first steps toward achieving a deeper understanding of the world as seen through children's eyes and using those insights to build more desirable toys. In the late 1990s, such a thing was anathema to LEGO. Today, a dedicated consumer insights team plays a pivotal role in every LEGO product launch.

Further evidence of Bionicle's influence on innovation is that cross-functional product development teams are now the new normal at LEGO. "Every team has a triangle-type arrangement," said Søren Holm. "Design, engineering, marketing—they all work hand in hand." Additionally, the move by Bionicle's writers to glean guidance and feedback from consumers presaged a far more robust effort to cocreate with fans. And Bionicle's successful licensing business pioneered new pathways for partnering with the makers of complementary products.

The Bionicle team's rituals and practices for seizing on the full spectrum of innovation are now replicated all across LEGO, and that is Bionicle's most enduring legacy. It's no longer enough for development teams to simply propose a new product. LEGO management expects team leaders to plot it on the innovation matrix and demonstrate what other, complementary innovations will add to the concept's revenue stream. Having learned that complementary innovations are too important to be left to chance, teams use the matrix to create and deliver them.

Bionicle was not just the toy that kept LEGO from falling into bankruptcy in 2003. It taught LEGO a far more expansive definition of innovation, one that need not be confined simply to products. It showed that while not all innovations are created equal, even incremental innovations can be highly effective, especially when combined into a complementary suite. LEGO codified these insights by creating the innovation matrix and requiring every development team to map their ideas to it. As a result, the matrix ensured that a full spectrum of innovations wasn't an occasional outcome but a required result. And, as we'll see in Chapter Ten, the company later reorganized itself around the matrix, thereby making it plainly evident which business unit was responsible for each type of innovation. Thus, the Bionicle team provided LEGO with an enduring, best-case example for guiding an expansive innovation effort. By looking back at Bionicle, Knudstorp was able to cast a bright light into the future.

Early LEGO

Photo 1 (above). The duck, a wooden LEGO toy from the 1930s, occupies a special place in LEGO lore. When young Godfredt told his father that he had saved time and money by only using two coats of varnish on a batch of ducks, his father made him go back to the train station, get the ducks, and stay up all night adding the third coat. The story is used to illustrate the maxim "Det Bedste Er Ikke For Godt." (Only the best is good enough.)

Photo 2 (left). A LEGO Town set from the 1960s promised a play experience that was "real as real."

Photo 3 (below). One of the LEGO Group's many innovations under young Kjeld Kirk Kristiansen was the introduction of fantasy themes such as Space. The 1979 Space Cruiser (below) was a big hit.

Experimentation at LEGO: 1999–2002

Photo 4 (above). The LEGO & Steven Spielberg MovieMaker set was an attempt to find a "blue ocean" market opportunity.

Photo 5 (left). In the early 2000s, LEGO phased out the DUPLO brand in favor of the new LEGO Explore brand. The LEGO Explore Music Roller was one of the first toys to feature the new brand.

Photo 6 (below). LEGO Digital Designer, developed by Qube Software, allowed users to create virtual LEGO constructions and upload them to a LEGO website.

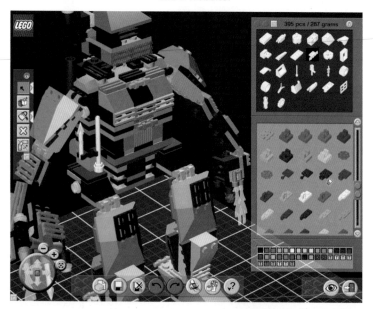

Photo 7 (right, and below). The Galidor action figure, introduced in 2002, had a full spectrum of complementary innovations, including a new building system, a TV show, and a video game.

Photo 8 (below). Between 1996 and 2002 LEGO launched three LEGOLAND theme parks in the UK, US, and Germany.

The Evolution of Bionicle

Photo 9 (above, right). The Slizer line, launched in 1999, was the toy world's first buildable action figure and a precursor to the Bionicle figures.

Photo 10 (above, left). The RoboRiders line, launched in 2000, never took off and was pulled from the market after little more than a year.

Photo 11 (below). Building on the success of Slizer and RoboRiders, LEGO sketched early concepts for Voodoo Heads, the toy that would become Bionicle.

The Birth of Bionicle

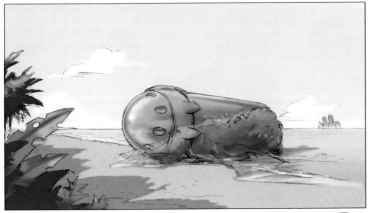

Photo 12 (above). Two of Christian Faber's early concept sketches from 2000 for the toy that would become Bionicle. Note the pill-shaped container that delivers the Bionicle heroes to the island of Mata Nui.

Photo 13 (below, right). The canisters used to package the Bionicle toys in 2001 were very similar to the concepts drawn by Christian Faber.

Photo 14 (below). The innovations tracked in these two pages culminated in Bionicle, a line that was far darker and more violent than anything LEGO had offered before and was an immediate hit with boys around the world.

Open Innovation at LEGO

Photo 15 (above). The four original Mindstorms User Panel members (standing) were selected from the LEGO fan community and invited to help the LEGO team develop the next generation of the product. In the back (from left to right) are Steve Hassenplug, John Barnes, David Schilling, and Ralph Hempel. Kneeling in front are the LEGO Group's Søren Lund (left) and Paal Smith-Meyer.

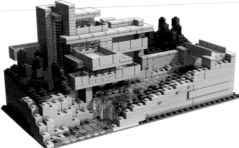

Photo 16 (left). Adam Reed Tucker, a Chicago architect who had created massive LEGO models of famous buildings and landmarks, worked with Paal Smith-Meyer at LEGO to develop the Architecture line of toys.

Photo 17 (above). The LEGO Architecture Fallingwater kit.

LEGO, Minecraft, and 3D Printers

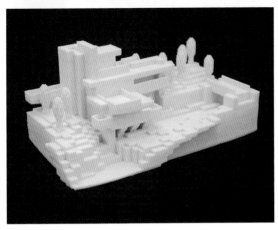

Photos 18, 19, 20. LEGO fans can now design and replicate kits in their homes. Above is a re-creation of the LEGO Architecture Fallingwater kit in the online game Minecraft. Using a fan-created conversion program, that model was sent to a 3D printer to create a physical version, shown left next to the original LEGO Fallingwater kit. Finally, the fan-designed re-creation was "printed" using a Makerbot 3D printer, shown bottom left.

The Birth of LEGO Games

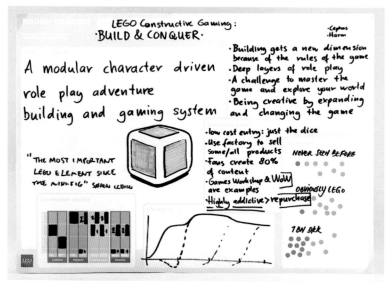

Photo 21 (above). The original proposal for LEGO Games. Notice the Innovation Matrix in the lower left and the management team's votes in the lower right. Management was asked to rate each concept according to how well it met the criteria of "never seen before," "obviously LEGO," and its potential to achieve annual sales of DKK one billion (about $200 million) per year.

Photo 22 (above). LEGO dice prototypes. The final version is shown in the lower right of the photo.

Photo 23 (left). Ramses Pyramid, one of the first sets in the LEGO Games line.

7

Fostering Open Innovation

Mindstorms, Architecture, and the Wisdom of the Clique

You can't fire them, because you haven't hired them.

—Søren Lund, director, Mindstorms NXT

IT WAS LATE APRIL 2010, AND THE GEORGIA DOME WAS rocking. Thousands of LEGO Mindstorms fans had packed the vast arena in downtown Atlanta to witness the world finals of the FIRST LEGO League robotics competition, a kind of Junior Olympics for math and science athletes from every part of the planet. Pioneered by Segway inventor Dean Kamen and his nonprofit organization, FIRST (For Inspiration and Recognition of Science and Technology), the three-day tourney featured a rollicking series of showdowns between eighty-one teams with a total of eight hundred Mindstorms wizards ages nine to sixteen, and hundreds of adult volunteers supporting them. Those eighty-one teams were the best of the best—the regional and national winners from a worldwide contest involving well over sixteen thousand teams.[20]

Each team's goal: design and program a Mindstorms robot—consisting of LEGO components, motors, sensors, and an "intelligent" brick—to weave through an obstacle course and perform a series of complicated tasks, all while sprinting against other teams' bots. Combining the earsplitting thunder of a World Wrestling smackdown with the thrill and mechanistic glory of a NASCAR race, the FIRST World Championship was an amped-up celebration of brains over brawn, as thousands of kids demonstrated what's possible when their imagination and technical prowess were yoked with LEGO and digital technology.

When the kids weren't competing, many swarmed the LEGO Mindstorms booth, where LEGO staffers delivered coaching tips on the finer points of building a better bot and expert adult hobbyists showed off their over-the-top creations, such as Mindstorms Moon Rovers and an astoundingly faithful, LEGO-ized re-creation of Wall-E, the famous robot from the Disney/Pixar movie of the same name.

For a couple of hours, a group of LEGO software developers and other staff members slipped away from the booth and into a vacant hallway, where they met with a thirteen-year-old college student and FIRST LEGO League competitor from Beaverton, Oregon, named Tesca Fitzgerald. Instead of delivering a demo, the LEGO crew witnessed one, as Tesca unveiled the massive artificial-intelligence program she had written for her team's Mindstorms robot.

Outfitted in the red wig and Day-Glo orange T-shirt that were the uniform of her robotics team, the Fire-Breathing Rubber Duckies, Tesca told the LEGO developers of how she had spent 440 hours creating, testing, and modifying a complex algorithm for her AI-based pathfinding software. The program allowed her robot to navigate through a typical hospital environment on its own. With more than twenty feet of flow charts spread across the hallway's floor, Tesca walked the LEGO developers through her program and answered their questions about her code, as well as what improvements *she* wanted to see in the Mindstorms software. When she finished, the duly impressed LEGO crew invited the precocious programmer (and her parents) to present her AI work at the LEGO Developers Conference in Billund the following year.

Tesca Fitzgerald's foray into artificial-intelligence software development via LEGO was, as Mindstorms marketing manager Steven Canvin later put it, "pretty mind-blowing. It's very likely that this young girl created the largest program ever written in our software." At the same time, Tesca's achievement was one more milestone in a remarkable journey that has seen LEGO transform itself from a remote, highly insular organization, where only the public relations manager spoke for public consumption, to one that has adroitly managed to open up to its most inventive customers, learn from them, and thereby harness their creativity.

Birthing the First LEGO Bot

To appreciate just how insular LEGO has been in the past, consider what transpired in 1998, when LEGO debuted its first Mindstorms set. Sporting a retail price tag of $199, the original kit consisted of a software application that customers could use to program a microcontroller-based brick, dubbed the RCX (Robotic Command Explorer); three motors; three sensors; and a collection of roughly seven hundred LEGO bricks, beams, gears, axles, and wheels for building a wide range of robots.

In those first, crucial months following the launch of Mindstorms, the LEGO Group's brain trust was taken aback when it learned through surveys that 70 percent of Mindstorms hobbyists were adults, not kids. Intended for children, Mindstorms was enchanting tens of thousands of grown-up geeks.

Soon after the Mindstorms release, a Stanford University graduate student cracked open the RCX brick and revealed to the world what was inside. He reverse-engineered the RCX brick's microcode as well as the firmware and put his discoveries up on the Internet.

With the Mindstorms proprietary code spreading across LUGNET (the worldwide network of LEGO user groups) as well as robotics and computer discussion groups, a software engineer whose day job was programming for Motorola Inc. worked off the now public RCX code to create a programming tool called Not Quite C (NQC), a text-based language that allowed skilled hobbyists to add more detailed features for controlling the Mindstorms hardware.* Almost simultaneously, a computer science graduate student at Germany's University of Karlsruhe developed an open-source operating system, legOS, which among other things allowed developers to program a version of the RCX brick that was four times as fast as the original.

Not surprisingly, some LEGO managers fretted that the hacking outbreak, which spread across the Internet in a matter of weeks, would lead to people pirating the code and creating robotics kits that would bite into the Mindstorms market, which was still in its infancy. The company's lawyers were even more alarmed. They pushed to hit the hackers with cease-and-desist letters ordering them to stop mucking with the company's intellectual property. "The legal department went nuts," recalled Søren Lund, who led the 2006 Mindstorms team. "They were like, 'They're showing the code to the world! It will be copied!' "

But rather than sue, LEGO decided to let the hackers have their way. Unlike the LEGO Group's lawyers, the Mindstorms development team believed the hacking signaled that they had come up with a winner. Adult hobbyists wouldn't take the trouble to dig into the RCX brick and write alternative code if they didn't think the Mindstorms platform was worth developing. After Mindstorms discussion groups popped up across the Internet and more software developers began to write their own applications, LEGO sought to catalyze the burgeoning community's creativity by adding a "right to hack" to the Mindstorms software license and creating a Mindstorms website

---

* LEGO used an icon-based programming language, RCX-code, which was less powerful than NQC but easier to learn and use and therefore more appropriate for kids.

with its own discussion forum, a heady move for a company that had always sought to tightly control its image. LEGO wasn't thinking about harnessing the crowd's creativity at that point. It just wanted to get out of the way of a rapidly building success.

Nevertheless, some LEGO executives' worst fears were realized when the company hustled out a Mindstorms accessories kit that was less than warmly received. "[Customers] were posting on our message boards, saying the [accessories kit] was overpriced and basically a piece of crap," recalled Tormod Askildsen, who heads up the LEGO Community Development team. "And the reaction from at least some people in the higher levels of the company was that we can't let people say things like that on a LEGO site—we needed to remove the negative comments. We argued that we could take the forums down, but we couldn't edit them. And if we did close the forums, the discussions would just move to another site. So why don't we just open up, admit there's a problem, and do something about it?"

LEGO wisely left the forums alone and even used the Mindstorms site to release a free, downloadable software development kit that further enabled adept hobbyists to dream up their own applications for Mindstorms. In doing so, LEGO switched from contemplating lawsuits against hackers to actively encouraging them to reinvent Mindstorms in ways that LEGO itself had never imagined.

The results were dramatic. Customers lit up the LEGO Mindstorms site—as well as LUGNET and dozens of fan-created Mindstorms sites—with postings on a mind-boggling array of LEGO-ized bots. Along with photos and videos of their Mindstorms MOCs (My Own Creations), fans from around the globe put up hundreds of Web pages with detailed instructions for replicating their inventions. Their zeal for all things Mindstorms sparked a cottage industry of how-to books for building and programming the LEGO bots, as well as a plethora of start-up companies selling third-party Mindstorms sensors and hardware.

Seemingly overnight, an entire ecosystem of customer-generated

Web forums, books, microcompanies, and competitions such as the FIRST LEGO League tournaments had evolved around Mindstorms. Recalled Askildsen: "People were improving on the product and making it accessible to niche needs that LEGO couldn't serve." Buoyed by its fans' creativity with Mindstorms, which drew new customers into the Mindstorms orbit, LEGO sold eighty thousand kits over the first five months of the RCX robot's inaugural year. The set was so popular, it outstripped the company's forecasts and left LEGO out of Mindstorms inventory for the Christmas holidays. Despite that nearly unforgivable sin, Mindstorms would go on to become the best-selling single product in the company's history. It would also dramatically reshape the company's approach to managing innovation.

Through Mindstorms, LEGO began to see the advantages in not just allowing but *encouraging* its customer community to come up with complementary innovations to its toys. When customers wrote new applications for Mindstorms, they helped grow the market by enabling other customers to come up with buzz-generating Mindstorms creations, such as an assembly plant that custom-builds a LEGO car, or a vending machine that takes money, dispenses candy or soda, and gives correct change. With the posting of each new application, innovative customers expanded the possibilities that Mindstorms offered. In the late 1990s, the notion of tapping into a virtuous web of volunteer innovators was "a totally different business paradigm," as Mads Nipper later described it. "Although users don't get paid for it, they enhance the experience you can have with the basic Mindstorms set—it's a great way to make the product more exciting."

At the same time, Mindstorms powerfully demonstrated to LEGO managers and developers that there was much they could glean from skilled adult hobbyists and from child prodigies such as Tesca Fitzgerald. That notion was powerfully underlined in the fall of 1999 when LEGO and the MIT Media Lab organized a gathering, called Mind-Fest, of roughly three hundred Mindstorms enthusiasts, including robotics geeks, teachers, and master builders of all ages. (Since the mid-1980s, LEGO had collaborated with the Media Lab's Seymour Papert—one of the pioneers of artificial intelligence and author of the book *Mindstorms*, which gave the LEGO toy its name—on research into how children learn through experimentation and play.) The MindFest conference's big-picture focus was on the future of learning; for the LEGO Mindstorms development team, the conference offered abundant opportunities to do some learning of their own.

The most powerful learning moment occurred during a panel discussion among a "dream team" of hackers that included Kekoa Proudfoot, the Stanford University grad student who reverse-engineered the RCX microcode, and Markus Noga, creator of the legOS operating system. The LEGO team listened slack-jawed as the hackers described the RCX brick's potential to enable kids and adult hobbyists to build contraptions that LEGO developers hadn't imagined. Then it was Ralph Hempel's turn to talk. Hempel, an embedded-systems engineer from Owen Sound, Ontario, had written a memory-conserving programming system, pbForth, for Mindstorms. Citing complaints from some robotics geeks that the RCX lacked sufficient memory, Hempel recalled one of technology's greatest achievements, NASA's first lunar landing. With the RCX, said Hempel, developers held in their hands the same computing power that had put a man on the moon. His message: *Shame on us, as a community, if we can't create great code for the brick.*

"It was the first time we met face-to-face with the hackers, and we were all thinking, 'This is too good to be true,' " recalled Mindstorms team leader Søren Lund. "Afterward we took them out for some beers, and it immediately felt like we were a team of equals brainstorming together."

Exploiting the Wisdom of the Clique

Six years later, just when LEGO was attempting to pull out of its financial free fall, the company began preparing for a return to the wired world with Mindstorms NXT, the next generation of its robotics kit. Recalling the stirring debut of the original Mindstorms, LEGO decided to tap the talents of the world's most creative Mindstorms customers by inviting a handful of them to codevelop the new kit. Such a move was unprecedented at LEGO. Although LEGO had invited expert adult fans to contribute ideas and prototypes for Factory sets, never before had it allowed outsiders into a secret project's core development process. Nevertheless, the business logic for inviting customers to codesign the future of Mindstorms was inescapable. "It was obviously relevant to engage them," said Nipper. "They knew stuff that we didn't."

So began the LEGO Group's disciplined bid to amplify one of the past decade's most talked-about business innovations—tapping the "wisdom of the crowd" to create breakthrough products. Keep in mind that LEGO launched its experiment with crowdsourcing in 2004, a full year before James Surowiecki came out with his groundbreaking book *The Wisdom of Crowds*, in which he posited that because groups of people are "often smarter than the smartest people in them," a crowd's "collective intelligence" will produce better outcomes than a small group of experts. Since the publication of that and other books on customer cocreation, initiatives ranging from LINUX to Wikipedia to more than 240,000 open-source software development projects (according to SourceForge.net) have amply demonstrated that crowdsourcing opens an organization up to a broad swath of insights and ideas that it could never muster by itself.

For more conventional companies, however, crowdsourcing remains a conundrum, and a scary one at that. How can a company open up to the crowd yet still protect its most vital secrets? How can developers separate out the mass's few genuinely inspired insights from its many genuinely loopy ideas? And how can managers capture customers' creativity while ensuring that their fervor doesn't bust budgets and deadlines and ultimately sink the project? Despite those challenges, LEGO managed to leverage outsiders' talents and thereby launch a new generation of Mindstorms that surpassed its predecessor's impressive performance. Indeed, the LEGO Group's disciplined approach to leveraging the talents of citizen developers helped it overcome many of crowdsourcing's underlying challenges.

> **Challenge:** In established companies, many managers are skeptical as to whether the risk that comes from opening up to the outside world is worth the benefits.

In 2004, as Knudstorp and his new management team were struggling to pull LEGO out of its crisis by selling off assets and shutting down money-losing lines, they also were attempting to build a profitable product portfolio for 2006. (Back then, it took LEGO an average of two years to develop and launch a new line.) Despite the remarkable success of Mindstorms during its first two years, a next-generation Mindstorms did not immediately appear to offer much promise.

During the first years of the last decade, even though melding the brick with the bot seemed like a powerful strategy for keeping LEGO relevant in the digital age, the company largely abandoned Mindstorms as it invested in big-budget lines such as Explore and Galidor. In 2001, after releasing a modest update to Mindstorms, LEGO closed down the line's development team and scuttled its marketing effort. Although LEGO kept manufacturing a comparatively small number of sets, it wasn't long before bloggers began writing an obituary for Mindstorms and speculating on why Mindstorms had been a hit with everyone except LEGO executives. "We tried for years to kill the product," Lund recalled ruefully, "because we did absolutely nothing to support it."

But when Knudstorp and Nipper gave the robotics line a second look in 2004, they concluded there was much to commend a Mindstorms revival. Even though LEGO had lost its enthusiasm for the Mindstorms line, customers hadn't.

Since its debut in 1998, the FIRST LEGO League Mindstorms tournaments had grown from sixteen hundred kids participating in the inaugural year to fifty thousand competitors in 2004. Adult hobbyists' passion for Mindstorms hadn't waned substantially, either, as evidenced by countless fan websites and the publication of more than twenty Mindstorms-related books by authors who were unaffiliated with LEGO. The line continued to sell about forty thousand units a year, without any advertising. Moreover, the concept of encouraging open-ended play through buildable, brick-based robots adhered to Knudstorp's back-to-the-brick strategy for rescuing the company, with the added benefit that the Mindstorms microcomputer brick would help LEGO stand out in a digital world of MP3 players and video games. Based on those positive leading indicators, Nipper asked Søren Lund and Paal Smith-Meyer, who was then a LEGO creative director, to lead the development of a new Mindstorms kit.

Almost from the start, the pair agreed that cocreating with the most skilled Mindstorms hobbyists, some of whom they knew personally, was the logical next move. Nevertheless, some LEGO managers, concerned about competitors finding out about their new plans, hesitated to embark on such a precedent-breaking path. "In research and development, you just don't tell strangers what you're working on," said Lund. "In hindsight it sounds easy, but at the time it was a huge cultural barrier, trying to cross that line." A nondisclosure agreement provided little real protection, since the source of a leak is often hard to identify. And the remedy—in this case, suing one of your most influential and respected customers—is unpalatable.

Before Lund and Smith-Meyer took the irreversible step of inviting outside innovators into the inner sanctum of the Mindstorms development team, the pair sought to map out the core business logic for cocreating Mindstorms. First, they bet that tapping into outside experts' knowledge and insights would radically increase the odds of breaking out a hit kit. Second, by engaging expert customers—people who were semicelebrities in the Mindstorms world—those customers could in turn act as persuasive ambassadors for the next generation of Mindstorms. They might even help build a more trusting bond between LEGO corporate, which was widely viewed as having grown indifferent to Mindstorms, and a skeptical fan community. Third, just as Apple would later do with its iPhone app developers, so Lund and Smith-Meyer wanted to do with Mindstorms citizen developers—give them the tools and support they needed to create complementary innovations, from sensors to programming languages to building instructions, that would enhance and expand the Mindstorms platform.

Finally, because LEGO was still mired in its financial crisis, the new Mindstorms would have minimal marketing support. So Lund and Smith-Meyer turned to a resource-conserving, PR-based marketing strategy. If customers helped them codesign a breakthrough product, the pair believed they'd have a buzz-generating story for the business and high-tech press, at a total cost to LEGO of next to nothing. Concluded Lund: "We were on such a limited budget we *had* to work with the fans."

Taken together, those four factors—building a better product, catalyzing fans, launching an accessories market, and creating a tantalizing story for the media—amounted to a due-diligence checklist for engaging outside collaborators. If there was pushback from within the company, the checklist would act as a clarifying reminder of why the benefits outweighed the risks.

Challenge: Volunteer developers are smart, but they're not always right. They can take over a project and turn it in the wrong direction.

The design managers for Mindstorms drew a bright distinction between how the crowd could help and how it couldn't. Although they were determined to engage citizen developers in a soup-to-nuts reinvention of their robotics kit, Lund and Smith-Meyer made a number of fundamental design decisions before soliciting any input from outsiders. Despite the remarkable knowledge and creativity of the most elite Mindstorms customers, none had expertise in designing compelling building experiences for children. That remained the company's responsibility.

Lund had seen how the first-generation Mindstorms sets were challenging for ten- and twelve-year-olds to build by themselves, without help from adults or more experienced kids. For the next-generation kit, he wanted kids to have a much more intuitive first-time building experience. Thus, the developers set themselves a goal: create a kit where kids could build a bot within twenty minutes of opening the box. To that end, the team decided to include only LEGO Technic studless components in the kit. Technic components, which lack the knobs found on classic LEGO pieces, gave kids greater flexibility when building and ultimately made for a sleeker, less chunky-looking bot.

Other early design decisions that came without any input from customers included the move to forgo a product face-lift and instead develop a full-on next-generation product. Making a clean break with the past meant the new Mindstorms set would lack backward compatibility with the first-generation Mindstorms set. On the other hand, the programmable brick and the software that controlled the original Mindstorms could be replaced with an updated intelligent

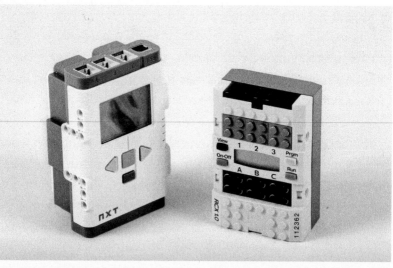

The 2006 LEGO Mindstorms NXT brick (left) used Technic connectors (which fit into the holes in the side) to connect to other pieces in the set. The earlier-generation RCX brick (right) could connect using either Technic connectors (on the sides) or traditional LEGO studs (on the front).

brick, dubbed NXT. Recognizing that LEGO lacked the resources to develop Mindstorms software internally, Lund and Smith-Meyer partnered with Austin, Texas–based National Instruments to build a kid-friendly software platform.

By nailing down such key reference points as studless components and overhauling the robot's brain before fans had a chance to weigh in, Lund and Smith-Meyer lowered the risk that the citizen developers would drag the project off course. With those big-picture decisions behind them, they were prepared to engage lead users in codeveloping the Mindstorms NXT.

Challenge: Controlling the crowd eats up the clock and diverts vital resources.

One of the biggest challenges in any cocreation effort is finding ways to work the crowd without letting it grow into a rule-busting mob. The Mindstorms team's solution was to put a velvet rope around the crowd and admit only a very small, very elite clique into the design team. By limiting the number of codevelopers to only the cleverest Mindstorms hobbyists, Lund and Smith-Meyer believed they'd reap a higher percentage of helpful ideas. The question was who, out of the scores of skilled Mindstorms users, should the team let through the door? "If we had chosen the wrong people," said Lund, "we would have ended up in the wrong place."

Mindstorms managers found the right people by getting guidance from the line's customer community. The managers monitored Mindstorms Web forums and discussion groups with an eye toward identifying those people who were most often cited as masters in their fields. After generating a list of twenty names, they pared the candidates down to a final four, each of whom had expertise in an area deemed vital to Mindstorms. Steve Hassenplug, a software engineer from Indiana, was heralded for his remarkable building skills; John Barnes, who ran a company in upstate New York, Hi-Technic, which developed ultrasonic sensors for the original Mindstorms, was the clear choice to be the "hardware guy"; Ralph Hempel, the hacker who had wowed Mindfest, was selected for his prowess in developing firmware; and David Schilling, a home-school educator from Minneapolis, was renowned for using Mindstorms to teach math and physics. (Insert photo 15 shows the four original Mindstorms User Panel members with Søren Lund from LEGO.)

In late 2004, a LEGO staffer sent an email to each of the four, as well as to a fifth person who never responded: "We'd like you to join a group of AFOLs for an über-top-secret project. Which project? I'm not telling! At least not until you sign and return the NDA [nondisclosure agreement] attached to this email."

The email invited the stellar Mindstorms users into a closed Web forum, where they formed a Mindstorms User Panel, or MUP, to help LEGO conjure up the next-generation kit.* LEGO didn't offer the four men a paycheck, only the opportunity to spend the next year collaborating with the Mindstorms R&D team. In return for voluntarily contributing countless ideas and critiques to Mindstorms NXT, the MUPs would receive a few free kits, plus the street cred that came from becoming de facto LEGO employees and helping to develop sets for the entire world. Within a few hours of receiving the note, all four citizen developers had signed on. The next note from LEGO, in December, said, "Merry Christmas. A package is in the mail to you." The MUPs opened it to find an early-stage prototype of the next generation of their beloved Mindstorms kit.

At first the MUPs believed LEGO wanted them to test prototypes for which the principal features were already locked in. When they learned that in fact LEGO hadn't even settled on the design specs, the MUPs were ecstatic. "When they told me I was going to help develop the next-generation Mindstorms while it was still on the drawing board," recalled Hassenplug, "it was more than I could have dreamed."

---

* The term *MUP* evolved, and the individual members of the panel became known as MUPs themselves.

The MUPs were free to do whatever they wanted—answer questions, lobby for certain features, critique design drafts. "We didn't try to organize their time in any way whatsoever," said Lund, who worked hand in glove with the MUPs. "But they were not to be treated as an alien group. They were part of the team." Nevertheless, cocreating was hardly a frictionless effort. The Mindstorms team continually struggled to channel the MUPs' boundless capacity to generate ideas. For their part, the MUPs never ceased to run up against the company's deadlines, its budget, and the core dictum that the new set must appeal to kids, not just adults.

Striking the right balance between the MUPs' fervor and the company's constraints resided in understanding the difference between "you must" and "I can." As Lund explained it, LEGO employees, like most in the corporate world, work in a "must" culture where, more often than not, work is assigned and commitments are binding. The MUPs, on the other hand, come from a "can" culture where they have the freedom to opt in—or opt out. "They can help, and they can also decide not to help. And guess what: you can't fire them, because you haven't hired them."

By managing the tension between "must" and "can," Lund and Smith-Meyer exploited the power of voluntary commitment. They understood that people are far more willing to give their all when they sign on to a project, as opposed to when they're appointed to it. Because the MUPs worked only on what they wanted and were rewarded with reputational capital by their peers, LEGO reaped a fat payoff: the MUPs' ever-growing zeal and commitment to the success of Mindstorms. "Their enthusiasm, paired with their insight and technical skill set, was just such a winning cocktail," said Lund. "That was the biggest reason for [engaging them]."

Challenge: There's almost always a key manager or team member who believes that outsiders distract and detract from the project.

Although Lund and Smith-Meyer were unabashed advocates for working with the MUPs, the rest of the project team was less than welcoming. One engineer, in particular, protested that "chitchatting on a website" with adult fans was a waste of his time. Lund proposed a compromise: that for two weeks the engineer spend thirty minutes a day talking with the MUPs. If at the end of those two weeks the engineer still believed the MUPs had nothing to offer, he wouldn't have to work with them. "That particular engineer ended up spending more time on the forum than anyone else," Lund recalled. "He saw that they were very clever and there really was a lot of value in talking with them."

The MUPs' biggest contribution resided in their unsparing critiques of Mindstorms prototypes, which helped the design team gauge the true progress of their development efforts. During the project's first months, the MUPs dug into all of the proposed improvements for Mindstorms NXT. They contributed dozens of ideas for upgrading the model's sensors and overhauling the software and firmware. They helped persuade the team to shift to a 32-bit processor, which was necessary for serious robotics. They demanded more powerful motors. And they successfully lobbied for a wireless module that allowed the NXT brick to communicate with Bluetooth devices.

LEGO didn't accommodate all of the MUPs' suggestions, of course. The MUPs pushed for a DC power pack (instead of the much less common AC charger that Mindstorms uses) and more memory for the programmable brick, for example, but LEGO deemed both suggestions to be budget busters. And therein resides a critical lesson for any organization that wants to tap the wisdom of the clique: *cocreators are not necessarily coequals.* Although Lund valued the MUPs' unbridled creativity, at the end of the day LEGO was the ultimate arbiter.

"A lot of people call this consumer-led innovation," said Lund. "But this was not consumer-led, this was innovation led by LEGO. Yes, it was cocreation. But no one was in doubt about who would make the final call." Nevertheless, the MUPs' relentless advocacy for the innovations that mattered most sometimes prevailed, even after LEGO had delivered a thumbs-down.

Take, for example, what happened in April 2005, when Hassenplug and Schilling traveled to Billund to compete in a Mindstorms contest at the company's headquarters. The trip marked their first face-to-face meeting with the Mindstorms R&D team. On the day after the tournament, the pair were escorted into the Global Innovation and Marketing building, which is strictly off-limits to everyone except LEGO staffers. Upon entering the Mindstorms research sanctum, Hassenplug was somewhat taken aback. "I saw my picture on the wall—they had our [the MUPs'] names and faces up there. It was kind of scary. They really knew us."

Lund gave the pair of MUPs their first close-up look at prototypes for the NXT circuit boards, as well as the set's assortment of studless Technic pieces. Hassenplug was disappointed to find that the proposed kit lacked a 90-degree joint. On a piece of paper, he sketched out a small L-shaped joint, which would enable Technic beams to be connected at right angles in one seamless move. Without it, he argued, it would take an unwieldy combination of seven Technic beams to do the same job. Lund loved the idea but told them he couldn't make it happen. The company's internal FMC targets wouldn't allow it, he explained to the MUPs. The cost of building a new injection mold to manufacture Hassenplug's proposed piece would put Mindstorms over its budget. "But they kept coming back," Lund recalled. "They kept pushing."

Four months later, at a gathering during a BrickFest fan convention in Washington, D.C., the Mindstorms R&D team presented the MUPs with the first working prototype of Mindstorms NXT.* Hassenplug was delighted to find that the set included his proposed piece. While investigating other options, Mindstorms designers

* During the first half of 2005, the original group of four MUPs expanded to eleven. For example, Hassenplug, who often worked with his friend John Brost to create ingenious Mindstorms models, persuaded the LEGO team to admit Brost into the clique. The original four referred to these new team members as the MUPpets.

Steve Hassenplug's "Hassenpin," a piece that allows two Technic beams to connect at right angles.

discovered that a mold had long ago been developed for an L-shaped Technic piece that precisely fit their needs. Lund had easily obtained permission to add the piece to the assortment. The community dubbed it the "Hassenpin."

"It turned out to be a key piece for building in three dimensions," said Lund. "Had it not been for [the MUPs], the element would not have been in the set."

Challenge: The right crowd for the early stages of a project may not be the right group for the later stages.

In January 2006, LEGO surprised the tech and toy worlds when it unveiled a showcase prototype of Mindstorms NXT at the Consumer Electronics Show in Las Vegas. Even after a year of working on the project, none of the citizen developers had spilled their secret to the press or their peers. Their silence was a crucial part of the project's success. "If anyone had talked," explained Smith-Meyer, "it would have killed the project." A leak also might have throttled any future crowdsourcing initiatives at LEGO.

That January, LEGO also announced it needed a hundred more lead users for the beta-testing phase, the final debugging prior to the new line's August launch. Unlike the original group, the new volunteers wouldn't get to work alongside the company's developers and they'd have to pay for their kits. But they would get discounted kits and the peer recognition that came with helping LEGO perfect a robot that just might rock the world. According to Smith-Meyer, the team expected about a thousand users to apply for the openings. Instead, in a clear sign that the new Mindstorms line would be a hit with adult hobbyists, more than ninety-six hundred pitches poured in. To land a coveted spot on the testing team, candidates had to

The Mindstorms NXT robot, which was unveiled at the Consumer Electronics Show in Las Vegas in January 2006.

demonstrate how their contributions would expand the Mindstorms NXT platform.

"You had to have built great robots and put them up on the website," said Lund. "Or you had to be writing a Mindstorms NXT book. If you couldn't convince someone that your work was adding value, you couldn't sign up."

Given that the original clique of volunteer developers had swelled into a real crowd of a hundred-plus testers, who were dubbed Mindstorms Community Partners, or MCPs, LEGO brought in Steven Canvin, a design manager on the original Mindstorms team, to coordinate with the burgeoning group and answer the volunteers' questions. On the first day of testing, he was nearly overwhelmed by the cataract of emails from anxious MCPs who were itching to get started. Canvin was savvy enough to realize that neither he nor any LEGO staffer could rein in an oversize group of accomplished, opinionated geeks. But he could harness the fanboys' passion by organizing the MCPs into forums, each of which would test the robot's critical features, such as the firmware, sensors, and components. To moderate the forums, Canvin tapped the community's most respected members, the MUPs. Essentially, LEGO recognized there were leaders among the crowd, and it relied on those leaders to exercise at least a minimal amount of crowd control.

"We called it an open-source community," said Smith-Meyer. "But it was really more of a society with its own kind of hierarchy, ranks, and roles." The four pioneering MUPs sat at the top of the hierarchy's pyramid, followed by the small army of volunteer testers who also acted as ambassadors for Mindstorms NXT. And then there were the ninety-six hundred fans who registered on the LEGO Mindstorms website.

The Mindstorms hierarchy—or, to be more accurate, the Mindstorms meritocracy—was always in flux. People ascended the pyramid based on their Mindstorms innovations and their contributions to the group, whether it be hacking new code or squashing a record number of bugs. As word of their eye-popping achievements—such as the CubeStormer, a Rubik's Cube–solving robot that beat the human record for cracking the puzzle—spread across the far larger web of LEGO fans and even tech-heads who previously had been indifferent to LEGO, the buzz built upon itself and attracted thousands more converts to Mindstorms. By opening up the Mindstorms NXT development process, not only did LEGO build a better product, but it grew the Mindstorms brand by eliciting the goodwill of volunteer hobbyists who were more than willing to proselytize for a toy they had helped create.

In fact, the next-generation Mindstorms kicked up more buzz than Lund and Smith-Meyer had believed possible. LEGO estimates that the open-source development story, which was picked up by *Wired*,

Forbes, CNN, and numerous other outlets, resulted in millions of dollars' worth of free publicity, a substantial boost for a product that relies mostly on word-of-mouth marketing. Mindstorms NXT was an immediate hit: LEGO sold more than $30 million worth of kits in NXT's first year. Together with the original Mindstorms kit, Mindstorms NXT went on to rack up sales of more than two million units. And yet Mindstorms NXT's most lasting impact might well have been on LEGO itself.

After the arrival of Mindstorms NXT, LEGO went on to tap the wisdom of the clique in new and surprising ways. For example, when LEGO decided to close down its nine-volt train line and replace it with battery-powered trains—a decision that infuriated devotees of the older line—the company turned its most ardent critics into collaborators by inviting a group of fifteen of the most skilled enthusiasts to come to Billund and workshop improvements to the next-generation set.

Cocreating with customers obviously requires a different management mind-set. So let's recap the Mindstorms team's clever approach to sourcing the wisdom of the clique.

- Lund and Smith-Meyer first built a convincing case for reaching beyond the company's internal product development process. Had they not proven to themselves that the MUPs would help build a better bot and inspire the LEGO legions to get behind it, Mindstorms NXT would have been developed in-house.

- The Mindstorms team was realistic about what citizen developers could and couldn't contribute. Before enlisting the MUPs, the team first identified design features that would remain off-limits to the outsiders.

- The LEGO team carefully chose what crowd to source from. And LEGO didn't expand the team before all the major design decisions were locked in.

- The Mindstorms cocreators weren't coequals. Though the citizen developers' contributions were highly valued, the team's leaders were clear that LEGO would make the final calls.

- LEGO realized that crowdsourcing required crowd control. As the project grew and the clique took on more members, Lund tapped the original MUPs to lead the effort to test and tweak NXT.

Given its success with Mindstorms NXT, LEGO might have grown its outside innovation efforts by working with larger groups. Instead, the company proved itself fully capable of going in the opposite direction, from tapping the talents of four adept hobbyists to harnessing the acumen of one inspired entrepreneur. The company's bid to exploit the wisdom of one was born out of its desire to bring new, authentically LEGO innovations to the brick while retaining its discipline and focus. By learning how to locate and work with one black-belt entrepreneur, LEGO developed a successful, highly original product line and opened up a whole new channel to market.

A Crowd of One

By 2006, the LEGO Group's leaders began to worry that their laserlike focus on rebuilding the company's core product lines and running the day-to-day business was leaving them shortsighted. Although Mindstorms NXT was an unequivocal success that had staked out a new market for LEGO, at the end of the day it was just one set. LEGO was still devoting far more of its resources and mind share to "more of the same" than to "new and different." Such a narrow approach to pumping up the business meant that LEGO might well miss out on other growth opportunities.

The LEGO Group's dilemma was one that every forward-thinking company must inevitably face: how to ensure that the effort expended on profiting from the core doesn't shortchange the future.

Google, for example, answered the challenge by developing an explicit formula for innovation, which it calls "70–20–10." Google puts 70 percent of its engineering resources into enhancing its base business, while 20 percent is concentrated on developing services that extend the core and the remaining 10 percent is allocated to fringe ideas that might prove critical for the long term. The policy ensures that as Google strives to continually evolve its core search and advertising business, it still devotes substantial resources to growing new services and launching experimental products.

Had LEGO done the math for its own innovation efforts, the numbers would have skewed closer to 90–10–0, with 90 percent of its resources devoted to advancing core product lines and 10 percent aimed at extending the base with genuinely new play experiences. As for speculative efforts that might one day yield a breakthrough, LEGO just didn't go there. "If you take R&D, we did D," quipped Smith-Meyer, who helped lead the Mindstorms NXT codevelopment effort. "Before the [financial] crisis, we did a lot of big research projects that just didn't amount to anything. After the crisis, it was almost like all efforts were meant to launch."

In 2006, LEGO sought to strike a better balance between innovations that enhanced the core business and those that opened entirely new markets. Knudstorp and Lisbeth Valther Pallesen, who headed up the company's Community, Education, and Direct (CED) division, asked Smith-Meyer to lead a "front-end innovation" unit that would focus exclusively on developing initiatives to take LEGO into unexploited markets. The brief from upper management was undeniably ambitious: within one year, uncover two new opportunities that could potentially grow to make up 10 percent of the company's revenue.

Although Smith-Meyer was eager to take on the challenge, he soon began to doubt whether he or anyone else would know a big opportunity when they saw one. Seeking some inspiration, one day he dug into the birth stories of several resilient companies. He found that while the stories differed wildly in the details, there was a common thread. Whether it was Nike cofounder Phil Knight selling running shoes from the trunk of his car, a young Michael Dell marketing PCs made from stock parts out of his University of Texas dorm room, or even Ole Kirk experimenting with his injection molding machine, these were entrepreneurs who relied as much on passion as on acumen to build industry-defining businesses.

Smith-Meyer decided his new-business initiative stood a better chance of getting to the future first if he reached outside Billund and enlisted entrepreneurs whose zeal for LEGO was taking the brick in entirely new directions. "The idea," he recalled, "was that they would help us start businesses that are impossible to start within LEGO."

Smith-Meyer had already seen firsthand how an outside group of smart, accomplished brick masters had burnished Mindstorms NXT and reignited the adult fan community. But this time he decided to tack to a course that varied by several degrees from NXT's cocreation effort. Rather than exploit the wisdom of a crowd or even a clique, now the strategy was more a matter of leveraging the wisdom of one—one passionate entrepreneur who had identified an opportunity for a new product line. "If we could mix in a little venture capital with that 'start-up in the garage' mentality, we just might create a successful business."

Smith-Meyer returned to Knudstorp and Pallesen and won their backing to revise his brief. Instead of taking a year to find two potentially big growth opportunities and then invest significant resources to develop them, the front-end team would align with entrepreneurs who were already working on nascent but promising projects. Within a matter of months or even weeks, the team would use the LEGO Group's know-how to help these entrepreneurs test the market, make necessary revisions, and test again. The idea was to avoid making bet-the-farm mistakes by launching a series of low-cost, low-risk experiments, which would increase the odds that one might grow into a runaway success.

Then came the next challenge. Having convinced LEGO to back his unit-of-one approach to cocreation, Smith-Meyer had to find the right entrepreneur.

Finding a Master Builder

About a year before Smith-Meyer assembled his front-end innovation team, a Chicago-based architect named Adam Reed Tucker began to feel the pull of the brick. Tucker had built a healthy practice designing high-end homes, but he hungered to do something more meaningful with his life. In the aftermath of the destruction of the World Trade Center towers during the 9/11 terrorist attacks, he had seen how iconic structures such as the Empire State Building and the Sears Tower endured dramatic declines in tenants and tourists. He began to explore ways of using his architectural experience to help laypeople understand that the stunning human accomplishment called the skyscraper is something we should celebrate rather than fear.

One day, while thumbing through a book titled *The World of LEGO Toys*, Tucker came across a 1970s Scandinavian architect who had showcased his designs by building models out of LEGO bricks. Recalling the countless hours he had spent building with LEGO as a child, Tucker wondered whether the brick might be a powerful medium for demonstrating the complexity of skyscraper engineering while making it easier to view up close.

Tucker immediately decided to "get reacquainted" with the brick. He drove to a nearby Toys "R" Us store and bought nearly every LEGO set he could find, which amounted to thirteen shopping carts stuffed with boxes of LEGO *Star Wars*, LEGO *Harry Potter*, and much, much more. Once home, he tore through the boxes, threw out the instructions, and began to build in a very big way. Working nights and weekends, he first pieced together a six-foot model of Chicago's Sears Tower, comprising five thousand bricks. He was immediately struck by the juxtaposition between the "sincerity and seriousness" of the tower and the playfulness and naïveté of the brick.

"From ten feet away, it looked like a cool, somewhat imposing model of a building," Tucker recalled. "And then you get closer and you're like, 'Wait a minute, those are LEGO bricks!'"

Over the next few months, Tucker snapped together tens of thousands of bricks to create more model skyscrapers, which ranged from eight to twelve feet tall. (Insert photo 16 shows some of Tucker's creations.) As images of his large-scale creations spread through the adult fan blogosphere, a few people suggested that he show his work at BrickFest, the annual gathering of the LEGO tribes. It was there, surrounded by his soaring interpretations of the John Hancock Center and the Empire State Building, that Tucker first met Smith-Meyer, who'd come to the event to scout out potential collaborators. Tucker was planning on selling his LEGO sculptures to art galleries and corporations, but Smith-Meyer left him with a different thought: shrink the models down to souvenir-size boxes and sell them at retail.

Fired up by his fifteen-minute conversation with Smith-Meyer, Tucker spent the next year delving into all things LEGO. He continued sculpting his towering interpretations of famous city buildings, such as the World Trade Center and the St. Louis Gateway Arch, some of which soared up to eighteen feet high and incorporated as many as 450,000 bricks. Inspired by BrickFest, he founded the Chicago area's first fan convention, Brickworld, which would launch the following June. And he worked long nights "scratching out" designs of miniature models of iconic tall buildings, made entirely of bricks. As summer approached, he shot Smith-Meyer a cryptic email: "Come and see us at Brickworld. I'll have a surprise."

When Smith-Meyer arrived at the convention, Tucker handed him an event kit that was presented with a holographic sticker and the Brickworld logo. Smith-Meyer was taken aback by the box's amateurish design but enthralled by what he found inside: a package of LEGO pieces, with a booklet featuring step-by-step instructions showing how the bricks could be assembled into a miniature model of the Sears Tower. The booklet included archival photographs of the tower, along with a brief profile of its architect, the origin of its design, and its architectural features. Taken together, the bricks and the booklet captured Tucker's ambition: "I wanted to tell a story, not just sell a box of bricks."

At that point, Smith-Meyer decided that Tucker was for real. Clearly, Tucker possessed the "crazy entrepreneurial gene" that Smith-Meyer was looking for. Equally important, he had an original idea that grew out of the LEGO heritage but potentially took the brick into new sales channels. Moreover, the thousands of enthusiasts who were wending their way through Brickworld and the 250 kits of mini Sears Towers proved that Tucker made things happen.

Over the next two days, the novice entrepreneur and the LEGO executive worked out a plan for a proof-of-concept test. With LEGO providing bricks and the power of its brand, Tucker would create and sell a thousand kits of his LEGO Sears Tower. They would call the new line LEGO Architecture.

Creating a Test Plan

After returning to Billund, Smith-Meyer presented the LEGO Architecture idea to his new-business investment board, which consisted of Knudstorp, Pallesen, senior vice president Per Hjuler, and several other executives. He first sketched out a pathway to test, launch, and grow the new line. It was a simple stage-gate development process that was built around a series of major investment points, or MIPs—except in Architecture's case, it was more a matter of *minor* investment points, as LEGO would absorb only shipping charges and the cost of manufacturing the bricks for the test run. If Architecture made it through the test gate, MIP I, it would move on to MIP II—a minuscule but real pilot launch of four thousand Architecture sets.

The kicker came when Smith-Meyer pitched the review board on the business logic for the new line. He predicted that Architecture would take the company into such new-to-LEGO channels as souvenir stores, museum shops, big bookstore chains, and even high-end

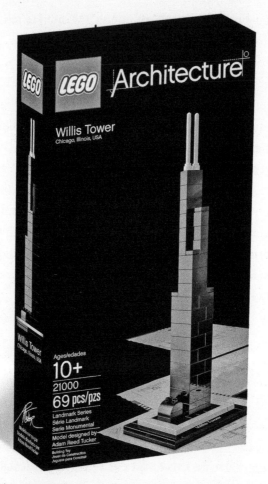

The LEGO Architecture Willis Tower (formerly Sears Tower) kit.

clothing stores. What's more, the line would sell at a premium price. Whereas a simple box of seventy LEGO bricks retails at $7.99, an Architecture box containing the same number of bricks would retail for $19.99. At that, the board's reaction was swift and unanimous. "Everyone was like, 'You can never charge $20,' " said Smith-Meyer. " 'That's just crazy.' "

Despite the new-business investment board's skepticism over Architecture's rich price tag, the opportunity presented so little downside that LEGO green-lighted the test. With that, Architecture became a true start-up effort that took LEGO back to the garage, literally as well as metaphorically. Just consider:

- Tucker's first "contract," as he put it, was essentially a back-of-the-napkin agreement with Smith-Meyer that was "nothing more than a leap of faith to say we want to do this together."

- Seeking to tamp down development costs, Smith-Meyer bypassed the company's in-house artists and crafted Architecture's initial packaging design himself. Tucker also wore many hats: he not only designed the Sears Tower set but lined up an offset printer to produce the boxes and leveraged the LEGO brand to strike a licensing deal with the owners of the Sears Tower.

- When it came time to deliver the LEGO bricks and boxes for the test run, a tractor-trailer pulled up in front of Tucker's suburban home and unloaded four pallets of packages into his garage, much to his neighbors' consternation. Thus Tucker's garage became LEGO Architecture's first distribution center.

It took Tucker and his wife two weeks to sort the tens of thousands of pieces and bundle them into a thousand sets of LEGO Sears Towers. He then turned the lot over to a souvenir chain, Accent Chicago, with a handshake understanding that if the kits didn't sell, the company wouldn't owe Tucker a dime. Ten days later, he got a call from the chain's buyer.

"He'd already sold through half the line," Tucker reported. "He's like, 'You're on to something here. Polish it up and let me know when you're coming out with more sets.' "

Having proven that consumers wouldn't flinch at Architecture's heady markup over a simple LEGO set, Smith-Meyer took the line to the next stage gate, MIP II: a pilot launch of two thousand kits each of a Sears Tower and John Hancock Center. Only this time, he brought the development effort in-house.

Launching the Line

Smith-Meyer recruited an ad hoc team consisting of a dozen LEGO designers, engineers, and operations veterans. Working only during their downtime—staffers still had to fulfill their day-job responsibilities—they perfected Tucker's brick selection and assembly instructions for each kit, crafted Architecture's logo and a sleek white-on-black packaging design, coordinated approval for images and text from the Sears Tower and John Hancock owners, and readied the production run, which was so small the boxes were packed by hand. The goal was to spend the least amount of time and money to test whether the product would sell on its own. Starting only with Tucker's design models, it took the team a mere eight weeks to perfect the line and produce the finished boxes. Total cost to LEGO: $10,000.

"Every time a problem came up, we just made a decision right there and then," said Smith-Meyer. "There was no time for debating."

In November 2007, LEGO shipped the two Architecture products to nine gift shops in Chicago. This was Architecture's proof-of-concept test. The sprawling U.S. souvenir store industry includes about thirty thousand stores with combined annual revenue of nearly $200 billion. If the line sold well in those nine Chicago stores, LEGO would take Architecture from the pilot test to a small but real launch of ten thousand sets. Smith-Meyer's two-year plan was to grow the Architecture businesses in large markets across the United States and then start experimenting in markets overseas.

Within a matter of weeks, the matter was settled. The John Hancock sets were moving quickly, while the Sears Tower was a complete sellout. At least within its test market, Architecture was a hit.

By the time we caught up with Tucker, he and his wife had moved into a new home in Arlington Heights, a Chicago suburb. There was a notable lack of furniture in the house, though his garage and more than a few rooms were packed with bins of LEGO bricks—roughly *ten million* bricks in all. And then there was his studio, which was overflowing with his LEGO-driven explorations of the aesthetics of engineering: a half-completed model of a swooping, curvilinear roller coaster, made entirely of bricks; intricate studies of Chicago bridges; and, of course, test models of the next generation of Architecture. Having taken the LEGO Architecture series from replicas of the White House and Seattle's Space Needle to a lovingly detailed, eight-hundred-piece rendering of Frank Lloyd Wright's masterpiece Fallingwater, Tucker and Smith-Meyer were shifting their focus to iconic architectural creations in Asia and beyond.

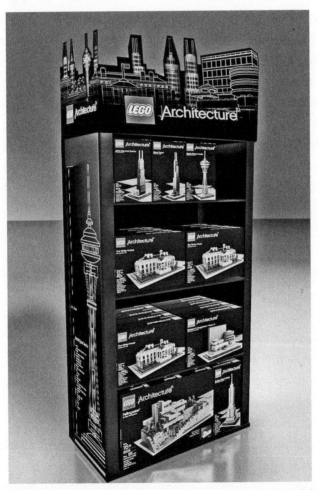

A LEGO Architecture store display showing the White House kit (middle) and Fallingwater kit (bottom left).

"There are so many landmark structures, both ancient and modern, throughout our built environment," Tucker proclaimed. "Architecture transcends race, religion, age—it really knows no boundaries. So the possibilities for LEGO Architecture are almost limitless."

Although LEGO doesn't break out revenues by toy line, it's safe to assume that LEGO Architecture has hit the DKK 1 billion in sales that the company prioritized in its first brief to Smith-Meyer. Since its 2008 launch, the line's sales increased 900 percent in 2009, 350 percent in 2010, and 200 percent in 2011. With popular, advanced kits such as Fallingwater (see insert photo 17) retailing for $99.99, LEGO Architecture is "very, very profitable," according to Smith-Meyer. Not only has the series taken the company into upscale channels such as Hammacher Schlemmer and museum stores, as well as almost-new-to-LEGO chains such as Barnes & Noble, it's also a hit with adults and it's pulling in new fans. Surveys showed that more than 60 percent of those who buy a LEGO Architecture

The LEGO Architecture Fallingwater kit.

kit are over eighteen (and intend to use it themselves); more than 15 percent have never previously purchased a LEGO kit of any kind.

Just as it did with Mindstorms NXT development partners, LEGO went on to ever so slightly expand Architecture's codevelopment effort, enlisting architects who worked in parallel with Adam Reed Tucker to create brick-based versions of famous European buildings. For example, the Slovenian architect Roc Z. Kobe designed the iconic Big Ben Clock Tower kit, while the German architect Michael Hepp created the French Villa Savoye set. By encircling Architecture with a velvet rope and admitting just a few more architects into its exclusive club of talented contributors, LEGO reaped their creativity while still exerting enough control to deliver profitable sets.

Lessons in Crowdsourcing, Sourced from LEGO

Taken together, Mindstorms NXT and LEGO Architecture taught LEGO some valuable lessons about open innovation.

Set a fixed direction; stay flexible in the execution. Although their original brief to Smith-Meyer's front-end innovation team was unequivocal, the LEGO Group's leaders understood that launching a search for unformed business opportunities likely would increase the need for midflight corrections. When Smith-Meyer pushed back with his "leverage the wisdom of one" cocreation strategy, Knudstorp and Pallesen were flexible enough to adapt. No doubt this was in large part due to Smith-Meyer's standing within the company: he was a battle-tested innovator who had earned leadership's trust. And that was key. The CEO didn't consign the open-source effort to a talented but unproven MBA. In Smith-Meyer, he tapped someone who had the throw weight to challenge first assumptions.

With Mindstorms NXT, Søren Lund never lost sight of the peak goal, which was to create a LEGO robotics kit for *kids*. Thus, he was uncompromising in his insistence that a twelve-year-old must be able to have a satisfying play experience within twenty minutes of opening the box. But like Knudstorp and Pallesen, he recognized there was more than one trail to the summit. Even though Steve Hassenplug's pitch for an L-shaped joint threatened to bust the project's budget, Lund didn't reject the idea out of hand. He worked the problem until he found a way to manufacture the Hassenpin without building a new mold, which saved LEGO upward of $50,000 and ultimately delivered a better building experience for kids. Lund remained open to the MUPs' suggestions, so long as they kept within the project's design parameters and recognized that the primary customers were children, not adults.

Though they have different expectations, outsiders and insiders share responsibility for the ultimate outcome. Both the Mindstorms team and the outside codevelopers had to recalibrate their expectations of what each side could deliver. At the outset, the MUPs and Tucker bumped up against the company's unyielding quality and safety standards. They had to work within the LEGO ethos of "only the best" and remember they were designing for children, not adults. They also had to deal with such unfamiliar terrain as learning to cap the cost and complexity of their designs. For its part, LEGO had to learn how to channel the adult users' creative zeal without choking it off. Lund and Smith-Meyer soon found they had to be both enforcers and advocates. They had to press the outside contributors to recognize the company's rules, even as they argued within LEGO to let the outsiders push the company's limits.

Open-innovation efforts require new roles. In an established company, open-innovation projects require managers to take on some unfamiliar challenges. Smith-Meyer had to set limits around Tucker's expectations—he couldn't strike an agreement to produce the Architecture line without first putting the concept through some rigorous tests. At the same time, he had to represent Tucker's interests within the company and help him overcome internal skeptics.

So it went for Mindstorms NXT. When the NXT project scaled from the four MUPs to the one hundred testers, Steven Canvin had to assume the role of community organizer. That meant educating the community of testers about the company's design goals and limits, setting deadlines, representing them internally, and, above all, demonstrating that LEGO was listening. Roles could act as effective controls for guiding open innovation.

Less than two decades ago, LEGO was a fortresslike company whose public position was "We don't accept unsolicited ideas." By 2006, the company had upended both the policy and its above-the-fray mind-set. LEGO had recruited expert adult fans to help reinvent Mindstorms, its most successful stand-alone product. Paal Smith-Meyer had begun collaborating with Adam Reed Tucker to create LEGO Architecture, which brought the brand into retailers that had never before carried LEGO. The company had even started developing a "toys for adults" line, the ultrachallenging LEGO Modular Buildings series, which was originally suggested by AFOLs through a poll the company had organized.

To be sure, LEGO continued to develop the majority of its products in absolute secrecy. The company opened up its innovation process only when it concluded that outside collaborators possessed a particular area of expertise that staffers lacked. Or the company would enlist entrepreneurs whose acumen helped identify an emerging business opportunity. As those efforts yielded successes, LEGO rolled out other platforms for sourcing the crowd, as we will see in the final chapter.

LEGO came to realize that while open-source innovation can be managed, it can't be controlled. The process is best understood as an ongoing conversation between the company and its vast crowd of fans. Like any good dialogue, LEGO-style sourcing was built on the principles of mutual respect, each side's willingness to listen, a clear sense of what's in play and what's out of bounds, and a strong desire for a mutually beneficial outcome. For outside collaborators, the reward could be intrinsic—such as recognition from peers and access to LEGO—as well as financial. As for LEGO, the conversation almost certainly tightened its ties to the fan community. And in some instances, it delivered products that LEGO itself had never imagined.

Attempting a Disruptive Innovation

Aiming for the Stars with LEGO Universe

This is the largest and most complex project that LEGO has ever undertaken. It touches every part of the company.

—Mark Hansen, project lead, LEGO Universe

THE EMAIL FROM DENMARK WAS TANTALIZINGLY CONCISE. "There was just one line: 'Would you be interested in working on an online world project for LEGO?' " recalled Scott Brown, the cofounder of NetDevil, a developer of massively multiplayer online (MMO) video games, where thousands of players connect, cooperate, and compete in a virtual world. The NetDevil studio, situated in Louisville, a suburb north of Denver, Colorado, had just begun casting about for a big brand with enough muscle to help them create and market a new MMO game. They never imagined the opportunity would come winging across five thousand miles of ether, from the Danish maker of innocent little plastic blocks.

"When we got the email from LEGO," said Brown, "we were all like, 'This is it!' "

It was October 2005, when LEGO was back in the black. By year's end, the company would post sales of DKK 7.0 billion ($1.2 billion) and a pretax return on sales of 6.5 percent; in 2006, sales would rise only slightly, to DKK 7.8 billion ($1.3 billion), but profitability would more than triple, to 20.2 percent of sales. Revitalizing core brands such as LEGO City and DUPLO had helped the LEGO Group boost its earnings; the relaunch of Mindstorms exceeded the company's most optimistic forecasts.

By refocusing 90 percent of the company's resources on enhancing its core products, Knudstorp and his senior management team had clearly put LEGO on a path to profitability. But the journey had barely begun. To sustain its momentum, LEGO couldn't simply refine and adjust its product portfolio. The third and final phase of "Shared Vision," Knudstorp's road map for transforming the business, set a goal of markedly increasing profits and market share, all in a bid to make LEGO "the world's premier toy company." That meant creating visionary toys that changed the way kids play. To build new growth drivers, LEGO would once again seek out untapped, blue-ocean markets. (We will trace that effort in the next chapter.) And it would attempt to unleash a disruptive innovation—a low-end, low-quality product that improves over time and eventually upends the industry incumbents.

In a *New Yorker* profile, Clayton Christensen cited the pint-size transistor radio as a prototypical example of a big, disruptive innovation. Launched by Sony in the late 1950s, the tinny, tiny radios, using the then-new technology of the transistor, had nowhere near the same sound quality as the big vacuum-tube RCA and Zenith consoles found in many middle-class homes. But the radios' easy portability and low price made them a hit with teenagers. By the time the radios' sound quality improved enough to pull in adults, RCA and Zenith were too far behind to catch up.[21]

In 2005, the LEGO Group's brain trust believed the digital brick could be another disruptor, just like Sony's little radio. An online LEGO game, where kids from all across the globe could connect and create their own virtual LEGO worlds, would offer a low-cost alternative to plastic bricks. And as the technology improved, so would the play experience, potentially pulling in the masses of kids who loved gaming but were indifferent to brightly colored plastic blocks. Digital bricks might even become as ubiquitous as plastic bricks. Based on those insights, LEGO decided it would disrupt its own business model before another company did, and thereby create a new platform for growth.

Hence the email to NetDevil, which kicked off one of the company's most ambitious bids to create a break-the-mold play experience. Developing the game, dubbed LEGO Universe, would consume countless person-hours and $30 million in start-up costs. Along the way, LEGO discovered that of all the seven truths, the toughest challenge was to launch a disruptive innovation. Unfortunately for LEGO, it failed to heed the bright red warnings that it was taking a flawed approach to disrupting its plastic brick business.

First Warning: Don't Jump into a New Business Before You Understand It

The LEGO Group's foray into global video gaming, an industry of which it knew little, was fraught both with risks and with potentially outsize rewards. As Universe's development team imagined it, the concept was decidedly immodest: millions of children from across the globe would enter an online world, interact with other kids through avatarlike minifigs, do battle with a dark force called the Maelstrom and its evil architect Baron Typhonus, and collect bricks with each successful mission. Because it was a virtual world, kids could do almost anything they could imagine: fly their minifigs over mountaintops, leap across vast canyons, or drive a car into a head-on collision with another car. Best of all, they could use their stashes of virtual bricks to build castles, dragons, spaceships, and forts whose scale and complexity far exceeded anything they could assemble with plastic bricks. At least, that was the idea.

To surmount the difficult technical challenges of creating such a vast virtual world, LEGO would have to seek out and successfully collaborate with an unfamiliar partner such as NetDevil, which had deep expertise in developing MMO games but knew nothing about building with the brick. Creating and launching the game would directly or indirectly involve more than 350 stakeholders across LEGO—staffers from the corporate IT department, marketing and sales, LEGO.com, product design groups, operations, finance, and customer service, as well as most of top management and thirty outside suppliers. That was an early sign of trouble, as it's tough for a bloated project team to create a low-end, disruptive product. At the outset, LEGO estimated it would take three years to develop the game. It ultimately took five years and three missed deadlines.

"Building an MMO is like launching a space shuttle," said LEGO Universe chief Mark Hansen. "It's the largest and most complex project that LEGO has ever undertaken. It touches every part of the company."

At first glance, Hansen seemed an unlikely choice to be the point man for bringing LEGO Universe to life. Whereas many video game developers have the beanpole physique of teenage skateboarders and the clothes to match, Hansen stood well north of six feet tall, was built like an NFL linebacker, and preferred polo shirts to tie-dye. In a company where the majority of the managers are Scandinavian, Hansen was an American, a former Navy SEAL who spent twelve years in the United States military.

Hansen, however, was a bit of an old LEGO hand. He was the original architect of LEGO Factory, which bridged virtual design with real-world construction by allowing anyone to create DIY LEGO models online that could then be ordered as a set for assembling offline. Moreover, his imposing presence frequently inspired others to get things done. Those were qualities that served him well in his role as the force behind LEGO Universe.

Some LEGO executives required a good bit of convincing that investing prodigious amounts of capital, talent, and executive attention would produce a breakthrough business. They took the view that the video game market was a big sinkhole, given that roughly 70 percent of new launches failed to do better than break even and just a minuscule 3 to 4 percent of MMO games managed to soar into the rarefied world of certifiable megahits.

By launching Universe, LEGO would face off against media giants such as Disney—and, later, Nickelodeon and the Cartoon Network— whose marketing platforms let them kick out new MMO game titles every six to twelve months. LEGO, on the other hand, had never produced a single successful video game for solo players, let alone a 3-D game that could simultaneously handle thousands of kids the world over.* In fact, more than a few LEGO managers were still smarting from the pounding they had endured during the Darwin debacle, their previous big push into the digital world.

Nevertheless, Hansen and a dedicated group of like-minded managers kept pressing the case. Their pitch rested on three reasons for launching LEGO Universe.

First, developing Universe would evolve the LEGO System of Play on a vast scale. In the online world that LEGO envisioned, kids would not only build and create but socialize. Universe was really

---

* Through a worldwide licensing agreement, the British video game developer TT Games—founded by former LEGO staffers who had been let go in the 2003 downsizing—created popular console games such as LEGO *Star Wars* and LEGO *Batman*.

about bringing legions of kids into the LEGO play experience, where they could engage in construction, competition, and collaboration, all in a safe online environment.

Second, the business logic for gambling on Universe was persuasive. Although most MMO game launches quickly fizzle, there are some that strike it very, very hot. One of the most popular titles among MMO games, Blizzard Entertainment's World of Warcraft, wowed the video gaming industry by capturing twelve million monthly subscribers and generating more than $2.2 billion in subscriptions between 2005 and 2012. With more than twenty million unique visitors clicking into LEGO.com every month—by far the most in the toy industry—LEGO had the magnetism and the hosting capacity to build a massively successful online world of its own. And once LEGO did the heavy lifting of developing an underlying code base that would allow customers to create whatever they could imagine, LEGO could leverage the Universe platform to regularly launch new MMO titles, just like Disney.

Finally, there were the disruptive possibilities that came with launching a digital building platform. A team of software engineers had already developed the LEGO Digital Designer (LDD), the computer-aided design program that allowed customers to go online and create one-of-a-kind LEGO models using virtual LEGO bricks. LDD, which was at the heart of LEGO Factory (later renamed Design byMe), was a powerful tool, but it was difficult to use. Any four-year-old can snap together two plastic LEGO bricks. But even twelve-year-olds who used the Digital Designer found it difficult to build anything complicated. Like the transistor radios of half a century ago, the LDD was an inferior technology with lots of upside potential. If the first iterations of Universe proved good enough for early adopters, LEGO just might capture greater numbers of kids as the virtual play experience improved.

After nearly forty meetings, the LEGO Group's brain trust felt confident enough to give Universe the green light. So it was that in the spring of 2005, LEGO began to take its first big stab since Darwin at building a digital future.

Unbeknownst to the NetDevil founders, theirs was not the only company that LEGO had reached out to. LEGO identified fifty-one MMO game developers throughout Europe, North America, and Asia; Hansen and a technologist visited every single one of them. It made for an exhausting—and exhaustive—lap around the world. Hansen met the NetDevil team in their Colorado headquarters on an early November morning; he then flew to a meeting in Texas and finished in California that night, in what was a typical day on the road. But to Hansen's mind, there was no other option. To find the right partner, he needed to get an up-close look at every potential team and its technology.

"We saw every part of the game industry," he recalled. "We had one guy who just put his feet up on his desk and said, 'Give me $10 million and get the f___ out of my office.' There's a lot of interesting people in this business, to say the least."

After spending two months visiting MMO outfits, Hansen slashed the list of potential partners from fifty-one to eight. He then assembled a five-person team of LEGO managers—including executive vice president Lisbeth Valther Pallesen, as well as managers from purchasing and marketing—and paid a return visit to the eight semifinalists. Although much of the visit to NetDevil was dedicated to digging into the company's culture, financials, and technology, Scott Brown kicked off a discussion of Universe by running a trailer for Gears of War, which was initially released as an exclusive title for Microsoft's Xbox 360.

Developed by Epic Games, Gears was a "third-person shooter," a 3-D video game in which a player's on-screen avatar blasts away at other avatars, with much mayhem and bloodletting. The game focused on a squad of hulking, heavily armed, armored warriors who battle to save the last human holdouts on a fictional planet from a swarming subterranean enemy called the Locust Horde—not an obvious model for a LEGO game that would feature kid-friendly minifigs. But the trailer's ability to quickly establish characters of consequence gave the LEGO team a feel for how heroic personalities could be a compelling draw. With a running time of barely a minute, the trailer delivered an oblique glimmer of what Universe might become.

After the trip, LEGO narrowed the list of potential partners to NetDevil plus an MMO developer in Seattle and another in Norway. NetDevil emerged as the winner, but one event foreshadowed a little problem that would eventually loom large. LEGO sent out a request for proposal (RFP) to the three finalists. The highly detailed document, which totaled hundreds of pages, focused mostly on policy and procedure. There were very few questions about the actual game, which surprised the NetDevil founders. They could conclude only that LEGO hadn't developed a deep sense of the kind of experience it wanted to deliver. LEGO, it would seem, was seeking to disrupt an industry that it hadn't figured out.

Second Warning: Don't Demand That a Young Technology Deliver a Near-Perfect Experience

Hansen believed that NetDevil couldn't build a great LEGO MMO without deeply delving into LEGO itself. So in early 2006, he took a dozen NetDevil staffers to Billund for a week. They met with developers and marketers, visited the design studios and the LEGO factories, and immersed themselves in all things LEGO.

"It was the most inspirational week I've ever had on a project," said Ryan Seabury. "People assumed that LEGO was into heavily childish designs with these rainbow-colored bricks. But when you see the level of sophistication that can be achieved with LEGO bricks, it absolutely just sparks your imagination."

Accurately rendering a virtual version of the LEGO brick, however, proved to be a formidable undertaking. LEGO insisted that

Universe deliver the cleanest, most detailed bricks of any video game on the market. It took a team of eight engineers working flat out for six months to produce a brick that met the LEGO design specs. The result was that a single Universe brick, with its lovingly rendered tubes and studs—each imprinted with the LEGO logo—was more technologically complex than a fully decked-out World of Warcraft character.

Although they had created an authentic, virtual version of the brick, NetDevil's developers discovered that it took just a few bricks to exhaust a computer's ability to display them. In a typical Universe scenario, such as when a minifig walks toward a car, a player's computer would drain all of its available horsepower by drawing and redrawing the vehicle as the minifig moved closer and closer to it.

Only after running down many dead ends did the developers find a way to work around the problem. They created a system that made the car look hazy and blocky in the distance; because bricks viewed from afar had less detail, the computer could conserve more of its memory when rendering them. The bricks grew sharper only as more of the car came into view. It was a clever solution, but the demand for greater detailing ultimately reduced the number of illustrations—cars, minifigs, spaceships, and more—that the game could display at any one time. The LEGO Group's quest to deliver a more beautiful virtual brick had the unintended effect of making the game less visually interesting.

"That was one of those things where we just never agreed," said Brown. "But what could we do? It was their IP, and LEGO would never give in on the quality of the brick rendering."

The push for perfection breached the logic of a disruptive innovation. At first it's fine if the disruptive product is low-end and low-quality, so long as it's easy to use and works well enough to attract less-demanding customers who don't care if, say, a LEGO logo is etched into each stud of every brick. It's better to put a cheaper price tag on the product, launch it even though it's less than ready for prime time, and then make improvements (and charge more) as it moves upmarket. LEGO, however, spent years working to get Universe just right, which cost it the disruptor's advantage.

The LEGO Group's insistence that Universe deliver an ultra-premium play experience even showed up in the RFP we mentioned earlier. A LEGO lawyer inserted a provision that Universe, upon its release, must be entirely free of bugs. It was a preposterous demand, especially for a game that would require somewhere between half a million and a million lines of code. The request signaled that the LEGO Group's innermost value, "only the best," would bump up against the disruptor's "good enough" ethos, perhaps best expressed by a maxim credited to Facebook cofounder Mark Zuckerberg: "Better done than perfect." In the months and years to come, LEGO and NetDevil would ceaselessly struggle to smack back bugs and achieve a rough equilibrium between less than perfect and better than merely done.

The disconnect between NetDevil and LEGO over Universe's quality loomed larger as development got under way. At any one time, there were thirty or more programmers working on Universe, all changing code in different parts of the game. As Stephen Calender, a former Universe developer, put it in an interview with the blog *MMO Fallout*, producing a flawless game with nearly one million lines of code "would be like getting a perfect score on a math test with that many questions."[22]

Five years later, when Universe was finally launched, the development team had slashed the game's most bothersome bugs to well below the industry standard. Nevertheless, seven months after the game's release, Ronny Scherer, a LEGO veteran and Universe's project manager, still wasn't satisfied. "My house here in Colorado has all these nice features, but its questionable quality means it's going to need a big overhaul in ten years," he told us. "NetDevil was making software the same way. And fundamentally, LEGO doesn't think like that. We want to make sure that when we build something, we build it to last."

Third Warning: Insulate the Project from
the Demands of Other Business Units

Had Universe been a physical LEGO product, the game would have been "locked down" as soon as the development team defined the core concept and play experience. That is, no major design changes would have been permitted, since the team would have begun the process of readying the product for manufacture. But because LEGO had a remarkably underfocused view of what the game should be, Universe remained unlocked for months, which eventually grew into years. As a result, it was subject to the influence of many product lines throughout LEGO, each of which had a stake in the MMO.

As originally envisioned, some of Universe's "worlds" would be designed around classic LEGO play themes. For example, one world would feature knights and castles, another ninjas, while a third would have traditional LEGO City buildings. Getting those play experiences to work in the MMO meant that the Universe development team had to coordinate with the leaders of those product groups back in Billund and ultimately get their sign-off.

Every Billund product group scrambled to ensure that Universe wouldn't dilute its sales. The result: managers from other business units pulled the Universe development team in different directions. To reduce that risk, LEGO should have separated Universe from the main business and essentially run the Universe development process in parallel with the LEGO Development Process. Big companies that attempt to launch a disruptive innovation are better off setting up something akin to a spin-off unit far away from headquarters, where associates can do what is best for the product, even if it means breaking some company rules. But that never happened with Universe. Even though Colorado-based NetDevil was an ocean plus half a continent away from Billund, it was never permitted to act independently from the mother ship.

"We had to work with everybody, and everybody wanted a say," said Brown. "The game kept changing. And because the game was a little bit amorphous as to where it was going, we'd get even more requests." As the requests and changes accumulated, the Universe team found itself drifting from a course that it had never really set in the first place.

Setbacks almost always invite greater scrutiny; LEGO was no exception to that rule of thumb. Hansen soon found himself making repeated trips to Billund to report in on Universe's delays and to continue championing the project to an increasingly skeptical management. Over Universe's lifetime, he estimated he made more than a thousand presentations to senior management and other constituencies throughout LEGO. "This project," he later said, "just Power-Pointed you to death."

A big-company mind-set likewise thwarted Hansen's attempt to open up the Universe innovation process, as LEGO had done with Mindstorms NXT. In 2007, Hansen recruited a small group of dedicated AFOLs to contribute to Universe. He even riffed off the Mindstorms MUPs moniker to conceive an appellation for Universe's volunteer developers, who came to be called the LEGO Universe Partners, or LUPs. In the months that followed, Hansen concluded that Universe's scale required far more volunteers, and so the LUP team grew to include nearly one hundred members—a crowd, not a clique, that proved devilishly difficult to manage.

As Universe's development dragged on for months past its deadlines, many LUPs grew discouraged and nearly half dropped out of the program. When it was finally launched in October 2010, Universe included at least three worlds that were created entirely by LUP teams. Even so, the LUPs' contribution was considerably less than originally envisioned.

"When a project takes five years to complete, it's very hard to keep people motivated," concluded Hansen. "We probably didn't get as much out of it as we would have liked."

Fourth Warning: Make the Product for Customers, Not Managers

Despite Hansen's frequent visits to the LEGO Group's headquarters, he and the NetDevil team still found it difficult to bridge the five thousand miles and eight time zones separating Colorado from Billund. A problem that normally would require a two-minute telephone conversation to resolve often dragged on for two or three days, simply because, say, a NetDevil developer couldn't quickly connect with the right IT staffer in Billund. As the number of missed connections multiplied, little setbacks grew into big delays.

Equally problematic, each partner had made assumptions about the other that ultimately failed to hold up. "We thought Mark had this team of [LEGO] experts who knew everything about online gaming," said Brown. "As it turned out, they didn't know much at all." More months were burned through as each side struggled to get a clearer line of sight into the other's shortcomings and shore them up. Increasingly, more and more deliverables were delivered late or not at all. By the spring of 2008, LEGO had deep doubts that the "build" and "socialize" pillars of the Universe experience were articulated enough for the game to hit its 2009 launch date.

In an attempt to bridge the communications chasm between the NetDevil studio and Billund, Lisbeth Valther Pallesen and a handful of other LEGO managers flew to Colorado every six weeks to review the project's progress. The check-ins garnered decidedly mixed reviews.

Hansen believed the meetings were invaluable for making timely decisions and ensuring that the project kept its momentum. Others took a different view. NetDevil's Chris Sherland, who, as lead producer, worked to keep the project focused and moving toward its deadlines, believed there were times when LEGO and NetDevil never achieved sufficient trust and confidence to truly expose the project's problems and make hard decisions.

"There was a lot of, 'LEGO's coming, let's put lipstick on this pig and gussy it up as best we can,'" Sherland recalled. "Part of the problem was born out of the culture of third-party game developers, where we've got to impress the publisher so we can keep the contract. It was never that blatant, but there was certainly that undercurrent. The founders of NetDevil had to mortgage their entire lives to make this company work. Those check-ins were very important for them. And so we did that dog-and-pony thing."

The result was that even though the Universe development team did extensive focus testing with kids, the review sessions with Pallesen and other executives made the play experience less appealing for gamers. During an early stage of Universe's development, the NetDevil team brought in a group of LEGO managers for a demo, the purpose of which was to show off the game engine and the multiplayer environment. They watched as a handful of kids clicked into a network through separate computers and entered a game where they could hit a LEGO monkey with a hammer. With each whack, the monkey would run off and then return for another blow. The kids loved it. The LEGO execs were horrified. One stood up and essentially asked if the NetDevil team had lost their minds: "Do you really think we're going to go out publicly and have kids smacking monkeys?"

Billund's stipulation that Universe must be free of any hint of violence was deflating for NetDevil, which, as the creator of unabashedly brutal titles such as Auto Assault and Warmonger, knew well that violence is a turn-on. But once NetDevil began focus-testing some Universe demos, kids delivered an unequivocal verdict: the game was too babyish. The level of conflict just had to be amped up.

There then ensued months of debate between LEGO and NetDevil over just how scary or dark the game should be. The problem was somewhat resolved when TT Games came out with the *LEGO Star Wars II: The Original Trilogy* single-player video, which proved that chunky minifig versions of Luke Skywalker and Princess Leia battling Stormtroopers could be humorous in an off-kilter kind of way.

More important, parents were okay with the video's blockheaded form of conflict, so long as there wasn't any bloodletting.

For all that, Universe's dark-versus-light problem never completely dissipated. In an interview with *PC Gamer*, former Universe concept artist Mike Rayhawk recalled that he often had to "tone down" images that were deemed too frightening. "I was always pushing to make the look of the game more epic and scary, because I wanted to give real weight to the struggles of these boxy rainbow-colored plastic figures," he said. "In general, I was more successful selling [management] on the epic than on the scary."[23]

When NetDevil would demo a new Universe feature for a review session, one of the most persistent criticisms from the Billund side of the table was that the feature "doesn't feel like LEGO." Such feedback was less than helpful, largely because no one could vividly define the LEGO play experience in an MMO context. It was agreed that the game should stand on three pillars: build, play, and socialize. But translating those themes into bits and bytes was a trial-and-error undertaking. "We found out pretty quickly that LEGO didn't understand what LEGO Universe should be," said Sherland. "They could only tell us whether we were or weren't hitting the mark."

Each time the steering committee rejected a feature that wasn't "LEGO enough," NetDevil had to dump at least some of the underlying code and start over. The team would then spend months rebuilding entire maps—the game's locales, stages, and missions—in hopes that this time the new feature or play zone would pass muster. And with every do-over, the project would veer just a little more off course. "We'd go off in a new direction, and then everyone would realize that was a mistake," said Brown. "Then we'd go backward again."

It took years rather than months to get the game to a place where LEGO managers deemed Universe to be authentically LEGO. Even more troubling than the delays was the fact that LEGO was pursuing the wrong customers. Transistor radios were disruptive because they appealed to a new customer segment—teenagers—who lacked the money and the desire to buy big, luxe radios. Universe might well have been a truly disruptive innovation—the transistor radio of its time—had Billund allowed the toy to become dark enough and aggressive enough to attract kids who could care less about brightly colored plastic blocks but who just might like the prospect of building and competing in an exciting, somewhat sinister LEGO world. Instead, LEGO targeted kids who loved plastic blocks—and never gave them a compelling enough reason to go digital.

Final Warning: Price the Product to Meet What the Market Will Bear, Not to Recoup Your Investment

LEGO Universe finally launched in October 2010, to decidedly mixed reviews. Although many commentators were thrilled to see the LEGO brick come to life in an MMO environment, they complained that the game had an unfinished feel. *Macworld* pretty much summed up the consensus view when it opined, "It doesn't seem that Universe has really arrived yet."[24]

A big part of a disruptive product's appeal is that it's low-end and therefore cheaper than the industry standard. LEGO, however, never gave Universe a disruptive price. Whereas most MMO publishers attract consumers by letting them play a few levels for free—the idea being that once they get hooked on the game, people will pay for more challenging levels—LEGO Universe had a forbidding entry process. Before children could try the game, their parents first had to order a DVD for $40, install it, and then sign up for a $10 monthly subscription. For most parents, that was simply too high a barrier. It took nearly a year for LEGO management to realize its mistake and restructure the game by giving kids a no-cost entry to a couple of Universe's worlds.

When we visited the NetDevil studio in Colorado a few months before it closed, the LEGO Universe team tried to summon some cautious optimism, though the underlying mood was as dark as the afternoon thunderheads that swept over the Front Range's snow-capped peaks. On one hand, Universe had achieved a resubscription rate of 87 percent, which far exceeded the industry standard of below 20 percent. But it had registered just thirty-eight thousand subscribers, not nearly enough to sustain the business.

Unfortunately for its staff of more than a hundred, plus the tens of thousands of kids who loved the game, LEGO Universe never came close to meeting the company's sales targets. Just fifteen months after its launch, LEGO quietly pulled the plug. On January 30, 2012, the company shut down Universe's servers. With that, Universe became the one major product failure during Knudstorp's seven-year effort to turn around and transform LEGO.

LEGO Universe's collapse shows how difficult it is for any big company to change its product development system so as to deliver a disruptive innovation. As it turned out, the strategies that worked for the LEGO Group's plastic brick business hindered its efforts to build a disruptive digital brick business, as Christensen himself might have predicted. Rather than let NetDevil act like the start-up that it really was and ignore what counted as prudent in Billund, the Danish company's senior management pushed the Colorado coders to develop Universe the LEGO way.

LEGO, largely an analog company, failed to adapt to a digital world where change is unrelenting and noncompliant. LEGO jumped into the MMO business before fully understanding it. Because executives took many months to fully define Universe's play experience, the game's design specs kept changing, resulting in further delays and cost overruns. Then, instead of tailoring the game to what the underlying technology could actually deliver, LEGO executives demanded that Universe create an "only the best" play experience. When the satellite studio failed to do so, the number of miscommunications and misunderstandings between Billund and Colorado spiked upward. And when LEGO finally launched Universe, it didn't price the product to meet what the market would bear, but instead sought to quickly recoup its investment. No doubt LEGO will keep chipping away at the big, important challenge of creating riveting digital play experiences. But after that fifteen-month run, the company's patience for Universe ran out.

A video on the LEGO Universe website announced the closing by proclaiming that the game had "shot for the stars and reached the planets." Not a bad epitaph, given that Universe extended the fun of the physical brick into the virtual realm but never became a sustainable business.

An Innovation That Might Well Disrupt LEGO

In May 2009, a little more than a year before LEGO released Universe, a Swedish video game programmer and designer named Markus "Notch" Persson posted the first crude version of a game he'd created. Like Universe, the game let players freely roam a virtual, 3-D world and build complex creations such as spaceships and volcanoes. Like LEGO, it featured textured building blocks reminiscent of the brick, though Persson's were not nearly as complex. It also had a survival challenge that proved to be a magnet for kids and adults. Each game began at dawn, with nightfall coming eighteen minutes later. Players had to quickly build a shelter to protect themselves, because at night monsters came out—zombies, skeletons, and (later) green "creepers." Persson called his game Minecraft.

Based on feedback from users, Persson steadily expanded Minecraft, adding new building materials, new monsters, a multiplayer capability, and the capacity for users to create "mods," their own DIY versions of the game. He started charging for the game soon after releasing it, and steadily increased the price as the game's features expanded and its popularity exploded. As it worked its way upmarket, Minecraft began to take on all the hallmarks of a disruptive innovation.

When it launched, Minecraft was decidedly a low-end product. Its crude, blocky look and feel had none of the LEGO brick's precision and Universe's attempt at perfection. Early on, Minecraft's "building experience," which involved hitting things with an axe, offered none of the brick's limitless capacity for creative play. And the characters—zombies and creepers—were barely recognizable. But Minecraft was inexpensive. An unlimited, lifetime license for Minecraft cost just $13, which was far cheaper than a typical themed LEGO set consisting of plastic bricks and just a little more than the price tag for a month's play on LEGO Universe. And the gameplay, where the primary goal was to escape attacks by monsters, proved addictive. Minecraft spread like World of Warcraft through the global gaming community.

In January 2011, Minecraft passed one million purchases. By April 2011, Persson estimated that Minecraft had made $33 million in revenue. By August 2012, Minecraft claimed more than thirty-six million users, nearly seven million of whom had purchased the game. That translated into a sales rate of about $100 million per year for the game's PC-based version. At the time, Minecraft was the fastest-selling game on Microsoft Xbox, and it featured an extensive catalog of merchandise, including a partner product with LEGO.

With the explosion of 3-D printing tools in 2012, Minecraft moved further into LEGO territory. The MakerBot Replicator, just one of more than a dozen new 3-D printers introduced in 2012, can make objects out of ABS plastic—*the same plastic that LEGO bricks are made of*—in any shape, up to about the size of a small loaf of bread. At the time of this writing, 3-D printing is roughly equivalent to the digital photography of the late 1990s. Back then, the price of a digital camera was comparatively high and the picture quality was inferior to film-based photography. But the benefits were clear—you could take as many pictures as you wanted for almost nothing, and print out only the images you liked. Similarly, 3-D printers are expensive (in early 2013, the MakerBot Replicator cost $1,749) and the quality of the product is decidedly on the low end. But the cost to "print" a single 3-D copy of a LEGO model is 5 to 10 percent of what it would cost to buy that model in a store.

With a program called Mineways, developed by a Minecraft fan named Eric Haines, Minecraft users can "print" their creations in plastic, stone, ceramic, silver, or gold-plated steel. The program starts with a Minecraft creation and automatically produces a file that can be sent directly to a 3-D printing company such as Shapeways or to a personal 3-D printer such as the MakerBot Replicator.

To illustrate the Mineways/Minecraft threat to LEGO, Gordon Robertson (the author's son) built the LEGO Fallingwater kit (part of the Architecture series we described in the previous chapter). He then used it as a model to create a version of the famous Frank Lloyd Wright house in Minecraft, a four-hour project on a rainy weekend afternoon. (Insert photos 17 and 18 show the LEGO Architecture kit and Gordon Robertson's Minecraft version.) Using the Mineways tool, he then "printed" a physical reproduction of the virtual Minecraft version of Fallingwater, both using Shapeways (see insert photo 19) and the author's MakerBot Replicator (see insert photo 20). The cost of the MakerBot model is about one-tenth of the LEGO kit, which retails for about $100.*

So now, using a combination of Minecraft, Mineways, and a MakerBot Replicator, kids can create any model they want using as many blocks as they wish, and print out a half dozen copies for less than the cost of a similar LEGO kit. Just as with digital photography, the price of the machines is dropping fast and the quality is improving. Although the machines are designed for sophisticated hobbyists, it won't be long before anyone will be able to build, print, and rebuild any block-based plastic model they wish, for a fraction of the cost of a LEGO kit.

---

* The cost of the LEGO Fallingwater kit is about 15¢ per gram, which is three times the cost per gram of the plastic used in the MakerBot. But with the MakerBot you can hollow out the inside of a model, reducing the amount of plastic used to make the model.

To be sure, the LEGO Architecture Fallingwater set offers a beautiful re-creation of Wright's iconic house. But Adam Reed Tucker's kit includes just the pieces and colors he believes will create the best reconstruction. If you want to add Wright's guest house (which sits above the main house) or create your own modifications to Fallingwater, it's difficult and expensive to find the right LEGO bricks. With Minecraft, Mineways, and the MakerBot Replicator, you can build many different versions of the house and print the best four or five, all for less than the cost of a single LEGO kit. It's easier and faster to redo a room in the Minecraft version of the house than it is with the LEGO version. With LEGO, you'd have to disassemble the model, find the bricks you need, rebuild the room, and then reassemble the floors above it. With Minecraft, you simply "walk" into the virtual house, make your changes, and print out the new version.

Minecraft is a long way from posing a serious threat to LEGO. It lacks the sweeping variety of LEGO play offerings. It hasn't come close to matching the LEGO brand's global appeal. And it can never duplicate the essential thing that's drawn millions to LEGO—the tactile pleasure that comes from making two bricks click. But LEGO executives have long known they had to disrupt their plastic brick business with a digital brick business, lest a competitor do it for them. Minecraft, however, got to the digital future first. In 2012, the year LEGO shuttered Universe, Mojang—Minecraft's parent company—earned $90 million on sales of $235 million. As 3-D printing improves, LEGO might one day find that Minecraft (or something like it) has jumped the digital divide to become a more compelling, richer, and easier way to construct plastic buildings, characters, and vehicles. As many disrupted companies have learned, what was low-end yesterday can be mainstream tomorrow.

One of Clayton Christensen's most counterintuitive arguments is that managers sometimes fail because they are smart, not because they are stupid. They abide by the same management strategies that have worked so successfully in the past. As a result, the disruptive effort goes wrong. Such was the case with the LEGO Group's handling of Universe.

The company's management concluded that digital brick-based play experiences might one day overthrow physical brick-based play experiences. So it raced to get to the future first with Universe. In doing so, Lisbeth Valther Pallesen and her managers reverted to the very same practices that had helped revive LEGO itself. They insisted that the Universe team stand in the customer's shoes, through rounds and rounds of focus testing, to truly understand what core LEGO kids wanted out of the game. They built a full spectrum of LEGO experiences into the game—including a new pricing scheme and physical models of virtual creations—which meant coordinating with many business units in Billund. And they opened up the development process to expert AFOLs, just as LEGO had done with Mindstorms NXT. Taken together, those innovation strategies, which had helped LEGO succeed so well in its traditional markets, burdened the company's effort to thrive in unexplored territory.

With a novel product such as an MMO game, at first it's uncertain what the technology can and can't deliver and what market will ultimately want it. LEGO might well have been wise to let its Universe team act like an independent start-up—in other words, like a Minecraft. Freed from excessive executive attention and the demands of other LEGO product groups, the team might have launched a far more modest, less costly version of Universe. Compared to other LEGO products, Universe would have been low-end, a little shoddy, and in almost every way inferior—all the hallmarks of a truly disruptive product. Some kids would have been drawn to the novelty of a LEGO MMO, which would have allowed the Universe team to see what worked and what didn't, and thereby refine the play experience even as it "lived" in the market. As Universe improved, it likely would have attracted more customers and moved upmarket, just as Minecraft has done. Universe might even have become the transistor radio of its time, a product that ascended from the bottom of its market and eventually became ubiquitous.

What's certain is that Universe's failure and Minecraft's success demonstrate that to create a low-end disruptor, it's far more effective to put a tight lid on resources, free the development group from outside distractions, kick the product into the market before it's completely "finished," learn from customers' feedback, and make improvements in real time. What's surprising is that LEGO, as we'll see in the next chapter, had already set itself up for exactly that approach to innovation.

Sailing for Blue Ocean

"Obviously LEGO, but Never Seen Before" and the Birth of LEGO Games

*It was a one-in-a-million shot that we'd
actually hit something. But should we hit it,
we'd have done something amazing.*

—Cephas Howard, lead designer, LEGO Games

IT WAS DECEMBER 2005, AND SØREN HOLM, WHO HAD helped lead the effort to create Bionicle, was on the hunt for a new senior concept designer, one of the more difficult-to-fill positions at LEGO. There's no curriculum or career path for a job that requires people to imagine wholly original toys that are rooted in LEGO and will generate millions of dollars in sales. The company's executives had to rely on their own intuition to recognize an untested but promising concept designer when they saw one.

Holm's search had taken him to London, where he and Flemming Østergaard, a LEGO innovation and marketing executive, had lined up ten candidates. Their fourth interview of the day was with a loquacious, moon-faced man named Cephas Howard, a commercial design manager at the *Guardian* and *Observer* newspapers. With his spiky haircut, stubbly beard, and black-framed glasses, Howard certainly had the look of a LEGO designer. And while creating display ads and Web products for the British papers' advertisers was a long way from fabricating dynamic play experiences out of little plastic blocks, Howard's success inside a large corporation was a mark in his favor. So was his vivid entrepreneurial streak. Working nights and weekends, he had conceived and created two original board games and was seeking to bring them both to market.

Since he was a child, Howard and his two brothers had entertained themselves by playing a myriad of board games. They also dreamed up their own bespoke games and shared them with friends. Although he went on to pursue a graphic design career within the publishing industry, Howard never shook off his fever for inventing games. He continued to concoct games and kept detailed notes on all his ideas. His two most recent inventions held enough promise for him to solicit quotes from manufacturers and build a website to self-publish the games. Howard brought one of those games to the LEGO interview, where his zest for creating enticing play experiences burned brightly.

"Cephas seduced us completely with that game," recalled Holm. "He had this fantastic passion that just shone through. It took all of five minutes for Flemming and me to realize that yeah, this is the guy."

Four days later, Howard met with Per Hjuler, Holm's boss. Whereas Howard's session with Holm and Østergaard was full of the light and laughter that come when creative minds connect, Hjuler was all business. Howard recalled that Hjuler told him LEGO had a team whose brief was to create a line that would generate 10 percent of the company's sales each year. That group, said Hjuler, had thus far failed to deliver on its assignment. He then fired a get-to-the-point question at the job candidate: *Are you telling me that if I hire you, this team, plus you, will deliver on this brief?*

Howard swallowed hard. And then he nodded. "I had to say yes," he later recalled. "If such a man existed, I couldn't believe he'd be any better situated than I was. It was a one-in-a-million shot that we'd actually hit something. But should we hit it, we'd have done something amazing. And that's an opportunity you don't often get."

That spring Howard and his wife moved to Billund, where he joined the Concept Lab, a team of developers charged with creating revolutionary play experiences that were rooted in the brick's DNA but amounted to a whole new kind of LEGO. Søren Holm ran the Lab's day-to-day work and reported to Per Hjuler, who was also responsible for the product group that developed toys for older children, such as Bionicle and Technic.

Howard's arrival came at a time when LEGO, having accomplished the first phase of its "Shared Vision" strategy—stabilize the company and manage for cash—was moving into the second phase: build a "defensible core" of products and manage for profit. There would then come a third and final phase, which would commence in 2009: revitalize the brand and manage for growth. Management had already green-lighted one ambitious project, LEGO Universe. But Knudstorp didn't bet the house on Universe. He spread the risk by assigning the Concept Lab the formidable task of creating and bringing to market, by 2009, another entirely novel play experience—one that also aimed to spark the company's growth for years to come. After several false starts, that product line would eventually become a collection of board games called LEGO Games.

Early on, when Games was little more than an idea, the company's brain trust was deeply skeptical of the toy's prospects; some executives even refused to countenance the notion of giving the go-ahead to develop the line. There was also the not insignificant matter of the Concept Lab's abysmal track record. Though the Lab had thrown off hundreds of ideas over the years, it had failed to bring a single one of them to market. The Lab was a deeply moribund group when Knudstorp assigned it the task of inventing the company's next growth driver. Given that the Lab's design team hadn't delivered by the time Per Hjuler interviewed Cephas Howard, it's not hard to understand why the LEGO executive had nearly run out of patience.

How, then, did LEGO go on to match its ambition—to discover and claim a blue-ocean market—with sufficient discipline to conceive, design, and develop such a value-creating product? It did so by surmounting the obstacles that come with any attempt to create a new market space. How do you shield a blue-ocean team from the demands and distractions of your company's other product development groups, which must continue to fend off attacks from red-ocean competitors? Out of the mind-bending array of possibilities you can pursue, where do you find a promising opportunity that no other competitor has explored? And when you encounter the inevitable headwinds, what's the best navigational system for getting your initiative back on the right course?

In developing Games, the Concept Lab found a way to steer around the shoals that so often sink attempts to invent a product that creates new demand. The result was that after so many fruitless ventures, the Lab discovered a market that (at least for a time) was truly uncontested. Here's what it did:

Assembling the Team

In 2005, when Hjuler was given oversight of the Concept Lab, one of his first moves was to recommit the Lab to its core purpose. Because the Lab had some of the most skilled designers in all of LEGO, they were often loaned out, on a temporary basis, to other project teams that were developing novelty toys. The practice leached the Lab of its most valuable asset—its talent—and left it chronically understaffed. Hjuler's response was to ring-fence the Lab from the rest of the organization. He gave the Lab its own studio, in a building that stands apart from the main design group, and won commitments from the heads of other product development teams to look elsewhere for resources. Henceforth, the Lab was to operate solely as a front-end team that would pursue only entirely new LEGO experiences.

Another drag on the Lab's performance was that its development team was remarkably unvaried. The group consisted solely of designers, most of them Danish men, who were deft at conjuring clever concepts. But their inability to translate those ideas into commercially successful toys was largely due to the fact that they lacked a vivid sense of what turned kids on. What's more, they didn't understand the competitive environments and cultural trends that shaped the many markets LEGO targeted.

Hjuler brought some diversity into the mix by recruiting designers from different cultural backgrounds, including India, Japan, and the United Kingdom. That's when he tapped Søren Holm, who'd helped make Bionicle such a wild success, to head up the Lab. And he drafted Flemming Østergaard to create a marketing function within the Lab, which had never been done before, as well as Finn Daugård Madsen, a veteran project manager. Thus the Lab evolved from a pure design team to a fully matrixed product development team, with marketing and project management disciplines as well as design.

Note that Hjuler avoided the trap of promoting diversity at the expense of clarity. Whatever their backgrounds or skill sets, the Lab's managers and associates had one vital thing in common: they had built with bricks since childhood and thereby had developed a deep understanding of what it took to invent dazzling LEGO creations.

"Some of the designers were self-made, some of them came from the best design schools, and some were from other countries," said Hjuler. "But all of them understood the LEGO DNA."

Exploring Different Directions

When Søren Holm was a senior director at the Concept Lab during the Poul Plougmann era, the Lab's mandate was so expansive—develop entirely new product offerings that redefine the LEGO play experience—it virtually ensured that the group's designers generated hundreds of blue-sky ideas that were so untethered as to stand almost no chance of being developed and taken to market. More often than not, the concepts weren't backed by a compelling business case; they were poorly executed; they were too radical a departure from the LEGO DNA; or they failed to excite kids. During a 2003 review session with the company's top executives, Holm grew so frustrated with management's hazy focus that he blurted out a desperate question: "What do you want us to do?"

Kristiansen's reply didn't clarify things: "What would you like to do?"

"I really didn't know how to answer," Holm recalled. "But I couldn't allow myself to admit that. So I just said, 'We'll try a bit of everything.' We then took a year to develop twenty different projects, which we presented to 150 managers. We used a full day of their time and absolutely nothing came out of it."

The Lab's designers found the constant round of creating LEGO play concepts that management ultimately rejected to be "very disenchanting and very demotivating," as Hjuler later put it. By 2005, he and the rest of the company's senior management team set about giving the Lab the structure and direction it needed to succeed.

The biggest challenge resided in pushing the team to imagine new LEGO play experiences, while ensuring it didn't lose its way among all the possibilities. Recalling the days when the Lab lacked sufficient guidance from senior management, Holm likened the experience to "standing outside on a clear night, looking up at the Milky Way. There are so many stars it's just overwhelming. So you frame just one particular area—say, just the stars around Mars. By shutting out the gazillions of other stars, you start to get some focus."

Such "framing," or direction setting, began when Knudstorp wrote the Concept Lab into the "Shared Vision" document, the three-stage strategy for the LEGO Group's turnaround. By designating the Concept Lab as a primary driver of the company's organic-growth phase, Knudstorp signaled that the Lab would look further into the future than any other product development group. That is, it would solely focus on developing beyond-the-next-generation LEGO toys. And by assigning the Lab a sales target of 10 percent of the company's revenue, Knudstorp ensured that even as the Lab's designers and marketers were developing a new LEGO play experience, they were building a business case for it. Whatever concept they conceived, it had to be big enough to make a dent in the market.

Then there was the matter of coming up with language that precisely communicated the kind of toy that would take LEGO into the future. The LEGO Group's leaders wanted a radically new play experience, but it could not be unmoored from the quintessential LEGO core. After many long conversations, the group came up with a one-sentence brief that captured the salubrious tension between classic LEGO and new LEGO. The Concept Lab, according to the brief, would conceive and develop toys that were "obviously LEGO, but never seen before."

No one can recall who authored that line, but it didn't matter. "Obviously LEGO" conveyed the notions that the new line must be rooted in the physical brick, must seamlessly click into the LEGO system, and must engage the core customer demographic of five- to nine-year-old boys. Within those boundaries, the Lab's designers were free to imagine and explore "never seen before" LEGO concepts. Though the direction-setting details had yet to emerge, the brief gave the Lab's designers enough room to roam while providing enough of a signpost to at least begin to help them find their way.

"The brief directed us to focus on the same consumers, the same platforms, the same markets," said Østergaard. "All things being equal, whatever we came up with had to have a new play dimension. We didn't know what it was, but we knew it had to be out there."

The Hunt for a Blue Ocean

Although "obviously LEGO, but never seen before" cleared a pathway into the future, the Lab's designers found that starting the journey was a struggle. Holm, in particular, was humbled by the project's vast scope. The team felt it couldn't simply build on what LEGO had done before. So, then, how should it begin?

Holm was wrestling with that question when he heard a lecture by Mikkel Rasmussen, a partner at a Copenhagen-based consultancy called ReD Associates, on using anthropological research methodology to deeply explore consumers' lives and in turn use those insights to fuel innovation. (In 2005, this was still a relatively new concept in Denmark.) Rasmussen put up a slide that made a memorable impression on the Concept Lab's leaders: "If you want to know how a lion hunts, don't go to a zoo. Go to the jungle."

Soon thereafter, Holm and Østergaard enlisted ReD Associates to launch an ambitious project called Find the Fun. As the title suggested, the project's aim was to take a deep look at twenty-first-century childhood and reveal the needs and desires that LEGO wasn't fulfilling. Working with ReD's ethnographers, the Concept Lab's designers logged lengthy in-home visits with families in the United Kingdom, the United States, and Germany, where they took extensive notes on the real-world dynamics of LEGO play. A designer and an ethnographer would arrive at a home early in the morning and watch as the family scrambled to get ready for the day. When the kids were off at school, the team would interview one or both parents. At day's end, the team would play with the kids or simply step back and observe. Although the Bionicle team had used desk research and detailed consumer profiles to help create a whole new world of LEGO stories and characters, never before had LEGO designers stepped so directly into the lives of the company's consumers.

The experience was both eye-opening and somewhat unsettling. For Østergaard, one of the more memorable visits was to a family living in a suburb outside London. The older brother, who was nine, was "totally into LEGO," Østergaard remembered. And the younger sibling, who was six, totally wasn't. Feeling left out, he did his best to upend his big brother's LEGO playtime.

"The younger kid was a bit of a pain in the ass—there was all this tension," said Østergaard. "That's something you just don't see in a traditional focus group setting. Coming from Denmark, where LEGO is such a big part of your upbringing, we never would have thought of LEGO in that context, where the kids end up fighting."

As they worked through their notes and reflected on their in-home observations, the Lab's designers realized their approach to creating new products had fallen into a deeply grooved pattern of thinking. They thought of LEGO largely as a solitary play experience, epitomized, in that London suburb, by the older brother's struggle to immerse himself in bricks. They rarely considered a social dimension to LEGO. How could they create something that drew in the younger brother, so that *both* boys could participate in LEGO play?

The Lab's ethnographic team also spied an omnipresent hierarchy in kids' lives. Whatever the activity—basketball, math, LEGO bricks—kids were acutely aware of how they compared to their peers. The ethnographers would ask a nine-year-old what he was good at, and he'd unabashedly tell them he was the third-fastest runner in his class but one of the worst at drawing. Because hierarchy is built on competition, where for every winner there's a loser, LEGO viewed it in a negative light. But for children, self-ranking was a natural, instinctive part of their day-to-day lives. And that surfaced another opportunistic question: how could the Concept Lab leverage hierarchy and competition in more of what it did, whether it was developing or marketing a product?

The team also observed a third characteristic, the notion of mastery, which seemed to yoke the social and competitive aspects of kids' lives. Whether it was flipping skateboarding tricks or obsessing over the design and history of warplanes, kids demonstrated an innate desire to dig into a discipline and conquer it. As they built their skills, they'd show off the results to their peers, so they could win status and move up the hierarchy that all kids share. The greater their mastery, the more social capital they accrued.

Social play, hierarchy, competition, mastery: those characteristics of kids' lives—or, to put it in LEGO terms, those "unmet consumer needs"—became the cornerstones upon which the Lab began to build out whole new suites of LEGO play concepts. By discarding the "LEGO knows best" aloofness that once characterized the company, and instead humbly learning from kids and their parents, the Lab's designers and marketers revealed growth opportunities that had been ignored for too long.

Navigating the Course

To help the Concept Lab ensure that its designers' efforts aligned with the studio's brief, Hjuler and Holm enlisted a stakeholder group, consisting of senior executives, to review, evaluate, and make go/no-go decisions on the Lab's projects and proposals. Realizing that the Lab's concepts were less likely to grow into hit products without the fertilizer of top management's attention, the pair recruited the heads of every LEGO product development unit to sit on the review panel. Thus the group benefited from the mix of different executives' skill sets and expertise.

"We had to train them, and they had to train us, in finding a language to talk about concepts," said Holm. "We had to make concepts tangible, and we had to create a way to discuss multiple opportunities and directions. So it came very naturally to say, 'Let's design a process.' "

That effort began when the Lab decided that it wouldn't rely on calendar-driven reviews, a prime feature of the core LEGO Development Process. Instead of using a predetermined timetable to drive a product from concept to reality, the concept itself would determine the launch date. If a promising idea took longer to develop than the twelve to eighteen months that were standard for every other LEGO product, so be it. Freed from the clock, a promising project would bubble along until it proved it was real—that is, it could deliver a unique LEGO play experience and merit a high enough price to yield a good margin. Only in the later stages of a concept's development, after all the important assumptions had been tested and the key uncertainties resolved, would a project win a launch date. At that point, the calendar would take over and the product would be readied for its rollout, just like every other LEGO set.

The Concept Lab also overhauled the review sessions' format. In years past, when pitching their ideas to senior management, designers put in long hours perfecting elaborate prototypes. (Recall, for example, the extravagant volcano that Søren Holm and his designers mocked up for Voodoo Heads, the concept that later became Bionicle.) Problem was, those big productions required excessive prettifying and gilding, which bit into the designers' time and resources without adding much value.

The Lab's designers tossed the prototype approach and instead opted for poster boards, which featured a rough sketch of the concept, accompanied by a headline that summed up the play experience and a brief description of the market opportunity. This stripped-down approach allowed the designers to put far more time and effort into conceiving, rather than presenting, promising ideas. And by utilizing posters, designers introduced their ideas in a standardized form, which made it far easier for stakeholders to compare and review twenty-five or thirty projects during an eight-hour meeting. (Insert photo 21 shows the original poster board used to pitch LEGO Games.)

In assessing each proposal, the stakeholder group would always put a fundamental question to the design team: how is the play experience relevant to a five- to nine-year-old boy? The question aimed to determine whether the concept sufficiently appealed to that "obviously LEGO" core consumer. The group would also weigh whether the concept captured one or more of the consumer attributes—sociability, competition, hierarchy, or mastery—revealed by the Find the Fun research. If, for example, the concept appealed to kids' competitive instincts, it stood a better chance of delivering a new LEGO play experience.

Often the review team also invoked the "100-minute rule." They'd guesstimate the amount of excitement the proposed toy might ignite during the first minute of play, how it would engage kids through the tenth minute, and whether it would keep them coming back after one hundred minutes. Even though the concept had to reveal a "never seen before" LEGO experience, it still had to adhere to the core LEGO value of delivering unlimited play potential.

If an idea got the go-ahead and moved beyond the poster board stage, designers might build a model of the concept, so as to evolve their thinking. But even then, they put only a minimal amount of time into the effort. More often than not, the models were raw assemblages of LEGO bricks, wires, and cardboard—rough, ready, and not at all elegant. The goal wasn't to finesse a close approximation of the finished product, but rather to create a tactile experience for stakeholders and thereby tap into their intuitive sense of whether the designers were headed in the right direction.

As the review process unfolded, it formed a kind of loop: generate lots of ideas, get feedback, and keep refining until the concept was shelved or combined with another idea for further exploration. The stakeholder group never killed an idea outright. If a proposal was too abstract or pushed the brand in the wrong direction, the Lab would instead consign the concept to its file of "101 Lost Opportunities"—promising concepts that had proved problematic and were never launched but might someday spark a glimmer of an idea for a breakthrough product.

"We have a fantastic library with all these binders, and in each binder there's 101 opportunities that never became anything," said Holm. "Even if the idea doesn't work, there are still some worthwhile nuggets in there. So we'll park it, and someday the idea might reappear in some strange new form."

Testing the Waters

Among the thousands of proposals that had been relegated to the Lost Opportunities library, there were several concepts for board games that had been proposed in years past but never developed. LEGO designers had tried on different occasions to develop board game themes, most recently in 2004. But they never found a way to turn the concepts into viable products. Instead, LEGO licensed a line of games, which were manufactured and distributed by an arts and crafts company called Rose Art, best known for its crayons. In 2005, one of the LEGO Group's foremost rivals, Mega Bloks, acquired Rose Art. Given the LEGO Group's poor track record in developing board games and its uninspiring history of licensing them, no one among the company's executives was enamored with the concept at the time Cephas Howard joined the Lab in the spring of 2006.

Although Howard had wowed Holm and Østergaard when he met them in London, he wasn't permitted to work on games when he joined the company. "The first month that Cephas was at LEGO, he was pushing games and I thought, 'Yeah, come on,' " recalled Holm. "We've been there before. Let's give it a rest and try something else, which we then did."

Howard was dispatched to develop concepts that would add a social dimension to LEGO play. Over the next few months, he and his colleagues generated dozens of ideas. Most, such as a platform for buildable outdoor toys—think of LEGO water guns—were soon shelved. Other ideas felt too familiar to qualify as "never seen before" but were deemed promising enough to migrate from the Lab to the Product and Market Development (PMD) unit, where core LEGO themes are brought to life. One such concept to come out of the Lab was Inner Earth, a germ of an idea that PMD's designers grew into Power Miners, a popular theme that hit the market in 2009.

Despite being waved off games, Howard persisted. Working nights and weekends, he investigated countless different game mechanisms that could be built out of LEGO bricks. The first challenge was to come up with an iconic element that announced, *This is a board game*. He quickly homed in on developing LEGO dice. His logic: when a boy pours a pile of bricks onto a table, if there is a die in the mix, he instantly knows it's a game. To make the die "obviously LEGO," it had to be buildable. And so he set about piecing together the first die prototype out of existing LEGO components. He then used LEGO bricks to build something that looked like a chessboard, which further served to signal "obviously board game."

Upon seeing Howard's creation, Holm was underwhelmed. Like all of his early-stage prototypes, Howard's model was remarkably unadorned. When first designing a game, he was solely interested in testing the game's inner logic. Only later in the design process would he build in enticing details and dress the game up with stories that create a sense of narrative play for children. "The model Cephas created was so naive, just a plate with standard bricks," said Holm. "I couldn't see the idea, and that held me back. I was looking for something with a lot more oomph."

Despite the rejection, Howard was undeterred, and he kept experimenting. Later, at a Concept Lab off-site in the Bavarian Alps, he unveiled another prototype. This time he'd added a castle theme, where players rolled a die to travel a challenging course and complete a mission. The game was quintessentially LEGO: buildable, changeable, and rebuildable. Players first had to construct the game, which created a greater sense of immersion and ownership. The game itself delivered a social (and often competitive) play experience, where kids could have fun with their friends and families—a marked departure from the far more typical solo style of LEGO play. And the game's "instructions" actively encouraged players to rearrange the board and reinvent the rules—"to not just play the game," as one reviewer later put it, "but to play *with* the game." As Holm recalled, he and the other designers gave it a try and were "completely, utterly sold."

Not long thereafter, Howard presented the concept to the Lab's stakeholder team. The company's senior managers were likewise taken with the idea. They believed Howard's board game might let LEGO tap into a potent but elusive demographic: moms. Although fathers and sons are the biggest consumers of classic LEGO kits, mothers are the prime purchasers of board games, precisely because games are a magnet for family play. If LEGO could launch a winning line of buildable, eminently playable board games, it just might lure many, many more moms into its fold.

With that, Cephas Howard got the go-ahead to spend all of his time concocting game concepts. As they walked out of the meeting, Holm took him aside. "Søren reminded me that LEGO had already tried a number of times to develop games and they always shut it down," said Howard. "He was basically saying, 'You have this one opportunity. If you don't nail it, you probably won't ever get to work on it again.' "

Inventing a Value-Creating Product

Over the next three years, Howard and five other designers worked out of a bunkerlike, belowground studio at LEGO headquarters. Because LEGO deemed it a completely covert operation, he and the other designers were required to sign nondisclosure agreements promising they wouldn't tell another living soul about the project. Howard couldn't even broach the project with his wife, who had also taken a job at LEGO. In an interview with the London *Telegraph*, Howard was quoted as saying, "I think she wondered if my LEGO story was a front and I was actually working for the CIA."[25]

Østergaard was convinced the security was necessary. He and other executives feared that if competitors learned of the company's plan to launch a buildable board game, they'd quickly knock out a copycat, inferior product that would turn kids off and pollute the market for LEGO. "We actually managed to take the line to market without the competition knowing about it," said Østergaard. "It became a new way of developing at LEGO."

Howard and the other designers came up with hundreds of ideas for board games, more than thirty of which were developed into prototypes. The variety of concepts was nearly limitless: games for younger kids, games that would also appeal to grown-ups, on-the-go games, party-gift games, themed games such as pirates and ancient Egypt, and much, much more. From the outset, the concepts were play-tested on a weekly basis with groups of kids from Denmark, Germany, the United Kingdom, and the United States. The concepts were then refined and retested, whereupon some were rejected and those that made it to the next round were refined and retested some more.

Howard's early-stage prototypes were rough and largely unfinished, usually just a die, a simple board, and a bag full of standard bricks. The big goal, in the first phase of a concept's development, was to test the core idea. Only if the focus group gravitated to the play concept would the designers then begin to evolve the game's theme and write the rule set. Every test group featured a fresh round of kids, so each child encountered a LEGO board game for the very first time.

One of the bigger challenges, for the twenty- and thirtysomething LEGO designers, was to create games that appealed to nine-year-olds rather than themselves. That accounted for the weekly rounds of play testing. The focus groups helped designers see the game through kids' eyes; the kids' unadorned feedback often revealed flaws that the designers had failed to anticipate.

"There was a lot of codevelopment with the kids," said Howard. "They couldn't tell you how to design the game or even how to redesign it. But they could very much tell you what works and what doesn't, just in the way they played. And that was a massive tool for evolving our thinking and improving the games."

Play testing in Germany soon surfaced a common flaw in many of the prototypes: the rule sets, as Østergaard put it, "sucked." When it came to LEGO, kids expected a premium experience, never mind that they were playing with prototypes. "The rules weren't living up to those expectations, and the kids just hammered us. It was like, 'Guys, you really need to step up here.' "

The kids' unvarnished critiques pushed LEGO to seek out a select, external group of expert advisors—including Reiner Knizia, widely regarded as one of the world's foremost game developers—to help transform Howard's inventions into hit products. Howard and his team first sought Knizia's help in improving the rules and infusing his philosophy of game play: "the goal is to win, but it's the goal that's important, not the winning." Knizia also worked on developing the line's flagship titles, Ramses Pyramid (at the time, the only LEGO board game to feature a designer's name on the box) and Lunar Command, and he served as a consultant to the entire project. (Ramses Pyramid is shown in insert photo 23.)

Before fully committing to commercializing board games, LEGO decided to take one more run at trying to capture a promising new play opportunity. The company enlisted Advance, the Copenhagen-based consultancy that had helped develop Bionicle, as well as three other design agencies. The four external firms were given the same brief—create an "obviously LEGO, but never seen before" play experience—as had been given to the Concept Lab. None of the firms had a clue as to what the others were working on. Yet three months later, all four returned to Billund and revealed their proposals, each of which included some variation on a board game. The proposals differed significantly from Howard's concepts. Taken together, however, they powerfully validated the notion that games might well amount to a robust, wide-open market opportunity for LEGO. "Our initial take," said Østergaard, "was that maybe this combination of LEGO plus games was really right."

As the project gathered momentum, Howard enlisted a wider circle of LEGO designers and engineers to develop and perfect the line's two most prominent, "never seen before" innovations, the die and a tiny LEGO man called a "microfig." Designed to fit a single LEGO stud when placed on a game board, the microfig is an armless character that has the same knobby feet, stud-topped head, and facial expressiveness as its bigger sibling, the minifig. Because of the component's prominence, its design went through eight major iterations before the final production microfig was fully born.

"We did rounds and rounds of challenge sketches," said Howard. "And then when we thought we had it right, we found the decoration machine needed the figure to have slightly bigger feet. We had to battle with the engineers over tenths of millimeters to end up at a place where the feet were big enough for the machine to grab on to but still small enough to retain the figure's proportions. It was fine-tune, fine-tune, fine-tune."

Developing the die required even more time and effort. Howard first tried building it out of existing LEGO components. But the clunky creation lacked sufficient weight to roll well and too often landed on its edge. So he tried again. He and his team huddled around a computer and used 3-D modeling techniques to create the new LEGO element's essential design: a die with an ABS plastic core and four LEGO studs protruding from each of its six sides, which are encased in soft rubber around the edges. The studs let players snap on decorated LEGO tiles that differ from game to game; the rubber casing abets the die's roll. It took just a single day to concoct the first prototype, but sixteen months to perfect it. The die (see insert photo 22) would go on to become an icon. The one physical element common to all LEGO Games, its image would be emblazoned across all of the line's packaging.

Claiming an Uncontested Market

While Howard and his design team engaged in the "create" phase of the board games project, Østergaard and a handful of marketers worked on the two other phases, "collect" and "commercialize." Because LEGO was unfamiliar with the board games market, Østergaard embarked on a deep, almost ethnographic exploration of the category. Just as the Concept Lab's designers had embedded themselves in families so as to generate ideas, the marketers took a long dive into retail stores and regional markets so as to collect the knowledge and insights that would help them reveal growth opportunities. They recruited the former president of Toys "R" Us, John Barbour, to help them navigate the board games category. And they put in long hours at different toy stores in and around Enfield, Connecticut (where the company's North American headquarters is located), to get a read on the business dimensions of board games: logistics, margins, promotions, and the mix of board game offerings.

They learned that the board games business is heavily back-loaded toward Christmas, by far the category's biggest selling season. Products that remain on the shelves after the holidays are heavily promoted and rebated. They saw how companies exploit popular evergreen products through "skinning," where a Hasbro will spin off dozens of versions of Monopoly and even skin the game for local markets, such as its Yankees Collector's Edition Monopoly for the New York tristate area. They found that the market varied wildly in terms of quality and profitability. And then there was the most encouraging discovery: the board game market was ripe for innovation.

"It's a huge category, but also a pretty dull category," said Østergaard. "They do things just as they'd done them for the past twenty years. Any newness is just in the reskinning of these evergreens. When something original does come along, like a Cranium, Hasbro would eventually buy it."

They also discovered that board games reached a wallet that differed from the one that LEGO traditionally dipped into. Mothers make the majority of all toy purchase decisions, and mothers regard the purchase of a game and a LEGO toy as two separate "occasions" drawing from two separate "wallets." In other words, if a boy and his mother go into a store with two LEGO toys on the boy's shopping list, he's less likely to get both items than if he has a LEGO toy and a game on his list. Children, exquisitely tuned to such nuances, figure this out quickly.

As the project entered the commercialize phase, where LEGO prepared to take Games to market, the team continued to test and refine. They set up a small assembly line, far from the LEGO factory, to test packaging and packing prototypes. "It was still extremely secret, so everything was done after hours," said Østergaard. "We did an awful lot of prototyping in all directions—an extremely laborious process."

A milestone test came when Howard gave a couple of board game prototypes to Knudstorp and Hjuler, who took them home to their families for a weekend of play. Hjuler had just bought his two young children the latest PlayStation game for kids. To his astonishment, they spent far more of their time playing with the board games. The games likewise bewitched Knudstorp's children.

"It's one thing to do a presentation to top management," said Howard. "But it's an entirely different thing when they actually experience the game with their own kids. Suddenly they're really invested in the project. That got us a lot of traction fast."

Once the development team could demonstrate, through its nearly endless rounds of play testing, that LEGO Games stood a good chance of landing near the top of kids' wish lists for toys, management gave the go-ahead to launch. So it was that LEGO, in its initial August 2009 release, decided to come out with not one but ten different board games. It was all part of a bid to swiftly stake out an entirely new market, and it had the desired effect. Soon thereafter, LEGO Games was rapidly ascending the year's list of the hottest Christmas toys. Largely through the efforts of one driven games designer and a handful of wingmen, the company had an "obviously LEGO, but never seen before" hit on its hands.

On the surface, LEGO Games and that other ambitious creation— LEGO Universe—shared several similarities. Both were rooted in the LEGO DNA of the brick and the System of Play. Both sought to deliver new types of LEGO play experiences. Both aimed to drive the company's organic growth and further burnish the LEGO brand. The difference was that with Universe, LEGO attempted to disrupt its core brick business by creating a platform for digital play. With Games, LEGO sought out an untapped, blue-ocean market by creating the world's first buildable and rebuildable board game—a game that nevertheless adhered to the core LEGO brick platform.

But what's truly striking are the disparities between the two teams' approaches to innovation. While the Universe project marshaled roughly 350 managers and associates from every part of the LEGO organization, Games took in just six Concept Lab designers led by Cephas Howard, plus a review panel of roughly a dozen LEGO executives. While inventing Universe meant that more than two thousand LEGO elements had to be rendered in digital form, 95 percent of the pieces in LEGO Games already existed. And while LEGO opened up Universe's development to a crowd of nearly one hundred skilled fans, the development of Games was enveloped in secrecy, with the project's professional LEGO designers working out of a tightly secured office in a building that stood separate from the offices that housed the company's other Billund-based development teams. In fact, even though the Colorado-based Universe team was five thousand miles away from the LEGO mother ship, the covert Concept Lab was far more distant.

The foremost difference between Games and Universe resided in their performance. Universe burned through $30 million in development costs and was shut down fifteen months after its launch, generating a huge loss for the company. LEGO Games, which was launched in the United Kingdom and Germany in 2009 and globally in 2010, was an instant hit. LEGO hoped Games would take 10 percent, on average, of children's board game markets throughout the world. It far exceeded those expectations by grabbing anywhere from 13 to 45 percent of the regional markets in which it competed. In 2009, Games "generated significantly higher sales than expected," according to Knudstorp, and helped power LEGO to a 56 percent increase in pretax profit and a 63 percent profit jump in 2010. Games not only earned back its own development cost, it helped cover some of the loss from LEGO Universe.

———————

With Games, LEGO invented a value-creating product line and thereby discovered an uncontested market. And yet, despite its blue-ocean success with Games, LEGO never forgot that for the most part it remained a red-ocean company. Even by 2009, most of the company's revenue still came from such perennial bestsellers as City and *Star Wars*. Beginning with the turnaround effort of 2004, LEGO rediscovered and redeployed its core assets of the brick, the building system, and its globe-spanning tribes of fans, all of which helped LEGO grow into the third-largest shark in the toy industry. And with such core capabilities as its tight relationships with retailers, its direct dialogue with fans, and its varied approach to reimagining profitable product lines, LEGO tore away market share from the industry's whales, Mattel and Hasbro, more than tripling its share of the market between 2004 and 2011.*

LEGO also understood a fundamental principle of blue-ocean strategy: no unsullied market space remains uncontested for long. The more quickly a break-the-mold product grows, the sooner it fulfills the promise of its original business model and loses its novelty. The result is that a dynamically different product such as LEGO Games eventually becomes less of an innovation and more of a commodity. In fact, in 2011 and 2012, sales of Games cooled—as is so often the case in the toy business—and then declined.

Nevertheless, commodities can still be profitable. So it was that soon after the launch of LEGO Games, the Concept Lab "loaned" Cephas Howard to the Product and Market Development group, which takes on the company's primary development efforts. He then cre-

———

* While LEGO does not report its global market share regularly, market analysts at the NPD Group measure its U.S. market share, which rose from 1.9 percent in 2004 to 6.2 percent in 2011. The company's global market share, when it reports it, tends to be about a point higher than its U.S. market share.

ated versions of Games that were based on successful LEGO themes such as City, *Harry Potter*, and Pirates. With that, LEGO signaled that what was initially blue ocean for them would now be managed as part of a larger, red-ocean market. But by melding board games with the LEGO building experience, the company had carved out a place for itself in yet another big profitable market.

Leveraging Diverse and Creative People

The Ninjago Big Bang

*People who come from different disciplines provoke
and challenge each other, which is a lot more fruitful
than working with people who think the same way.*

—Erik Legernes, senior LEGO creative director

THEY CALL IT THE "BIG BANG." THE MONIKER REFERS TO A
homegrown LEGO theme that's built around an arresting story, one that shows a high potential for creating a worldwide sensation and generating lucrative revenue streams from the Web, television, and spin-off products, just as Bionicle had done for the better part of a decade. A Big Bang is also a big bet. LEGO launches a Big Bang line about every other year, and when it does, nearly every unit within the company, from manufacturing to logistics, marketing, IT, and beyond, goes all out to get behind the

line and deliver a hit. If the Big Bang is a big bust, à la LEGO Universe, it lets much of the air out of the company's earnings.

By 2008, LEGO had instilled its product development teams with enough discipline and focus to regularly churn out profit-pumping hit toys. When senior vice president Poul Schou assembled a small concept team to create the next Big Bang, he had enough confidence to give the team's leaders, creative director Erik Legernes and marketing director Henrik Nonnemann, lots of leeway to invent the theme and set its financial targets. Schou's design brief was little more than a simple goal: "double the fun; double the consumers." That was Schou's shorthand for defining the team's ambitious stretch goal of doubling sales from the company's previous Big Bang hit, a series of underwater adventure sets called Atlantis.

Several months later, having sorted through scores of ideas and focus-tested them with kids, Legernes and Nonnemann proposed their new concept to Schou. Their team had concocted a ninja theme, replete with such kid turn-ons as battling shoguns, Spinjitzu weapons, and an army of evil skeletons. They called the theme Ninjago, and set a daunting target: the line would deliver 10 percent of the company's total revenue. No other LEGO-generated theme, not even Bionicle, had ever surpassed that milestone. It was, as Nonnemann later put it, a "dream scenario." But they had identified so many potential revenue streams, they believed they could make the dream a reality.

During a focus group session in New Jersey in late April 2009, the team had sketched out a full suite of complementary products for Ninjago. In addition to the actual product line, which would total seventeen sets in its first year, LEGO would develop a Ninjago board game for LEGO Games, create a Ninjago-themed world for LEGO Universe, work with the Cartoon Network to develop an animated TV series (which debuted in January 2011), and partner with TT Games to create a video game (which launched in April 2011). Ninjago iPad and iPhone apps, as well as a series of graphic novels, would follow.

Cole, one of the ninja heroes, battles Bonezai in the LEGO Ninjago Battle Arena.

When Ninjago: Masters of Spinjitzu launched in January 2011, it set new financial and innovation records for LEGO. The LEGO Group reported a 20 percent increase in sales in the first quarter of 2011, largely due to the overwhelming popularity of the Ninjago line, which went on to rack up the highest single-year sales of any LEGO-invented theme in the company's history. With that, Ninjago's front-end development team redefined the conventional notion of success at LEGO.

Most striking, Ninjago signaled that LEGO had flipped its top-down approach to managing innovation. During the company's do-or-die survival phase of 2004, leaders such as Mads Nipper had defined the company's direction (back to the brick), identified its core customer (five- to nine-year-old boys), set its return-on-sales target (13½ percent), and even picked the look and feel of new LEGO sets. After all, it was Nipper who, at that town hall meeting, used Henrik Andersen's fire truck to set a course toward a classic yet modern look for LEGO City. Back then, LEGO was very much a hierarchical organization, with the big dogs at the peak of the pyramid evincing a command-and-control leadership style and, as Knudstorp described it, "only one truth and black-and-white thinking."

Just four years later, LEGO was remarkably decentralized. Nonnemann and Legernes, not the company's senior management team, defined the Ninjago design brief, conceived the toy and its complementary products, developed the business model, and ultimately set their own ambitious sales targets. To be sure, Schou, Nipper, and other managers approved the brief and saw to it that the team followed through on its commitments. But the team had abundant white space to make the important decisions and lead the way.

What changed during those four short years? Knudstorp and his team skillfully twined the challenges that so often make innovation so difficult. They vividly defined the outcomes they desired, and then gave people absolute freedom to innovate "inside the brick." They reached for the stars with never-before-seen efforts such as Mindstorms NXT and LEGO Games, even as they put a premium on the smaller innovations that refresh serial moneymakers such as LEGO City and *Star Wars*. They knew that before they could transform the brand, they first had to rebuild the business.

Above all, they concluded that while strategies matter, the prime source of competitive advantage consists of diverse and creative people. After all, strategies can be copied; people can't be. Since the Poul Plougmann years, one of the LEGO Group's biggest changes resided in building a culture where the people who make and market LEGO toys can summon all of their passion and creativity.

The Rise of T-Shaped LEGO People

Recall how in early 1999, after reporting the first loss in its history, LEGO fired more than one thousand staffers. Among those forced out were veterans who held much of the institutional memory for creating and marketing brick-based products that conformed to the System of Play. Their replacements: talented designers who could concoct imaginative play experiences but knew little about creating LEGO toys that clicked. Plougmann dispersed the new hires to design outposts throughout the world but failed to harness their creativity. The result was a host of big-bet, "never seen before" product launches, such as Galidor and Jack Stone, that were *not* "obviously LEGO" and very nearly crashed the company.

One might think that in the wake of such disasters, a chastened LEGO would return to its old model of recruiting mostly Danish designers who'd grown up in a land where LEGO is bigger than Coca-Cola. But today's LEGO is more heterogenous than at any other time in its history. Walk through the LEGO cafeteria in Billund and you'll hear conversations not only in Danish but in French, German, and lots of English. Consider the team that created Ninjago: Legernes hails from Norway, Nonnemann from Denmark, and lead designer Phil McCormick from the United States, and they were supported in part by Japanese illustrators and prototypers.

LEGO product development teams are diverse not only in terms of nationality but also in the skill sets and expertise they combine. Years ago, the Bionicle team demonstrated that sustained innovation occurs when people of dissimilar talents and mind-sets are brought together in close physical proximity, where they can have frequent meetings and serendipitous encounters. Systematic innovation does not often come from a homogenous group of designers working in isolation. Thus, every LEGO development team now comprises a project manager as well as a handful of designers, marketers, engineers, modelers, and communications people. All are expected to contribute to every phase of the project, not just the parts for which they are functionally responsible. LEGO believes that when people from different backgrounds mix it up in a creative endeavor, there's a human friction that can spark real breakthroughs.

"People who come from different disciplines tend to think differently," said Erik Legernes of the Ninjago team. "They provoke and challenge each other, which is a lot more fruitful than working with people who think the same way."

In keeping with that logic, LEGO has gone out of its way to recruit what some call "T-shaped people."* The vertical leg of the T represents expertise in one particular area, while the horizontal bar signals a breadth of knowledge across multiple disciplines. This potent mix of depth and interdisciplinary skills increases the likelihood that T-shaped people will solve wickedly difficult problems, something that LEGO designers encounter all the time.

Today, the vast majority of the LEGO Group's developers share the same depth of competence: they are abundantly creative when it comes to inventing with and for the LEGO brick. At the same time, they are diverse in the range of experiences they bring to the job. Just consider:

- The chief designer of LEGO Games, Cephas Howard, has the brick in his blood and a genius for imagining clever board games. He is also a skilled commercial designer and, as evidenced by his days at London's *Guardian* and *Observer* newspapers, a successful salesman with enough leadership skills to have managed a large team.

- As we've seen, Mark Hansen, the original architect of LEGO Factory and the project leader in the development of LEGO Universe, is a former U.S. Navy SEAL who spent three years researching mass customization and holds a master's degree in engineering.

- Mark Stafford, a British AFOL, formerly worked as a marine cargo surveyor on the Amsterdam and Antwerp docks in the Netherlands. It was Stafford's girlfriend and fellow LEGO adept, Megan Rothrock, who encouraged him to apply to become a model designer for the company. The couple moved to Billund in 2006, and Stafford went on to design sets for best-selling lines including Exo-Force, Power Miners, and Space.

* The concept behind the T-shaped profile has long been a staple of McKinsey & Company, Knudstorp's former employer, as well as the design firm IDEO.

- Jamie Berard is a star designer who created extreme LEGO models for advanced builders, such as the four-thousand-piece replica of London's Tower Bridge. Berard is so devoted to the brick, he estimated that LEGO sets account for 70 percent of his earthly possessions. He's also studied civil engineering, holds a BA in English literature, and once worked as a monorail driver at Disney World.*

T-shaped people might be configured differently from others, but they aren't superheroes. They, too, are exposed to the same forces that derailed the LEGO designers of the late 1990s: kids are still getting older faster, and nine-year-olds are as fickle as they ever were. Today's LEGO designers are just as creative as their predecessors and just as capable of chasing fads and losing their way. So how does LEGO ensure that diversity's spark doesn't fuel a runaway conflagration, as it did during the Plougmann years?

Part of the answer resides in the fact that while the company has been aggressively hiring diverse and creative people, it's also recruited people whose primary responsibility is to bring focus and discipline to all that creative energy. There's the community organizer Steven Canvin, who collaborated with the expert AFOLs to make Mindstorms NXT such a success. Paal Smith-Meyer, the new business developer, seized on Adam Reed Tucker's vision to create LEGO Architecture. Bionicle's licensing group manager, Sine Møller, was the internal voice who worked with licensees to make Bionicle-branded clothing, books, and games. And then there are the Design Lab's system controllers, the grizzled veterans who have the ultimate say on whether a designer's newly created color or shape has enough LEGO DNA to be admitted into the LEGO System of Play. All throughout the LEGO Group's Billund headquarters, there are managers whose chief role is to bring more focus and discipline to the creative process.

---

* Gender is one area where LEGO developers are decidedly unvarying, as most of them are men.

Most important, LEGO has surrounded its creative people with guidance mechanisms that channel their work into profitable innovations. Such mechanisms gave people enough space to create and direction to deliver. If you had followed the team that created Ninjago, here's what you would have seen:

Restructuring the company to give people a sharper sense of direction. When Nonnemann, Legernes, and their colleagues set out to create the company's next Big Bang, they knew they didn't have to seek out a pristine market space, à la LEGO Games. Nor were they expected to step into the breach that LEGO Universe had created and make another run at a disruptive innovation. Their task was to invent a new play theme, but one that was rooted in the company's DNA and would appeal to core LEGO customers who loved to build. The Ninjago team's sense of what was in play and what was beyond the project's scope grew out of the companywide restructuring that had occurred three years earlier.

In 2005, after taking the company back to the brick and defining the types of innovation they would pursue, Knudstorp and his team sought to bring a clearer sense of direction to the LEGO Group's individual business units. During the Plougmann era, the company's new leaders had seen firsthand that when discipline and focus are lacking, profits can suffer even when creativity flourishes. Seeking a way to harness the talents of the LEGO Group's diverse and creative people without reining them in, the management team used the innovation matrix (which we described in Chapter Six) to plot the company's key initiatives, as well as which unit was responsible for each.

Knudstorp set up the main part of the business, called Product and Market Development (PMD), to focus on profiting from the company's core assets and capabilities. Its assets: the LEGO brick, the building system, and the beloved LEGO brand. As for capabilities, they included the company's expertise in designing and manufacturing brick-based play experiences and its capacity to sell those experiences onto global markets. This is where the Ninjago team lived. The team was free to create anything it could imagine, so long as it innovated within the PMD's boundaries.

Past experience had taught LEGO management that the metrics and processes that bring incremental innovations to such classic PMD lines as City and DUPLO wouldn't lend themselves to creating "never seen before" play experiences. So they carved out an area at the top of the matrix for the Concept Lab—the unit that developed LEGO Games—that focused solely on developing brick-based experiences that LEGO itself had not yet imagined. .

However, the innovation matrix revealed a yawning white space: no one group was directly responsible for the brand's globe-spanning community of passionate fans. LEGO, said Knudstorp, was treating this community of engaged users, which was entirely unique to the toy industry, "as a sideshow." He also saw gaps in the more experimental part of the business, which called for the creation of new business models, new channels to market, and new ways of connecting with customers. Strengthening ties with the community of LEGO users, building out the LEGO education business, selling directly to consumers through platforms such as Factory.com, and exploring new business models (as Paal Smith-Meyer did with LEGO Architecture)—no single group was accountable for those initiatives. So Knudstorp and his team carved out a new unit, Community, Education, and Direct (CED). PMD and the Concept Lab could focus exclusively on the core and revolutionary parts of the company's brick business; CED would take on everything else.

"The work we do in PMD is the same that goes on in all successful toy companies," said Knudstorp. "But what we do in CED, no other company is doing. No one else goes direct to the consumer, no one else has an education division, and no one else has that level of community involvement. Creating CED was a way for us to clean up and optimize the business model."

Although the Ninjago team worked within PMD's confines, Nonnemann and Legernes knew that to deliver a Bionicle-size hit, they'd also call on CED's experts to help shepherd the creation of a suite of complementary innovations that would tap into additional revenue streams. So while the product team set about creating a line that would light up the construction toy aisles of Walmart and Target, its partners in CED would help define ancillary products—board games, movies, iPhone apps, and video games—that customers could access through the Ninjago website and LEGO stores.

In this way, the company's restructuring served to compartmentalize the Ninjago team's effort. Since it sat within the PMD organization, the team could home in on developing brick-based play experiences for core (and potentially core) LEGO customers. It had to focus on that single task, to the exclusion of all else. Yet, so long as it worked within those limits and delivered on its stretch goal, the team was free to innovate whatever it could imagine. As we'll see, the team's results underscore Knudstorp's formulation that "innovation flourishes when the space for it is limited."

A box of direction-setting tools. When LEGO launched the third stage—manage for growth—of its "Shared Vision" plan, its senior management team had taken enough direction-setting steps to give designers and developers a vivid sense of where the company needed to go and the kinds of play themes that would take them there. They had refocused associates on winning back core consumers, principally five- to nine-year-old boys who loved to build. They had dramatically reduced the number of elements in the LEGO product portfolio, a "do more with less" strategy that channeled designers' creativity. They had equipped developers and marketers with the CPP financial tool, which calculated the cost implications of designers' decisions and helped them drive the LEGO Group's return to profitability. And they had developed a credo, "obviously LEGO, but never seen before," that reasserted the primacy of the brick, even as it challenged associates to invent LEGO sets that are magnets for twenty-first-century kids.

Having set a clear direction, senior managers could then leave it to project teams to navigate much of the journey, as Legernes and Nonnemann's concept team did with Ninjago. "Design DNA" was one of the navigational tools that helped point the way. Every LEGO product line has a specific DNA, which outlines the toy's target audience, the desired play experience, the toy's "expression" (realistic or fictional, sunny or dark, timeless or trendy), and other details. Explicitly identifying the various strands that make up the toy's DNA helps guide new efforts to refresh or refine the line.

To create a new theme, LEGO developers first define its DNA. At the Ninjago project's outset, Nonnemann sketched a simple two-by-two matrix that mapped out, in four quadrants, four distinct play characteristics: themes based on realism, fantasy, low conflict, and high conflict. (So, for example, LEGO *SpongeBob* would map as a low-conflict fantasy theme.) The matrix sparked discussions that helped the team home in on the zone in which it wanted to compete: high-conflict fantasy. Nonnemann reasoned that since the team would have to deliver sky-high sales volumes, "the safer bet was to be up there with the fantasy and high conflict."

The choice hardly ensured success, since a LEGO theme can win or lose in any of the four quadrants. Case in point: LEGO City became a franchise theme by succeeding in the low-conflict realistic quadrant. And Galidor, a high-conflict fantasy theme—just like Ninjago—was an abysmal failure. But the matrix did help the team begin to target the theme it would pursue and edit out all other options.

The matrix also served to remind the front-end team of the degree of innovativeness that the new theme would require. An evergreen franchise such as LEGO City typically relies on 90 percent replication (deliver what fans have come to expect) and 10 percent invention (add enough new details to make the next set feel fresh). A high-conflict fantasy theme, especially one that's a homegrown IP, reverses that formula. Ten percent of the new creation might replicate design features from an older, out-of-circulation LEGO kit. But 90 percent of the theme would have to have a novel look and feel.

With that, the concept team had a rough but ready schema of the line's Design DNA—maximum fantasy, conflict, and innovation—to serve as a starting point for creating the company's next Big Bang.

Time for "inspiration and exploration." One of the foremost challenges for sustaining any innovation effort is to carve out enough time and space to build for tomorrow's success when the organization is already running flat out to deliver today's results. Although patience and perseverance are critical to value creation, they are highly vulnerable to short-term pressures to hit financial targets and deadlines.

By 2008, when the team was developing the toy that would become Ninjago, Knudstorp and his managers had injected a big dose of urgency into LEGO; as we've seen, the design and engineering teams responded by halving the amount of time it took to develop and launch a new toy line. But the company's senior managers also knew that before there can be productivity, there must be creativity. And creativity takes time. LEGO hedged against expediency by sometimes adding more lead time, in the form of an idea generation phase, to its product development process.

When senior managers meet with project teams to refine an existing product line, they typically kick-start the effort at the LEGO Development Process's P0 review stage. That's when market opportunities are identified and business objectives are defined. But concept teams that are charged with developing new themes, such as the Ninjago team, are allowed an extra "exploration and inspiration" stage that runs prior to the LDP's P0.

During this prelude to the actual development process, a team's search for a promising theme will lead it to seek inspiration from a wide array of sources—competitors' offerings, children's TV shows, successful LEGO sets from the past. The Ninjago team, for example, went on a weeklong reconnaissance mission to Japan, where the LEGO designers and marketers traveled three hours north of Tokyo to visit the Iga Ninja Museum. As they walked through a fifteenth-century ninja dwelling, with its revolving walls and hidden compartments, the LEGO designers soaked up the telling details that might bring a ninja-related theme to life. They also began to orient themselves around the challenge of bringing the medieval world of ninjas into the lives of twenty-first-century kids.

"Cocreating" with kids. Every LEGO product development group now uses focus testing with kids to evaluate potential concepts. In most of those tests, a couple of designers introduce kids to a prototype and elicit their reactions, with an eye toward gauging the strength of children's interest in the concept. The front-end teams, however, take a more robust approach to play testing.

The Ninjago front-end team regularly convened in an office building in Fort Lee, New Jersey, where they'd spend several days ensconced behind a one-way mirror, watching small groups of eight- to ten-year-old boys gather in a conference room and react to storyboards illustrating potential Big Bang concepts. Megan Nerz, a market researcher who's worked with LEGO for nearly two decades, moderated the discussion. With equal measures of discipline and aplomb, she enticed the kids to reveal their impressions. The kids could be funny, canny, crabby, and kind, often within the space of just a few minutes. They could also be unusually insightful, if you knew how to read them.

Although the Ninjago front-end team sometimes called those sessions "cocreating with kids," the boys rarely delivered a creative idea that could be directly applied to a concept design. Rather, Nerz and the LEGO designers interpreted the kids' impressions by utilizing a set of clear-eyed standards.

As Nerz walked the kids through richly illustrated storyboards featuring themes such as cities of the future, underwater adventures, and ninjas, the front-end team ranked the kids' feedback against a specific set of categories: the kids' spontaneous reactions, their understanding of the story line, the concept's ability to spark sustained play, and the extent to which the concept delivered on its play promise. Thus, while the kids' impressions were highly subjective, the team's interpretation was more measured.

"The best way to rank a theme is to see if the kids keep talking about it," said Nonnemann. "If they keep coming up with stories about how they'd play in the world you're showing them, you know you're on to something big."

Another way the kids helped the Ninjago team was in the choice of the villain. If ninjas were the heroes, whom did they battle? The team developed six different options for the villains, including monkeys, robots, skeletons, and lizard people. The response from the kid tests was overwhelming: skeletons. Kids understood that ninjas were real historical figures and that skeletons were "real" fantasy villains. Fanciful creatures such as demon lizards didn't make sense to them. The team homed in on the skeleton idea in the next round, showing four different skeleton options.

The ninja theme elicited waves of stories from kids, but not enough to convince the team that the concept, by itself, would propel the line to its sales target of 10 percent of the company's revenue. To clear that bar, the team would have to come up with an element that would give Ninjago "schoolyard currency," as Schou put it. "We needed something that was competitive and cool. Something the kids would talk about at school." In fact, the Ninjago concept team's goal—left unstated to upper management—was for the toy to be so popular it would be *banned* from schools.

To hit upon a solution, the team organized a series of brainstorming sessions and invited LEGO designers, marketers, and prototypers from other departments to participate, in hopes of sparking some fresh insights. For inspiration, they investigated iconic toys such as marbles, yo-yos, and spinning tops, which had succeeded across multiple generations of children.

The design group ran with the notion of fitting ninja minifigs on top of LEGO versions of spinning tops. The idea was to spin a pair of tops so that the ninja minifigs would whirl around and collide, or

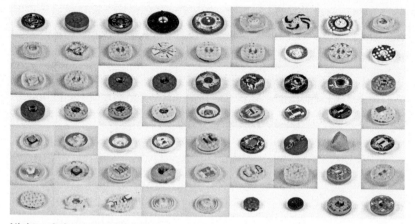

Ninjago Spinner prototypes.

"fight," just like real ninjas. The team went on to develop more than sixty different prototypes of the ninja spinners, until it perfected one that included an eject button: when two spinners struck each other, one of the ninja minifigs would pop off. "Suddenly there's a loser— the one that falls off—and a winner," said Legernes. "The winner gets the loser's sword, which turns it into a game where the kids compete for weapons.

"When we tested the spinners with kids, they almost blew the roof off the place," he continued. "They were so excited they started screaming. The moderator told us we were sitting on a treasure. She'd never seen such a strong response to a test."

By continually testing and retesting with kids, the front-end team concocted the varied play experiences—story (compelling heroes and villains), competition (between Spinjitzu spinners), and collectibility (the weapons)—that would make Ninjago such a rousing success.

Teams—rather than management—driving the review process. By the time the front-end team had fully developed the theme that became Ninjago, hundreds of kids, ranging from boys who were lukewarm to the brick to those who were gripped by it, had weighed in on the concept. The constant rounds of testing, refining, and retesting Ninjago reduced the risk that this new-to-LEGO fantasy theme would hit the market with a whimper instead of a bang. Moreover, the unbiased test results reassured LEGO management that the team was on track to produce a line that might actually hit its lofty sales target.

"To get the resources we needed, we had to convince the people in our organization that this was right," said Legernes. "The testing was not only a creative tool, it was a persuading tool."

Although Poul Schou, as the overseer of more than 70 percent of the company's products, sat in on many of the early rounds of testing the ninja and other themes, he participated mostly out of a desire to get a firsthand feel for which concepts were resonating with kids, given that the Big Bang project was such an overriding priority. Otherwise, the Ninjago front-end team drove the testing and development process. And as we've seen, it was the team itself—not upper management—that wrote Ninjago's design brief and set the line's sales target. For their part, Schou and other senior managers used the LEGO Development Process's stage-gate reviews to take a wide-angle view of *all* the projects under development, not just Ninjago. Their feedback helped to ensure that as specific themes evolved, they brought variety to the company's product assortment.

Essentially, the reviews were a form of addition by subtraction. The executives guided the development of stronger concepts by ruthlessly editing out those that duplicated other efforts or failed to deliver a promising play experience. Of the scores of LEGO ideas that were introduced at P0, just twenty made it to the P3 stage, where the final commitment is made to bring a toy to market. "It's very much a deselecting process," said Schou. "Survival of the fittest."

Prior to the company's turnaround, the LEGO Development Process was a hit-or-miss proposition. LEGO would bet big on themes early in the process and bring them to market when they were ready. Now it's like a Swiss railroad—a new set of products (the "train") heads to the market, reliably and on time, every year. LEGO management commissions teams to explore many different potential themes; only the best are allowed on the train. In fact, Ninjago was delayed a year, after management decided that while it was a good concept, another year's development would make it a great concept.

At the time of this writing, the LEGO Group's diverse and creative people have delivered a heterogenous mix of thirty-four product categories that take in not only Big Bang themes such as Ninjago but also board games, video games, kits for girls, kits for experienced builders, kits for preschoolers, two different robotics platforms, sets that combine bricks with digital devices, licensed lines such as LEGO *SpongeBob* and *Toy Story*, and more, much more. Like their creators, all of those lines are grounded in the brick and the "hands-on, minds-on" LEGO play experience.

The LEGO Group's front-line developers and marketers now have the incentive to do the right thing for profits. That's because, like the team that invented Ninjago, they have the freedom to set their own financial and innovation goals. Of course, having largely established their projects' objectives, people are responsible for delivering on them. This tight link between autonomy and accountability reduces the need for motivation-sapping interventions from upper management. The LEGO Group's diverse and creative people no longer have to seek out executives such as Mads Nipper for inspiration and direction. They need only look to themselves.

Transforming LEGO

The Rebirth of a Brand

To make the LEGO brand vital again, you first need to transform the whole business system.

—Jørgen Vig Knudstorp, CEO, the LEGO Group

LOOKING BACK AT THE LEGO OF THE LATE 1990S AND early 2000s, one can't help but wonder whether it possessed the same genetic mutation as the winner of the 1995 Darwin Award, which annually commemorates those who, by killing themselves in spectacularly stupid ways, unintentionally demonstrate Charles Darwin's theory of natural selection. That is, they enrich the human gene pool by removing themselves from it. Though later proved an urban legend, the story is irresistible: An amateur inventor attached a solid-fuel rocket engine to a Chevy Impala, motored out into the Arizona desert, and hit the accelerator. The vehicle surged to more than 250 miles per hour and achieved liftoff, hurtling nearly a mile through the air before smashing into a cliff. All that remained from the misadventure was a smoldering crater in a rock face some 125 feet above the ground.

Like that driver turned pilot, the late 1990s LEGO strapped on overamped engines of innovation and aimed for the stars, boldly declaring that in five years it would be the world's biggest brand among families with children. Disaster soon followed. Although it broke the sound barrier with LEGO *Star Wars* and *Harry Potter,* the company lost control of its dizzying array of innovation efforts and quickly found itself hurtling toward a crash.

When Jørgen Vig Knudstorp and his management team stepped into the corporate cockpit and attempted to pull LEGO out of its tailspin, they didn't overreact. They realized that while they had to continue to boost innovation at LEGO, they also had to turn their unguided missile of a company into a high-flying, on-target aircraft. That effort took seven years and played out in five stages.

LEGO 1.0. Throughout 2004, Knudstorp and his copilot, CFO Jesper Ovesen, engaged in a first-stage fight for survival, where the pair forced the out-of-control rocket that was LEGO into a white-knuckle emergency landing. They did so by focusing the company on three must-win battles: First, strip complexity out of the business by taking such cost-reducing steps as halving the number of components in the company's product portfolio, as well as the time it took to develop an idea and bring it to market. Second, restore competitiveness by making retail customers (rather than kids) their primary concern—boosting retailers' profits; speeding the rate of inventory turnover. Third, raise cash by selling off assets such as the LEGOLAND theme parks and carving costs throughout the organization.

Ovesen convinced Knudstorp that deciding what *not* to do was just as important as deciding what to do. By getting LEGO to zero in on just those three challenges and nothing else, they bought enough time to attempt a turnaround.

LEGO 2.0. There then came the second iteration, where the company's leaders did the metaphorical equivalent of jettisoning the rocket's thrusters and building a dependable, drivable workhorse of an engine. That is, they set a clear direction by taking LEGO "back to the brick." That meant focusing on core assets (the brick and the LEGO system), core products (such as LEGO City and DUPLO), and core customers (kids ages five to nine). If it wasn't core, it wasn't critical.

Knudstorp and his team further simplified managers' efforts by identifying the one metric that mattered most: the 13½ percent return-on-sales target. From a direction-setting standpoint, metrics are actionable and unambiguous. The 13½ percent ROS benchmark, prominently tracked on whiteboards in the corporate "war room" and reviewed in weekly meetings, pushed everyone to concentrate their efforts on just those product lines that promised profits—and to quickly kick over any line that was struggling. Thus, management dumped resource-draining lines such as LEGO Explore and Jack Stone and revived classic moneymakers such as DUPLO and LEGO City. By the end of 2005, LEGO could report that it had rebounded from a DKK 1.6 billion ($292 million) loss the previous year to a pre-tax profit of DKK 702 million ($117 million) and a 12 percent jump in sales.

LEGO 3.0. Having built a powerful yet controllable engine, Knudstorp and his team set about strapping wings and a tail on their revamped rocket and installing a navigational system that would shepherd its flight.

Managers clarified the company's direction by drafting a matrix that defined the different degrees of innovation, from incremental to radical. They then used the matrix to map which innovations they'd pursue with each product line. Management also overhauled the LEGO Development Process by instituting quarterly stage-gate reviews, where executives conducted in-depth checkups with the product development teams. By editing out those projects that duplicated other efforts or failed to deliver a distinctive play experience, executives concentrated the company's collective mind on launching only the most promising concepts.

And then there were those first steps toward opening up the development process to the LEGO community. By inviting the most inventive AFOLs to test and even codevelop lines such as Mindstorms NXT, LEGO gleaned insights it otherwise might never have been exposed to. With a clearly defined flight path and a navigation system informed by stakeholders as well as insiders, LEGO put itself on a track toward profitable growth. In 2008, despite a slowdown in the wider toy industry, the LEGO Group's sales rose 19 percent over the previous year and its profit jumped 32 percent.

LEGO 4.0. Once it achieved liftoff, the streamlined LEGO rocket swiftly began to gain altitude. And so LEGO pivoted from innovations that restored a profitable core business platform to innovations that aimed to fuel organic growth. That meant managing the trade-offs between expanding the product portfolio and continuing to drive profits, between delivering higher margins for customers and lowering costs, and between pursuing short-term performance goals while sowing the seed for long-term success. As Knudstorp put it in an April 2008 email to the company's corporate management, achieving those trade-offs would increasingly require a "bifocal perspective."

On one hand, LEGO increasingly took on riskier challenges. It refocused the Concept Lab on creating "never seen before" play experiences, which led to LEGO Games. The company also endured some very rough turbulence with the failure of the highly ambitious LEGO Universe. At the same time, LEGO maintained its dual focus by reimagining classic product lines such as LEGO City and LEGO *Star Wars*, which continued to dominate the company's top-ten list of best-selling kits.

More often than not, the company achieved a blend of "obviously LEGO" and "never seen before," which made for a remarkably revitalized brand. In 2009, the New York–based firm BMO Capital Markets declared LEGO "the hottest toy company." In a March 2010 email to senior managers, Knudstorp reported that after years of comparing LEGO to direct competitors such as Mega Brands (formerly Mega Bloks), Mattel, and Hasbro, the company's auditor, PwC, had begun to benchmark the brick maker against such world-class brands as Apple and Nike. While Mattel's and Hasbro's sales between 2007 and 2011 grew at an annual rate of 1 percent and 3 percent, respectively, the LEGO Group's sales surged at a rate of 24 percent per year. In 2012, LEGO reported a 27 percent increase in sales and a 36 percent increase in profits over the previous year, for a five-year average annual sales growth of 24 percent and annual profit growth of 40 percent. It's far from certain that LEGO can maintain that pace, but neither is it inconceivable that the company might someday become the toy industry's sales leader. Whatever happens, the LEGO brand, which was imperiled a decade ago, is closer than ever to realizing Plougmann and Kristiansen's dream.

LEGO 5.0. Since 2011, the metaphorical LEGO rocket has morphed into a high-flying mother ship surrounded by a growing fleet of small, experimental space probes. There's industry leader LEGO, a blockbuster machine. The majority of its revenue still comes from refining classic LEGO lines such as City and *Star Wars*, licensing more recent megahits such as *Lord of the Rings*, and inventing Big Bang themes such as LEGO Friends, the company's latest bid to compete in the voluminous market for toys that appeal to girls. Launched in early 2012, Friends was backed by years of ethnographic market research and a $40 million marketing campaign. That year, the company went on to sell twice as much of the Friends line as it originally forecast. When it wants to, LEGO can flex its brand and throw billions of bricks at an opportunity.

At the same time, there's the part of LEGO that has distanced itself from the mainstream and innovates from the fringe, conceiving and launching newfangled ideas quickly, systematically, and sometimes idiosyncratically. Through its cocreation effort with Adam Reed Tucker, LEGO continued to expand its Architecture line of minimalist models of iconic buildings. There was also the iPhone game Life of George, a clever mash-up of digital and physical LEGO play.

And then there was Cuusoo, another of the company's further adventures in geek-sourcing ideas. Launched in Japan in 2008 and globally in October 2011, LEGO Cuusoo invited users to submit—and vote for—DIY ideas for new LEGO sets. If a design won ten thousand votes, LEGO reviewed it for possible production; if the design was developed and launched, its creators got a 1 percent cut of the product's total net sales. In 2011, a Cuusoo concept for a LEGO set based on Minecraft—the online game that may disrupt the LEGO Group's brick business—racked up the requisite ten thousand votes in just forty-eight hours, an outpouring of support that compelled LEGO to announce that it would produce the set. Six months later (one-third of the company's average development time), LEGO Minecraft Micro World hit the market. With Cuusoo, LEGO moved from tapping the wisdom of a few elite cliques to sourcing the talents of massive crowds.

To be sure, some of those little LEGO start-ups might be wrong-headed. Some will never pay off. But that's no excuse not to experiment. Though some will probably fail, none is anywhere near large enough to sink the company.

The LEGO Group's leaders believe that to discover the next big growth opportunity, the company must adhere to a fundamental truth about innovation: the more experiments you launch, the more likely it is that one will strike gold. Today, LEGO continues to profit almost entirely from its core portfolio of brick-based toys. Tomorrow, the "core" might well be something that LEGO has not yet imagined. Experiments such as LEGO Architecture and Cuusoo are search strategies whose ultimate aim is to help LEGO discover unexploited markets.

The Seven Truths of Innovation and a Company That Clicks

In the late 1990s and early 2000s, Poul Plougmann and Kjeld Kirk Kristiansen defined success in terms of revitalizing the LEGO brand, declaring that by 2005, "our goal is for LEGO to become the world's strongest brand among families with children." That was an impossible dream even for a beloved brand such as LEGO, given that the company was in the midst of destroying economic value at the rate of almost half a million dollars per day.

For Knudstorp, the brand could never be elevated without first building a strong foundation for organic growth: that is, a financially sound balance sheet, a manageable level of debt, a defensible core business, and profitable product lines. Only then would people begin to believe that LEGO really is a rejuvenated, exciting brand. And that took time. "It starts with a financial turnaround, then it's a business transformation, and then you get brand revitalization," he explained. "To make the LEGO brand vital again, you first need to transform the whole business system."

The most difficult challenge in business is not to invent an innovative product; it's to build an organization that can continually create innovative products. Over an eight-year span, LEGO more than met that goal. The company found its way back to the brick, revived stalwart lines such as LEGO City, and concocted increasingly ambitious creations such as Mindstorms NXT and LEGO Games. Along the way, LEGO learned to control and direct the engines of innovation that once almost doomed the company—the seven truths—and turned them to its advantage.

What are some final lessons that you can take from LEGO and apply to your organization? Consider these three closing takeaways.

No Single Truth Stands Alone

The seven truths of innovation are not competing visions of what it takes to innovate successfully. Although the seven truths are usually presented as stand-alone models of innovation management, LEGO has shown that each can be integrated into a larger whole, and their joint power harnessed to create an innovation system that's consistently profitable.

But to make that system work requires an exquisite balancing act. Giving your teams enough space to create and direction to deliver means you must leverage the types of control mechanisms—such as extensive concept testing with kids and defining the Design DNA of every development effort—that we've seen LEGO utilize since 2005.

Admittedly, striking a healthy tension between freedom and control is no easy feat, as LEGO itself has amply demonstrated. From 1999 until 2002, LEGO boosted its innovation initiatives without counterbalancing those efforts with sufficient discipline and focus. And so the company rolled out a number of badly executed, unprofitable products and almost went bankrupt as a result. Yet with the LEGO Universe effort, LEGO exerted too much control over its attempt at a disruptive innovation and missed an opportunity to create the kind of online multiplayer building experience that Markus Persson exploited with Minecraft.

When LEGO succeeds, as it did with a Big Bang line such as Ninjago, it innovates from the inside out. That is, the development team starts with its core capabilities—its deep expertise in leveraging the brick and the System of Play—and then moves on to experiment with "never seen before" flourishes, such as the Spinjitzu spinners. And it continually tests ideas with kids, to ensure that it's moving in a profitable direction. However, the team never crosses over into territory that stands outside its charter. Truly revolutionary play experiences are left to the Concept Lab. Experimental efforts, such as Architecture, belong to Paal Smith-Meyer's new business team.

Whether it's attempting to launch a blue-ocean effort such as Games or an open innovation such as Mindstorms NXT, LEGO gives its development teams wide latitude to create, so long as they innovate "inside the box." Given the constraints that every company faces in these economically challenging times, perhaps it is time to reconsider our headlong rush to think "outside the box." Instead, we might follow the LEGO Group's example and climb back into it.

Resources for Innovators

For those interested in applying the lessons from LEGO to boost innovation at your company, we've assembled a set of resources to help you. They include:

- **A diagnostic survey.** Would you like to compare your company to LEGO and other best-in-class innovators? Fill out the survey and receive a free report with detailed feedback on your innovation management practices. Just click on "Take the Survey" at www .robertsoninnovation.com.

- **A generic innovation matrix.** One of the first direction-setting activities LEGO did was to define its own innovation matrix. The management team created eight categories of innovations that they used to spur creativity, guide teams, and, ultimately, organize all their innovation efforts. A generic matrix can be found at www .robertsoninnovation.com/innovation-matrix.

- **Innovation tools and techniques.** We've assembled the best anthropological, creativity, and prototyping tools available into a free iPad app. You can get it from www.robertsoninnovation.com or directly from iTunes at bit.ly/innovationtechniques.

- **The best books on innovation.** Our favorite innovation books can be found at www.robertsoninnovation.com/ favorite-innovation-books.

- **David's blog.** To see updates on our new research on innovation, go to www.robertsoninnovation.com/category/blog.

Sequence and Cadence Matter

Why did Knudstorp and his team succeed in leveraging most of the truths even though Plougmann and his team failed? Knudstorp didn't start by putting most of his emphasis on the more radical innovation strategies that call for disrupting the incumbents and sailing for blue oceans. And he didn't try to launch all seven innovation strategies all at once. Instead, he built a foundation for more ambitious innovations by first describing a very clear vision of where he wanted to take the company. He also broke the strangely self-satisfied culture that had brought LEGO to the brink in 2003, and he reconnected people with the fundamental values that had sustained LEGO for decades. At the same time, he reached out to core fans. They confirmed that his instinct to "get back to the brick" was the right course of action.

Having worked to build a culture that delivered profitable innovations and a company that had reoriented itself around its core customers, Knudstorp then looked back to Bionicle, the toy that saved the company. In Bionicle, Knudstorp and his team saw the value-creating potential that came with exploring the full spectrum of innovation. They defined the types of innovation they needed and opened up the company in order to bring complementary innovations to market. They extended the conversations they'd been having with adult fans in the Mindstorms NXT development process to incorporate the wisdom of the clique.

Only then, after exploring the full spectrum of innovation and opening up its development process to outside contributors, did LEGO take on the more out-there strategies of launching a disruptive innovation with Universe and seeking out an untapped market with Games. Universe, of course, was a failure. But LEGO hasn't given up. Some of the same strategies that work for a blue-ocean effort—adopt a start-up mentality, shield the team from the demands of other business units, realize that "good enough" is sometimes better than perfection—readily suit a disruptive effort. Having learned from its success with the blue-ocean strategy that was Games, LEGO can readily apply those lessons to its next attempt at a disruptive innovation, whatever it might be.

As with any innovation effort, seizing on the truths of innovation requires a certain sequence and cadence. It's best to start with the core and the customer, and work out from there. And you can't do too much too fast. It's highly unlikely that a company will possess the wherewithal to discover a whole new market if it first hasn't built a core business that knows how, as Knudstorp has put it, "to get stuff done."

Every Innovation Matters—Even Though They're Not All the Same

LEGO has demonstrated an impressive ability to recognize what types of innovation are most appropriate for a new product development effort. That's not an accident. Although break-the-mold innovations such as Mindstorms and LEGO Games garner a lot of attention, the company's most profitable lines are unsexy stalwarts such as LEGO City. Refreshing an evergreen line such as City won't generate any headlines, but it significantly plumps up the company's bottom line. Thus, LEGO puts as much of a premium on "adjusting" (to use its terminology) a classic bestseller as it does on creating a revolutionary line that "redefines" an entire toy category. Moreover, the company understands that those disparate efforts require different resources, strategies, and degrees of executive attention. To get a better sense of where and how it should marshal its assets, recall how LEGO plots its development efforts on the innovation matrix.

As we've seen, the matrix is especially useful in revealing the degree of innovativeness that LEGO should bring to a new initiative, depending on the overriding goal. And it prevents LEGO from ignoring the kinds of innovations that matter. Like many companies, LEGO once had a blind spot for innovation. It devoted much of its attention to product innovation, whereas the Bionicle team demonstrated that novel sales channels, a ramped-up development process, and new ways of marketing can also deliver outsize rewards. By mapping its innovation efforts on the matrix, LEGO can spy the white spaces—such as a compelling opportunity to partner with an outside company—it might otherwise have missed.

How many times has an innovation effort foundered at your company, all because the initiative lacked a clear direction and the control mechanisms that could help managers make midflight corrections? For LEGO, the matrix acts as a kind of GPS device, helping to keep most projects pointed toward their respective North Stars.

———————

No matter how or where it's innovating, LEGO is now driven by the same two desires. The first is to inspire imaginative play and creative expression in as many kids and kids-at-heart as possible, in as many ways as possible.

The second motivation, quite simply, is to outinnovate every company it comes up against. Or to put it another way, it's to strive to fulfill Ole Kirk Christiansen's founding value, "only the best." Odds are LEGO won't manage to continue its stratospheric growth rate, as every rocket inevitably yields to gravity's pull. The company might yet find itself in the thrall of outsize ambition as it takes on the heavyweights in its industry, Mattel and Hasbro. And it must continue to fend off a multitude of imitators, even as it strives to keep the brick enticing enough for twenty-first-century kids. Yet whatever the future holds for LEGO, its seven-year-long transformation offers two final messages for potential innovators.

Innovating at LEGO is not unlike building with LEGO. The LEGO brick is arguably capable of delivering anything the human imagination can conceive. In the space of one randomly chosen week (in February 2012), we came across reports that an American engineering student built a fully functional, eerily lifelike prosthetic arm and hand *entirely out of LEGO components*. There then came word that the brick had made it to the final frontier: a Japanese astronaut built a LEGO version of the International Space Station *while living in zero gravity in the orbiting station.* And to think that all of this inexhaustible creativity springs out of a precisely calibrated, highly engineered block of ABS plastic.

So it goes with the LEGO Group's approach to innovation. The company's wildly diverse array of play experiences, from stalwart classics such as DUPLO for the preschool set to the 5,200-piece, $500 *Star Wars* Millennium Falcon model, is born out of its highly disciplined, tightly focused system for guiding innovation. LEGO unleashes its associates' creativity and passion largely because its innovation process is so carefully scripted and clearly bounded. Just as you can build anything you want with LEGO bricks, you can create anything you want within the company, so long as you innovate "inside the brick."

Our final message includes a cautionary note. Although there's much to take from the LEGO Group's resurgence, there's also much to avoid. We've met many executives who want to emulate the company's success but fail to consider the trauma that forced the turnaround. Our advice to them is always the same: don't wait for a crisis to spur a drive for deep, systemic change. While hurtling toward bankruptcy, as LEGO did in 2003, focuses the mind, it's not necessary and it's certainly not desirable. Continuous innovation must be a product of an organization's capacity to learn and adapt.

LEGO opened its doors to us largely because its management team wanted to remind its thousands of associates and stakeholders of the dangers of complacency and the pitfalls of a blind adherence to management nostrums. It wanted to ensure that what transpired between 1998 and 2003 "would never happen again." We hope LEGO realizes that goal. We hope LEGO will continue to thrive, because a world with LEGO in it is a little smarter, a little more creative, and a lot more fun.

Notes

1. Portions of this chapter are based on material drawn from the following sources: *50 Years of Play* (LEGO Group, 1982); Christian Humberg, *50 Years of the LEGO Brick* (HEEL Verlag GmbH, 2008); Jesus Diaz, "LEGO Brick Timeline: 50 Years of Building Frenzy and Curiosities," *Gizmodo*, January 28, 2008, http://gizmodo.com/349509/lego-brick-timeline-50-years-of-building-frenzy-and-curiosities; Charles Fishman, "Why Can't LEGO Click?" *Fast Company*, August 2001; and Brickfetish.com's excellent account of the history of LEGO.

2. *50 Years of Play* (LEGO Group, 1982).

3. Christian Humberg, *50 Years of the LEGO Brick* (HEEL Verlag GmbH, 2008).

4. Gary Hamel with Bill Breen, *The Future of Management* (Harvard Business School Press, 2007).

5. Brandon Griggs, "10 Great Quotes from Steve Jobs," CNN.com, October 5, 2012.

6. Except where noted, all quotations are drawn from interviews conducted by the authors.

7. Charles Fishman, "Why Can't LEGO Click?" *Fast Company*, August 2001.

8. Sonia Purnell, "Picking Up the Pieces," *Independent*, December 20, 2000.

9. Nicholas Negroponte, "Where Do New Ideas Come From?" Wired.com, January 1, 1996.

10. Clayton M. Christensen, *The Innovator's Dilemma: When New Technologies Cause Great Firms to Fail* (Harvard Business School Press, 1997). This is the most well known of Christensen's books, but his ideas about disruptive technologies and disruptive innovation were first laid out in articles

before this book, and in later books, particularly *The Innovator's Solution* (with Michael Raynor, Harvard Business School Press, 2003)

11. Douglas Coupland, *Microserfs: A Novel* (HarperCollins, 1995).

12. The term "full spectrum" comes from George S. Day's *Growth Through Innovation*.

13. As quoted in Rosie Murray-West, "LEGO Wobbles as Star Wars and Harry Potter Sales Tumble," *Telegraph*, December 30, 2003.

14. Rosie Murray-West, "LEGO's Blueprint for Success: Build Bigger Bricks," *Telegraph*, February 3, 2004.

15. Christopher Brown-Humes, "After the Crash: LEGO Picks Up the Pieces," *Financial Times*, April 2, 2004.

16. Quoted from "How LEGO Caught the Cluetrain," presentation by Jake McKee, http://experiencecurve.com/archives/how-lego-caught-the-clue train-presentation-by-jake-mckee.

17. Some of the material from this section is drawn from Yun Mi Antorini, Alfred M. Muniz Jr., and Tormod Askildsen, "Collaborating with Customer Communities: Lessons from the LEGO Group," *MIT Sloan Management Review*, Spring 2012.

18. Jake McKee, "Behind the Curtains—LEGO Factory AFOL Project Team," November 16, 2004, www.lugnet.cc/lego/?n=2588.

19. Ira Sager and Peter Burrows with Andy Reinhardt, "Back to the Future at Apple," *BusinessWeek*, May 25 1998.

20. Portions of Chapter Seven are based on material that first appeared in the following publications: Patricia B. Seybold, *Outside Innovation: How Your Customers Will Co-Design Your Company's Future* (Collins, 2006); Brendan I. Koerner, "Geeks in Toyland," *Wired*, February 2006; Quentin Hardy, "Son of LEGO," *Forbes*, September 4, 2006.

21. Larissa MacFarquhar, "When Giants Fail," *New Yorker*, May 14, 2012, http://archives.newyorker.com/?i=2012–05–14#folio=086.

22. Connor Wack, "Stephen Calender Talks: LEGO Universe," *MMO Fallout*, July 24, 2011, http://mmofallout.com/2011/07/24/stephen-calender -talks.

23. Josh Augustine, "A Glimpse into What LEGO Universe Could Have Been," *PC Gamer*, January 31, 2012, www.pcgamer.com/2012/01/31/a -glimpse-into-what-lego-universe-couldve-been.

24. Chris Holt, "LEGO Universe," *Macworld*, February 19, 2011.

25. Tom Chivers, "LEGO Concept Lab 'Like Working for CIA,' " *Telegraph*, October 22, 2009.

Index

About the Authors

DAVID C. ROBERTSON was a professor of innovation and technology management at IMD in Lausanne, Switzerland, from 2002 through 2010, and was named the LEGO professor in 2008. As the LEGO professor, Robertson was given unique access to the company's management, partners, and customers. At IMD, he was the codirector of the school's largest executive education program, the Program for Executive Development, and directed programs for Credit Suisse, EMC, HSBC, Skanska, BT, and other leading European companies. Prior to IMD, Robertson was a consultant at McKinsey & Company and an executive at three start-up companies. Robertson joined the faculty of the Wharton School at the University of Pennsylvania in 2011, and lives in Chestnut Hill, Pennsylvania, with his wife and two children. To contact David, visit www.robertsoninnovation.com.

BILL BREEN is a founding member of the team that launched *Fast Company*, which gained an avid following among businesspeople and won numerous awards, including the National Magazine Award for general excellence. As senior editor, he edited *Fast Company*'s special issues on design and leadership and wrote many articles on competition, innovation, and personal success. He is the coauthor of *The Responsibility Revolution* and *The Future of Management*, which the editors of Amazon.com selected as the best business book of the year.